本书是广东海洋大学博士启动项目"基于事件语义的谓词性状语分析"（项目编号：102002/R20054）的阶段性成果；并得到校级人文社科项目"地点状语的语义标示不足"（项目编号：300702/C18035）的资助

现代汉语状位形容词的
事件语义分析

安丰科 著

A Study of
Adjectival Adverbials in
Mandarin Chinese:
An Event Semantics
Perspective

中国社会科学出版社

图书在版编目（CIP）数据

现代汉语状位形容词的事件语义分析：英文 / 安丰科著.
—北京：中国社会科学出版社，2022.8
ISBN 978 - 7 - 5227 - 0252 - 0

Ⅰ.①现…　Ⅱ.①安…　Ⅲ.①现代汉语—形容词—语义学—研究—英文　Ⅳ.①H146.2

中国版本图书馆 CIP 数据核字（2022）第 091657 号

出 版 人	赵剑英
责任编辑	张冰洁　李　沫
责任校对	郭曼曼
责任印制	王　超

出　　版	中国社会科学出版社
社　　址	北京鼓楼西大街甲 158 号
邮　　编	100720
网　　址	http://www.csspw.cn
发 行 部	010 - 84083685
门 市 部	010 - 84029450
经　　销	新华书店及其他书店
印　　刷	北京明恒达印务有限公司
装　　订	廊坊市广阳区广增装订厂
版　　次	2022 年 8 月第 1 版
印　　次	2022 年 8 月第 1 次印刷
开　　本	710×1000　1/16
印　　张	19
字　　数	325 千字
定　　价	108.00 元

凡购买中国社会科学出版社图书，如有质量问题请与本社营销中心联系调换
电话：010 - 84083683
版权所有　侵权必究

Abstract

This book details a study investigating the semantic property of adjectival adverbials (AA) in Mandarin Chinese in the framework of event semantics. Occurring as adverbial is a marked function of adjectives in Mandarin, which is reflected from the restrictions that adjectives are exposed to when they occur as adverbials. These restrictions come from prosody, morphology, syntax, semantics and pragmatics. The main focus of this work is to identify and represent the semantic restrictions that constrain adjectives to occur as adverbials.

There appears to be a syntax/semantics mismatch when some adjectives serve as adverbials, for some adjectival adverbials are not semantically related to primary predicates. The other mismatch, which is a temporal mismatch between the under adjective and the primary predicate is also vital to determining whether an adjective can occur as adverbial or not. In order to form a well-accepted sentence with an adjectival adverbial, both the primary predicate and the adjectival adverbial should receive stage-level interpretations. Individual-level predicate (ILP) differs from a stage-level predicates (SLP) in that an ILP introduces a Davidsonian argument which a SLP lacks. The ILP/SLP contrast is based on not only the meaning of the predicate per se, but highly context-sensitive. Some ILP adjectives are easily coerced out of the original interpretation and into an SLP reading.

The nature of adjectival adverbials is clarified by comparing them with adnominal attributives, *buyu* as well as the secondary predicates and predicational adverbs in English. Furthermore, based on the temporal relations between these two events denoted by the two predicates in a sentence with AA, the shared element of these two events, and whether the event denoted by AA is homogeneous or not, adjectival adverbials are classified into seven kinds. These seven kinds of AAs are analyzed in detail to reveal their semantic features and their requirements on the context in which they appear.

In this work, the structural subordinator *–De* is analyzed as a functional head in which all the information concerning the compositional pattern of these two events denoted by the two predicates in the sentence, including the temporal relation and the shared element between these two events. Seven kinds of AAs correspond to different functional head –*De* respectively. Lastly, the semantic derivation process is presented in detail with the revised pattern proposed by Rothstein in her predicate theory. This process reflects how the under adjective from the lexicon receives adverbial interpretation gradually. In this dynamic and incremental semantic derivation process, the morphological change, the meaning shift and the semantic orientation of the under adjective is clearly indicated. The syntactic-semantic isomorphism, compositionality principle and the context-sensitivity of the interpretation of adjectival adverbials are all represented in the semantic derivation process.

There are six chapters in this book. Chapter one is about the object of study. A brief literature review about the achievements of research related to AAs is given in chapter two. Chapter three focuses on the theoretical framework, particularly event semantics and the aspectual features of predicates. In chapter four, the nature of adjectival adverbials is clarified by comparing them with other downgraded predicates in Mandarin and secondary predicates as well as predicational adverbs in English. AAs are classified based on the features of events denoted by predicates in the sentence. Chapter five focuses on the semantic derivation process of each kind of adjectival adverbials. The compositionality principle and context-sensitivity of AAs is represented in this process. Conclusive remarks are given in chapter six.

Keywords: adjectival adverbial; semantic orientation; event semantics; individual-level predicate; stage-level predicate; *-De*

Abbreviations

AA	adjectival adverbial
Asp	aspect marker
CA	complex adjective
CL	classifier
de	attributive marker
De	adverbial modification marker
DE	post-verbal complement marker
Gen	generic quantifier
ILP	individual-level predicate
PAST	past tense
Perf	perfective aspect marker
p.n	proper name
REDUPL	reduplicated
SA	simple adjective
SLP	stage-level predicate
TOP	topic marker

Contents

Chapter One
Introduction 1
   1.1 Object of Study 1
   1.2 Problems Waiting for Answers 3
   1.3 Overview of the Book and Main Chapter Summaries 7

Chapter Two
Adjectival Adverbials in Mandarin 10
   2.1 Status of the Adjectives in front of Verbs 10
   2.2 Classification of Adjectival Adverbials 12
   2.3 Researches on -*De* 20
   2.4 Reduplication of adjectives 29
   2.5 Researches on AAs in Zheng (2000) 35
   2.6 Syntactic Research on AAs 38
   2.7 Semantic Research on AAs 40
   2.8 Summary 46

Chapter Three
Event Semantics and Aspectual Feature of Predicates 48
   3.1 Modification Relation 49
   3.2 Event Semantics 54
   3.3 Classification of Predicates 68
   3.4 The Nature and Basic Elements of Event 97
   3.5 Aspectual Shift 101
   3.6 Further Development of Neo-Davidsonian Approach 107
   3.7 Summary 114

Chapter Four
Clarification and Reclassification of AAs 116
   4.1 The Nature of Adjectival Adverbials 116
   4.2 Criteria for Classification of AAs 141
   4.3 Subject-oriented AAs 147
   4.4 Object-oriented AAs 169

4.5　VP-oriented AAs 176
　　4.6　Clause-oriented AAs..184
　　4.7　Summary 192

Chapter Five
Semantic Analysis of AAs 195
　　5.1　Features of Each Kind of AAs 195
　　5.2　Formalizing the Features of AAs 199
　　5.3　-De 226
　　5.4　Semantic derivation process of sentences containing AAs 246
　　5.5　AAs with Multi Orientations 270
　　5.6　Beyond Compositionality..273
　　5.7　Summary 274

Chapter Six
Conclusive Remarks 276
　　6.1　Important and Innovative Features of the Research 276
　　6.2　Further Questions 278

References...280

Acknowledgements 298

Chapter One

Introduction

1.1 Object of Study

The relationship between form and meaning is one of the focuses of linguistic research, for it is not always the case that the form rigidly corresponds to the meaning. Zhu (1985: 5) indicates that there is no a one-to-one mapping between the part of speech of a word and its syntactic function in Chinese. The functions of adjectives are especially complicated for adjectives can occur as subjects, objects, predicates, attributes and adverbials. This dissertation mainly focuses on adverbials which are composed of adjectives in Mandarin.

Generally speaking, although adverbs form a heterogeneous set, the function of adverbs is relatively unitary. Zhu (1982: 192) states that occurring as adverbial is the only function of adverbs. All adverbs can occur as adverbials which usually appear after the subjects (Guo 2002: 229). Yuan (2010: 73) provides the following syntactic environment that is compatible with adverbs, which means that adverbs can modify verbs and adjectives but not nouns.

(1) ___ V/A & * ___ N,

Compared with the function of adverbs, the functions of adjectives are much more complicated. It is a controversial issue to decide what the primary syntactic function of adjectives is. Some scholars state that to be attributive is the main function of adjective (Li 1924; Wang 1957; Zhang

1979; Zhang & Fang 1996). Li (1924: 114) states that the main function of adjective is to be attributive, and if the adjective is a primary predicate in a sentence, it is not an adjective any more, but a verb. Lyu (1966) states that being attributes and being predicates, are both the main functions of adjectives in Chinese. Hu (1993) basically supports this view. According to markedness theory, Shen (1997) makes a detailed statistical analysis based on a 60,000-word corpus to investigate the function of attributive adjectives and state adjectives respectively. He concludes that the unmarked function[①] of typical simple adjectives (SAs) is to act as adnominal attributives, while serving as predicates is the unmarked function of typical complex adjectives (CAs). However, Guo (2002: 196) states that primary function of adjectives[②] is to occur as predicate instead of attributive.

As for the adverbial function of adjectives, scholars also have different opinions. It is generally acknowledged that it is not the main function of adjectives to occur as adverbials. Guo (2002: 198) states that only 12% of simple adjectives can occur as adverbials directly. However, with the cilitc of -De, the proportion of adjectives that can occur as adverbials will increase to 40%. He suggests that acting as adverbials is not the primary function of adjectives, so it is reasonable to analyze these adjectives capable of occurring as adverbials as adverbs. As for complex adjectives—state words in Guo's classification, only 15% of complex adjectives can occur as adverbials.

Correlations between lexical items and their sentential functions are distinguished into 'natural' and 'unnatural' ones by Croft (1984). In a natural correlation, the lexical items appear in its original forms in the lexicon which is no more complex than any other form in less natural correlations. In unnatural correlations, lexical items will lose many of their own typical characteristics and would be taking on the

---

[①] Markedness in Shen (1997) is mainly judged on three criteria: firstly, the dependency on the aid of subordinator "de" (morphology criterion); secondly, the distribution of unmarked term is wider than that of the marked term(distribution criterion), and thirdly, the unmarked term is used more frequently than the corresponding marked term(frequency criterion).

[②] Adjectives in Guo (2002) refers to simple adjectives, for he includes complex adjectives into state words.

characteristics of other categories depending on what function they take in the unnatural correlations. According to such criteria, the correlation between an adverb and the sentential function of adverbial is natural, whereas an adjective and the sentential function of adverbial is an "unnatural" one.

Actually, scholars have noticed this unnaturalness long before. Many researchers have observed that the interpretation of the adjectival adverbials is different from the original meaning of the under adjective. Lyu (1966) states that when some adjectives modify verbs, the meanings of these adjectives usually shift, and sometimes, the changes of meaning are very dramatic. Hu (1991) concludes that, generally speaking, property adjectives, because of their semantic property, are not suitable for adverbials. Once they occur as adverbials, the meaning of these adjectives will change, which is the consequence of the contrast between the semantic property and the syntactic position.

The exclusive function of adverb in Mandarin is to occur as adverbial, whereas some adjectives also can occur as adverbials. However, it is not the primary function of adjectives to serve as adverbials. The unnaturalness between the adjectives and the syntactic function of adverbials will result in a series of restrictions on the adjectives that appear as adverbials. Any grammatical sentence is not formed at random, but a product that lives up to many requirements, including syntactic, semantic, phonologic and pragmatic requirements (Xu 1993). This work mainly focuses on exploring the restrictions on adjectives when occurring as adverbials. Restrictions on adjectives that occur as adverbials include morphological restriction, the restriction on the absence/presence of the structural subordinator *-De*, restriction on the semantic orientation of the under adjective, etc.

1.2 Problems Waiting for Answers

Typical examples of adjectival adverbials are given in (2). In these sentences in (2), the constituent between the subject and the primary predicate is composed of an adjective and structural subordinator *-De*. Such constituents are called adjectival adverbials (AAs for short) and they have never failed to arouse the interests of Chinese grammarians. For many years they have been contributing their wisdom to the research of AAs (Zhu 1956/1982, Lyu 1963; Liu1983; Zheng 2000; Zhou 2006; Liu 2011; Wang 2012; Xiong 2013; Li 2014).

(2) a. Xiaoming zaozao-De zha-le yi pan huashengmi.
　　　p.n　　early -DE　fry-Perf one plate peanuts
　　　"Xiaoming fried a plate of peanuts early."
　　b. Xiaoming xizizi -De zha-le yi pan huashengmi.
　　　p.n　　happy-DE　fry-Perf one plate peanuts
　　　"Xiaoming fried a plate of peanuts and he was happy during that process."
　　c. Xiaoming cuicui -De zha-le yi pan huashengmi.
　　　p.n　　crispy-DE　fry-Perf one plate peanuts
　　　"Xiaoming fried a plate of peanuts, and the peanuts became crispy."

The adjectival adverbials in these sentences indeed exhibit some particular features compared with adjectives appearing at other syntactic positions. At the same time, such adjectival adverbials are different from the adverbials that are acted by adverbs.

First, these adjectival adverbials, locating adjacent to the primary predicates, are semantically related to various constituents besides the primary predicates, whereas adverbial acted by adverb is usually part of the proposition involved the primary predicate in. The AA zaozao -De "early" in (2a), like normal adverbials, modifies the verb; in (2b), the AA xizizi -De "happily" modifies the subject; and in (2c), the AA cuicui -De "crispy" is semantically related to the object of the sentence. There are no morpho-syntactic markers to indicate the relation between the AAs and targets they are semantically related to, so the constituent that an AA is semantically related to only can be identified on semantic and pragmatic grounds. Many inflectional languages have morphological marker to indicate the difference between the VP-oriented reading and the participant-oriented reading of predicational adverbials. In English, there are two kinds of predicational adjuncts with the absence and presence of the suffix –ly as the marker: one is predicational adverb as in (3a), the other is secondary predicate as in (3b). Furthermore, the syntactic positions of the predicational adverbials result in different interpretation of the adverbials as indicated in (3c), in which the predicational adverb *happily* appearing at different positions contributes something different to the sentence.

(3) a. Tom left the room sadly.
    b. Tom left the room sad.
    c. Happily, John would happily play the tuba happily.
                                  (Jackendoff 1972)

In Japanese, the particle *-mo* can indicate the difference between VP-oriented reading and subject-oriented of adverbials:

(4) a. John-wa orokani odotta
    John-TOP stupidly danced
    "John danced stupidly."   (Manner reading only)
    b. John-wa orokani-mo odotta
    John-TOP stupidly danced
    "John stupidly danced." (subject-oriented reading only)

In Japanese, the variation of syntactic position does no affect the interpretation of the adverbial. When the adverb is fronted, the presence/absence contrast of the particle *-mo* clearly indicate the two different interpretations:

(5) a. Orokani John-wa odotta
    stupidly John-TOP danced
    "John danced stupidly."   (Manner reading only)
    b. Orokani-mo John-wa odotta
    stupidly John-TOP danced
    "John stupidly danced." (subject-oriented reading only)
                                (Japanese Matsui to appear)

The adverbial function of adjective is often compared with other functions of adjectives, such as adnominal attributives, primary predicates, *buyu*. What are the similarities and differences between these various functions of adjectives? In addition, some AAs are analyzed as secondary predicates (Zhang 2000, 2001, 2002; Lim 2004). What is the difference between AAs and secondary predicates and predicational adverbs in English? In Mandarin, is there an element having the function similar to that of *–ly* in English, or *–mo* in Japanese? If there is, what is it? In Chinese, is it possible to interpret an AA both as subject-oriented reading and a VP-oriented reading? If an AA can have different interpretation, how the VP-oriented reading and participant-oriented reading is distinguished?

Second, all these three adjectives in (2) are derived from the corresponding simple adjectives. Some adjectives must undergo morphological variation to occur as adverbials. Adjectives in Mandarin Chinese have various forms, and these forms exhibit different ability of acting as adverbials. In Mandarin Chinese, some adjectives are permitted as adverbials without any constraints, while some others are heavily restricted, and some adjectives are still forbidden to act as adverbials. In (2), "zaozao" and "cuicui" are reduplicated forms of the corresponding monosyllabic basic forms and "xizizi" is the basic form "xi"+ suffix "zizi". There are still a lot of other complex forms of adjectives derived from basic forms function as adverbials. The motivation of reduplication when occur as attributes and primary predicates has been researched intensively. However, what is the motivation for the reduplication of some AAs? Is the requirement for reduplication of AAs is the same as that of adjectival attributes and adjectival primary predicates? If they are not the same, what requires the reduplication of the under adjectives for some AAs? What is the difference between those can occur as adverbials with the clitic *–De* directly and those need morphological variation to occur as adverbials? Why reduplication can make some simple adjectives that originally cannot occur as adverbials permissible for adverbials? What motivates the reduplication of these adjectives?

Third, as it is indicated in (3c), predicational adverbial at different syntactic positions gets different interpretation in English. Whether the adjectival adverbials can have multi interpretations is a controversial issue. Scholars hold different opinions. Lu and Shen (2004) states that AAs are only likely to be semantically relevant to one constituent, while

Zheng (2000) holds that some AAs are semantically related to more than one constituent.

Fourth, the structural subordinator *-De* is sometimes compulsory and sometimes optional. What is the exact function of *-De*? What rule controls the absence and presence of *–De*? What is the difference caused by the contrast of the absence and presence of *-De*?

Furthermore, the meaning shift of the under adjectives has been observed. What is the motivation of the meaning changes of the under adjectives when occurring as adverbials? What is the nature of the meaning shift? How to express the semantic properties of AAs?

All these questions relevant to AAs in Mandarin have been attracting the attention of scholars, and the study on each of these topics has produced a wealth of empirical generalizations as well as some theoretical insights. In the research of this work, all these questions will be taken into consideration in order to get a more accurate understanding of AAs in Mandarin.

1.3 Overview of the Book and Main Chapter Summaries

A natural language like Chinese can be considered as an abstract system analogous to formal language of logic or mathematics. Both natural and formal languages are compositional in the sense that the meaning of any syntactically well-formed expressions is uniquely determined by the meaning of its constituent parts and the pattern used to combine these constituents. In this dissertation, AAs will be studied from the perspective of formal semantic in order to find out the constraints that the under adjectives undergo by investigating the semantic properties of the sentences with AAs. The semantic properties of adjective adverbials elucidated in this study are expressed in an underlying event analysis (Parsons 1980, 1990) and predicate theory (Rothstein 2001, 2004). In addition, it is of great interest to study AAs from a cross-linguistic perspective, since most analyses of depictive expressions of other languages appeal largely to morphosyntactic patterns of agreement and finiteness, which are not overtly marked in Chinese. This work will refer to the analogous constructions in other languages (mainly English) and take in the fruitful researches of other languages into the analyses of AAs in Chinese. Through the comparison with other languages, we will find that the adjectival adverbials in Chinese actually share a lot in common with the relevant constituents in other languages, and the features of AAs can be represented more accurately.

In order to accomplish this, a brief literature review of the researches relevant to adjectival adverbials will be first provided in Chapter 2. The contents include the identification of the status of the adjectives that occur in front of verbs, the classification of AAs and the characteristics of each subcategory of AAs, the function and the distribution of the structural subordinator -*De*, and the reduplication of adjectives. Researches on AAs form syntactic, cognitive, and pragmatic perspectives will be briefly introduced. Then the theory of semantic orientation analysis which is used in the analysis of AAs will be introduced.

Chapter 3 will be centered on the introduction of the theoretical framework that will be employed to analyze AAs, as well as the motivations for choosing such a theory. The relevant latest development of the theory will also be introduced. The aspectual classification of eventuality, the shift between different eventuality types, as well as the notion of coercion is introduced in this section to explain the unnaturalness represented in the correlation between adjectives and the syntactic function of adverbials.

In Chapter 4, the nature of adjectival adverbials will be confirmed by comparing with other constituents composed of adjectives in Mandarin, and by comparing with some constituents of similar functions in English. In this book, AAs will be analyzed as downgraded predicates introducing Davidsonian argument. AAs will be first classified according to the temporal relation between the event denoted by AA and the event denoted by the primary predicate, the aspectual feature of the event denoted by the adjective and its semantic orientation. Then the features of each kind of AAs will be analyzed in details.

In Chapter 5, the function of -*De* will be made full use in the semantic derivation of AAs. Comparatively speaking, the researches on -*De* is relatively weaker than those on -*de*. In this book, the function of -*De* will be explored in great details. Based on the initially proposed semantic analyses and the functional head -*De*, the semantic derivation process of each kind of AAs will be illustrated to verify the compositionality and context-sensitivity of AAs. Last, AAs with multi-interpretation will be explained to prove that different semantic orientation of AA is the result of different compositional pattern, not the polysemy of adjectives. The process of under adjective from lexicon to getting the adverbial interpretation in sentences will be presented dynamically and incrementally, which reflects the compositionality principle and the context-sensitivity of AAs. Furthermore, the meaning shift of the under adjective and the semantic orientation of AA will be clearly indicated.

The conclusion of the book and the direction of further researches on adjectival adverbials will be presented in Chapter 6.

Adverbials are a rich and as yet relatively unexplored system, and therefore anything we say about them must be regarded as quite tentative (Chomsky 1965: 219). In sum, I hope the research conducted in this book will shed light on understanding of the aspectual features of adjectives in Mandarin, the classification of AAs, as well as the dynamic and incremental process of the interpretation of AAs.

Chapter Two

Adjectival Adverbials in Mandarin

Adjectival adverbials in Mandarin have long been one of the focuses of research due to the abnormal performances of such constituents. Study on AAs has produced a wealth of empirical generalizations as well as some theoretical insights. In this chapter, the existing researches on AAs will be sketched and the organization of this chapter is as follows. Section 2.1 focuses on the identification of the status of the adjectives that appear in front of verbs. Section 2.2 includes the classification of AAs based on the semantic orientation and the morphological forms of AAs. The research on the function and distribution of the structural subordinator -*De* is introduced in Section 2.3. Section 2.4 is mainly about restrictions and consequences of adjective reduplication. The research on AAs in Zheng (2000) has been one of the most important and overall one, so his research and contributions are introduced in Section 2.5. The syntactic analysis of AAs is introduced in Section 2.6. Section 2.7 is about the semantic analyses of AAs. The theory semantic orientation analysis will be introduced and evaluated. Cognitive analyses as well as pragmatic researches of AAs are briefly mentioned in this section. A summary of this chapter is given in Section 2.8.

2.1 Status of the Adjectives in front of Verbs

The initial researches related to AAs are centered on the status of the adjectives when they appear in front of verbs. Lyu (1979: 60, 1986) notices the specialty of the following sentences:

(1) a. Yuan yuan De pai cheng le yi ge quan.
　　　round round De arrange become Perf one CL circle
　　　"arrange in a pattern of a circle."
　b. Women rere De lai hu cha he.
　　　we hot hot De come kettle tea drink
　　　"Let's drink a kettle of hot tea."
　c. Duo he dian shui.
　　　more drink some water
　　　"Drink more water."

There is an adjective appear in front of the verb in every sentence in (1), but these adjectives aren't always semantically related to the verbs. *yuanyuan-De* 'round' semantically relates to *quan* "circle", in (1a), *rere-De* "hot" is semantically related to *cha* "tea" in (1b), *duo* is semantically related to *shui* "water" in (1c).

As for the status of the adjectives in front of the verb, scholars have different explanations.

Some scholars suggest that these adjectives are adnominal attributes that have been relocated (Pan 1981; Lyu 1986; Zhang 1988; Zheng 2000). Lyu (1986) states that in these sentences, the words serving as adnominal attributes move to the adverbial positions. Zhang Jing (1988) states "Attributes most naturally stay before nominal heads, however, out of some needs of wording, attributes can be relocated. No matter where they are, the identity of being adnominal attribute will never change."

Some other scholars analyze such adjectives in these sentences as adverbials although some of them are semantically related to participants (Zhu 1982; Lu 1982; Dai 1982; Shao 1987). Zhu (1982) states that sometimes, adjectives can occur as adverbials in front of verbs and they are semantically related to the objects instead of verbs.

If the adjectives in front of verbs are analyzed as relocated attributives, it would be difficult to explain why not all adjectives in this position can be altered into adnominal modifiers, and not all adnominal modifiers can be moved to the adverbial position. Furthermore, the semantic difference between adnominal modifiers and modifiers in front of verbs should be taken into consideration (Lu 2003; Zhang 2005; Xiong 2013):

(2) a. Heihei   De ran le toufa.
       black black De dye Perf hair
       "dyed one's hair black"
    b. Ranle heihei de toufa.
       dye Perf black black de hair
       "dyed one's black hair"

(Lu Jian 2003: 103)

(3) a. Zhuoshang houhou De luo zhe xie zazhi.
       table on thick thick De stack Asp some magazine
       "There is a thick stack of magazines on the table."
    b. ?Zhuoshang luo zhe xie houhou de zazhi.
       table on   stack Asp some thick thick de magazine
       "There is a stack of thick magazines on the table."

In (2a), *heihei-de* "black" describes the color of hair after being dyed, and in (2b), *heihei-de* "black" describes the original color of the hair before being dyed. In (3a), *houhou-De* "thick" denotes the transitory thickness of many magazines being stacked together, while in (3b), *houhou-de* "thick" denotes the inherent thickness of every magazine. Conventionally, magazines are not very thick, which is the reason why (3b) is not a very good sentence. When adjectives appear at the syntactic position of adverbials, they carry on some transitory features, especially the temporal features of verbs (Zhang 2006; Xiong 2013; Li 2014), so it has been widely accepted that the adjectives in front of verbs are to be analyzed as adverbials (Zhu 1956; Zheng 2000; Lu 2003; Zhang 2006; Liu and Li 2011, Xiong 2013; Cong 2013; Li and Liu 2014).

2. 2 Classification of Adjectival Adverbials

After the statue of adjectives in front of verbs has been recognized as adverbials, scholars began to focus on the classification of adjectival adverbials. AAs are subcategorized according to different criteria and the characteristics of each kind of adjectival adverbials have been observed at great length (Liu 1983; Cheng 1987/1993; Zhang 1990; Dong 1991; Zheng 2000).

2.2.1 Classification Based on the Semantic Orientations

Liu (1983) conducted a macro study on the classification of adverbials and the linear order of different kinds of adverbials in Mandarin. He takes the grammatical meaning and function of adverbials into consideration and classifies adverbials into two groups: restrictive adverbials (FM adverbials) and descriptive adverbials (M adverbials).① All adjectival adverbials are descriptive adverbials.

(4) The Classification of Adverbials in Liu (1983)

	Types of Adverbial	Sample Words
descriptive adverbials (M)	M1　describing subject	*meizizi*, 'pleased'
	M2　describing verb	*kuai*, "fast", *chedi*, "thorough"
	M3　describing object	*luanpengpeng*, "disorder"
non-descriptive adverbials (FM)	time, mood, purpose, location, negation, degree, domain, relation,	*jintian*, "today" *yijing* "already", *gewai* "extremely", *bu* "not", *hen* "very", *quan* "all", *ye* "too"

M1 adverbials, usually relating to some perceivable properties of the subject, describe the agent's expression, gesture, psychological state when he/she conducts an action. Some adjectives such as: *gaoxing* "happy", *naixin* "patient", *jidong* "excited", *deyiyangyang* "proud", etc., exclusively act as M1 adverbials. M2 adverbials describe the manner and state of an action. M2 adverbial is so closely related to the verb that M2+verb usually forms a constituent. At the same time, M2 can be altered to be the predicate or *buyu* of the verb. Some adjectives, such as: *zixi* "careful", *xiangxi* "detailed", *chedi* "thorough", etc., can only

---

① Descriptive adverbials in Liu (1983) included adjectives, verbs, adverbs, noun phrases, number + classifier phrases, and onomatopoeic words. Adverbial Adjectival adverbial is just a subcategory of descriptive adverbials.

act as M2 adverbials. M3 adverbials are related to the objects of verbs. Some adjectives, such a *rere* "hot", *gulingling* "alone", *luanpengpeng* "disorder", etc., can act as M3 adverbials.

As for the question that whether adjectval adverbials in Mandarin can have more than one interpretation, Liu emphasizes that only few descriptive adverbials can have both M1 and M2 readings, such as, *renzhen* "careful", *nuli* "diligent", *jianjue* "resolute". Classification in Liu (1983) is of great influence on the following researches of AAs.

Chen (1987) is the earliest paper we can find that mainly focuses on adjectival adverbials. Compared with the classification in Liu (1983), the classification of AAs in Chen (1987/1993) is more concrete. He categorizes AAs into two kinds: VP-oriented AAs and NP-oriented AAs. VP-oriented adverbials express the situation, result, degree, domain, and time of the event denoted by the primary predicate, and NP-oriented adverbials express the states of the subject or the object. We can get a clearer picture of his classification from the following chart.

(5) The Classification of AAs in Chen (1987)

		Semantic Type	Sample Words
VP		state of action	*qiaomiao* "artful", *huanman* "slow"
		result of action	*yuanman*, "successful",
		degree or domain	*pubian* "overall"
NP		time	*zao*, "early" *changjiu* "long",
	agent-oriented	controllable mental state	*zhongshi* "loyal", *guoduan* "determined"
		uncontrollable mental state	*langbei* "akward", *jiankang* "healthy", *jingya* "surprised"
		evaluative	*buxing* "unlucky" *zhengque* "correct"
	patient-oriented	state	*sheng*, "deep", *wanhao* "intact",
		result	*yuan* "round", *hou* "thick"
	theme-oriented		*zaluan* "disorder", *zhengqi* "neat",

In addition to these two kinds of AAs, he also makes a detailed explanation on the evaluative function of AAs. When evaluative adjectives act as adverbials, they don't describe the state of the agent, but express the evaluation about the agent because of the happening of the event denoted by the verb.

(6) a. Ta   xingfu -De shoudao-le zongtong de jiejian.
       he/she fortunate De get Perf predident of meeting
       "Luckly, he/she was interviewed by the president."
   b. Yibai duo   ming chengke xingyun De huo le xia lai.
       one hundred CL passengers fortunately De live Perf on.
       "Fortunately, more than one hundred passengers survived the accident."
(7) a. Li Jinxi zhengque-De ba zhezhong mingci chuli cheng binyu.
       p.n   correctly De Ba this   noun analyze as object
       "Li Jinxi correctly analyzed such nouns as objects."
    b. Tamen cuowu -De pipan -le Ma Yinchu xiansheng.
       they incorrectly De critique Perf p.n   sir
       "They incorrectly critiqued Ma Yinchu."
                              Adapted from (Cheng 1987)

The structure of these sentences is: NP+A+VP and these sentences can be paraphrased as: because of VP, NP is A. The difference between (6) and (7) is that the verbs in (6) are not under control of the subjects, while in (7) the subjects can control the verbs.①

After that, Zhang (1990) and Dong (1991) go on working on the research of adjective adverbials. Zhang (1990) is the first researcher to introduce the term "semantic orientation" into the study of adjectival adverbials and he mainly focuses on complex adjectives (CA) in his research. Dong (1991) makes an even more detailed classification of the adjective adverbials. In her classification, there are four kinds of NP-oriented AAs and eight kinds VP-oriented AAs. In addition, she extends her research on adjectival adverbials into "Ba" and "Bei" constructions.

Zheng (2000) provides one of the most overall and detailed investigations into the classification and properties of AAs. He

---

① These sentences are ambiguous in the following analyses, for they can express the evaluation of the subject, and at the same time, they can also express the evaluation towards the whole proposition.

scrutinizes the constrains on the alternations between AAs and attributes, AAs and *buyu*, and he concludes that all participant-oriented AAs are derived from attributes of relevant NP, and only VP-oriented AAs are generated at the original place, so VP-oriented AAs are the most typical AAs in Mandarin (Zheng 2000: 240). His research will be introduced in details in section 2.5.

These classifications of AAs are mainly based on the semantic orientation of the under adjectives, as well as the semantic features of the adjectives, which has included almost all the potential functions of AAs. These researches are of great help for us to get an overall understanding of AAs.

2.2.2 Classification Based on Morphological Forms of AAs

The number of syllables and morphological forms of adjectives greatly influence the distribution and function of adjectives. Shen (2011: 8) suggests that the number of syllables of adjectives is the most important and reliable criteria to classify adjectives. Adjectives of different morphological features exhibit different ability to act as adverbials. Researchers conduct many statistical studies on AAs to find out the relationship between the morphological forms of adjectives and their ability to perform the adverbial function.

2.2.2.1 Monosyllabic AAs

Monosyllabic adjectives are the typical adjectives in Chinese, and most of them solely refer to certain property. It is clearly stated in literature that monosyllabic adjectives are extremely restrained in acting as adverbials. Zhu (1956) states that the number of monosyllabic adjectives that can occur as adverbials is limited and only a few monosyllabic adjectives can modify verbs freely.

As for the adverbial function of monosyllabic adjectives, He Yang (1996) investigates 198 monosyllabic adjectives and notices that only 22.7%, that is 45 of them, can occur as adverbials. Li (2005) investigates 700 lexical items derived from 388 monosyllabic adjectives and finds that 27.28% of these 700 items can act as adverbials. Liu (2007) conducts a similar research and the result is 21.7%. At the first sight, the results of these researches are not in agreement with the expectation that monosyllabic adjectives are not free to act as adverbials. However, the investigations of Li (2005) and Liu (2007) include a lot of compounds. Actually, the proportion of real monosyllabic adjectival adverbial is certainly much lower.

Zhu (1956) and Lyu (1966) state that most monosyllabic adjectives cannot act as adverbials freely and most combinations composed of a monosyllabic adjective and a monosyllabic verb have been lexicalized. The meaning of such combinations cannot be derived from the composition of their components, and these combinations have entered the lexicon as single words. Brinton and Traugott (2005: 18) states that the process of lexicalization means entering into lexicon and losing productivity. At the same time, the meaning of the combination has been conventionalized (Blank 2001: 1603). Take *qingchang,* 'sing a cappella' and *hongshao* 'cook with brown sauce' as examples, the former components are adjectives, but in the combination, the original meaning of these adjectives has mostly lost, and the meaning of combinations have been conventionalized as 'a particular way of performance' and 'a particular way of cooking' respectively. The productivity of such monosyllabic adjectives is extremely limited, and most of such monosyllabic adjectives can only combine with a few or only one monosyllabic verb. Some of such compounds are the remains of archaic Chinese, and are seldom used in Mandarin. In addition, some seemingly adjectives, when appearing in front of verbs, exhibit obvious meaning shift, are actually adverbs. Take *lao chaojia,* 'always quarrel' *zhi ku* 'cry continuously' as examples, in such combinations, *lao* 'old' and *zhi* 'straight' have lost the original adjectival meanings, so they are analyzed as adverbs (Zhu 1956).

Strictly speaking, only a few monosyllabic adjectives can occur as adverbials freely, and these monosyllabic AAs usually don't express the property of an individual, but relate to certain dimension of the properties of an event.

2.2.2.2 Disyllabic AAs

Disyllabic adjectives are always a problematic category, for they stay between the typical simple adjectives (SAs) and typical complex adjectives (CAs). Generally speaking, disyllabic adjectives exhibit stronger ability in acting as adverbials than monosyllabic adjectives. Zhu (1956) states that only a small amount of disyllabic adjectives act as adverbials freely in oral Chinese. He points out that in written language, combining with subordinator '-De', disyllabic adjectives, especially some relatively new adjectives, occur as adverbial freely and such usage is spreading into oral Chinese.

Zhu Dexi's opinion has been clearly verified in later researches. Statistical researches indicate that more and more disyllabic adjectives can extend to the sentential function of adverbials. Zhang (1993) investigates all the 868 disyllabic adjectives in the *Dictionary of Adjective Usage* (Zheng and Meng 1991) and gets 365 adjectives, accounting for 42%, which can serve as adverbials. Based on the same data, Shan tian (1995) investigates 918 lexical terms derived from the disyllabic adjectives in the same dictionary and gets 468 terms, accounting for 51%, which can serve as adverbials. After checking, we find that her conclusion mainly based on the examples listed in the dictionary. However, just as the editors of the dictionary claim, certain function of some adjectives has not been listed under the lexical entry, but it doesn't mean the adjective has no that function. Ling (2011) checks the materials of Shan tian (1995) again, and includes 182 words into the category that can act as adverbials. The final result is that among these 918 disyllabic adjectives included in the dictionary, 646 disyllabic adjectives, that is 71%, can occur as adverbials. There are two reasons for the difference: firstly, Shan tian's investigation is mainly based on the examples provided in the dictionary, but as the editors of the dictionary claim that not all functions of the lexical entry are listed in the dictionary. Therefore, some adjectives that can occur as adjectives are excluded in her research; secondly, language is constantly changing, more and more adjectives are admissible as adverbial modifiers.

Disyllabic adjectives also exhibit different degree of dependency on *-De* when they modify matrix predicates. According to Shan Tian (1995), among those 468 disyllabic adjectives which can act as adverbials, 143 are neutral to *-De*; 320 are in need of *-De*; and only 5 rigidly repel *-De*[①].

[①] Zhu (1982: 193) states that *De* after disyllabic adjectives changes the adjectives into adverbs.

2.2.2.3 Complex Adjective AAs

It is assumed that CAs naturally occur as adverbials. Lyu (1953: 6) states that "when adjectives modify verbs, these adjectives are often reduplicated." Ding (1961: 49) holds the view that "most adverbials[①] that expressing manner or state are in partial or complete reduplicated forms." Zhu (1956) states that simple adjectives (SA), including all the monosyllabic and most of the disyllabic adjectives, are not suitable for being adverbial modifiers, whereas complex adjectives (CA), especially the reduplicated forms, naturally act as adverbials. Actually, different subcategories of CAs exhibit various degree of freedom and reliance on -*De* when acting as adverbials.

According to the restrictions on adjectives of different morphological forms when occurring as adverbials, Liu (2007: 76-77) states that when occurring adverbials, reduplicated adjectives undergo less restrictions than disyllabic adjectives; and monosyllabic adjectives undergo most strict restrictions.

Guo (2002) and Yuan (2010) classify CAs as an independent word class: state words. According to the investigation over 43,330-word data in Guo (2002), 15% of 395 state words occur as adverbials, which is not as high as expected.

The classification based on the morphological features of adjectives and the data of the statistical study provide a macro perspective for us to get to know the relation between the morphological features of adjectives and their ability to occur as adverbials. Studies based on the targets of modification of AAs have presented an overall classification of AAs with all the potential functions in Chinese. Almost all the functions of AAs have been discussed: subject-oriented AAs include agent-oriented controllable mental states, and uncontrollable states, evaluative AAs; Object-oriented AAs include states and results and theme-oriented AAs; VP oriented AAs express the state, result, degree, time, reason, purpose, frequency, mood, manner of the event. Such classifications of AAs based on different criteria have provided a very good foundation for the research in this dissertation.

---

① The adverbial here includes various kinds: adjective, verb, noun, and number+classifier.

2.3 Researches on -*De*

Zhu (1961, 1993) divides "de"① into three morphemes de1, de2 and de3. They correspond to the 地 1, 地 2 and 底 in Tang and Song Dynasty: 地 1 is the suffix of adverb, 地 2 is the suffix of complex adjectives, and 底 is the nominalization marker that appears after verb, or adjective to derive NP-like phrases. In written system, de1, de2 and de3 are realized as -*de* and -*De*. -*De* usually appears after adverbs, and complex adjectival adverbials. The division of "de" in Lu Jianming (1963) is basically in agreement with that in Zhu (1961). Generally speaking, "-*de*" has been researched untensively, while the researches on "-*De*" are relatively weaker. The achievements of researches on "-*de*" is of great value for the research on "-*De*" due to the similar function of "-*de*" and "-*De*". Consequently, we can get some inspirations from the researches on "-*de*".

About the syntactic status of "-*de*", there are different opinions: some syntacticans treat it as the head of CP (Huang 1982; Ning 1993, 1996; Wen 1996); Xiong (2005) suggests that "*de*" can be a phonological realization of the functional category D. some argue that there is an independent *de*P projection in the syntactic structure (Si 2004).

(8) The projection of *de*P

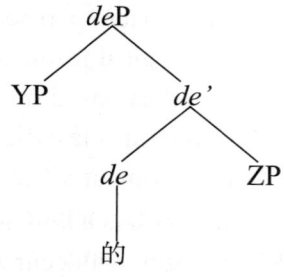

(Si 2004: 26)

Si (2004) states that "-*de*" is a functional syntactic head, which should be distinguished from semantic head. Pan & Lu (2013) propose that the "-*de*" triggers the projection a deP and form a deP with the preceding phrase.

---

① 'de'here just indicates the pronunciation of the subordinator, including the two written form '的' and '地'.

However, no agreement has been arrived at about what the primary semantic function of –*de* is. Some grammarians argue that the primary function of the unique -*de* is to make distinction (Yuan 1995, Shi 2000); whereas some support that the primary function of -*de* is to describe (Lu 2004, Xu 2004). Lu (2003) supposes that the basic function of -*de* is to describe, and the function to make distinction is derived from the descriptive function of -*de*.

Pan (to appear) proposes that different from the modification relation in English, the modification relation in Chinese needs to be marked by an overt marker. -*de* is a marker of adnominal modification, which can trigger the application of predicate modification rule:

(9) Predicate Modification (PM)
If α is a branching node, $\{\beta, \gamma\}$ is the set of α's daughter, and $[\beta]$ and $[\gamma]$ are both in $D_{<e,t>}$, then
$[\alpha] = \lambda x \in D_e. [\beta](x) = [\gamma](x) = 1$

(Heim and Kratzer 1998: 65)

Pan's analysis of -*de* is in agreement of Zhu (1956) and Huang (2006). The modifier and the head are matched in semantic type.

2.3.1 The Function of -*De*

The research on the structural subordinator -*De* is a very important subfield of the researches relevant to adjectival adverbials. The function of -*De* and the rule governing the presence/absence of -*De* is a controversial and unsettled issue. When adjectives occur as adverbials, often, the particle -*De* is necessary; sometimes it is optional; and sometimes it is repelled:

(10) a. Xiaoming wai (*De) dai zhe maozi.
 p.n slanting (*De)wear ASP cap
 'Xiaoming wears the cap slantingly'
 b. Xiaoming zaozao (De) zha-le yi pan huashengmi.
 p.n early DE fry-Perf one plate peanuts

'Xiaoming fried a plate of peanuts early.'
c. Zhang San renzhen (De) jiancha le zuoye.
   p.n   careful (De) check Perf homework.
   'Zhang San checked his homework carefully.'
d. Xiaoming xizizi *(De)   zha-le   yi pan huashengmi.
   p.n   happy -DE   fry-Perf one plate peanuts
   'Xiaoming fried a plate of peanuts and he was happy during that process.'
e. Xiaoming cuicui *(De)   zha-le   yi pan huashengmi.
   p.n   crispy -DE   fry-Perf one plate peanuts
   'Xiaoming fried a plate of peanuts, and the peanuts were crispy.'

About the exact function of -*De*, scholars have different ideas. Liu and Pan (1983) suggest that -*De* is a structural particle which links adverbial and main verb. Huang and Liao (2003: 93) states that -*De* is the marker of adverbial. Hu (1995) supports Huang and Liao (2003) and states that -*De* is a subordinator attaching to words or phrases to indicate the adverbial statues of the words or phrases in front of it. In the grammar text book *Modern Chinese* (2004: 294), -*De* is defined as a suffix, which is attached after adverbials to form a state word or an adverb-like constituent.

He Hongfeng (2012: 2) states that -*De* is both a descriptive structural particle and an adverbial marker. Exactly speaking, -*De* is a manner adverbial[①] marker. One function of -*De* is to make the descriptive function of adverbial more prominent, and the other function of -*De* is to alter these non-adverb constituents into adverbials.

Pan (to appear) suggests that the modifying relation in Mandarin must be overtly marked, and -*De* is an overt marker of modification relation between adverbial and verb. He further notes that such modification is not word-internal but at phrasal level.

These discussions mainly provide a very general description of the function of -*De*. However, as far as AAs are concerned, how and why

---

① The definition of manner adverbial in He (2012) is more general, including almost all with-*De* adverbials.

-*De* can permit adjectives to occur as adverbials has not been explained clearly.

2.3.2 The Distribution of -*De*

As is indicated in (10), it seems that the absence/presence of -*De* after adjectival adverbial is at random. However, extensive researches have been conducted to find out the rules that decide the distribution of -*De*. Lyu (1965, 1980) provides a description about the absence and presence of –*De*. His findings are listed in (11):

> (11) The distribution of -*De*
> I When monosyllabic adjectives modify verbs, -*De* is repelled. *kuai (*De) pao* "run fast" *jin (*De) wo* 'hold tightly'.
> II When disyllabic adjectives modify verbs, *De* is usually necessary. However, -*De* is optional when the combination of the adjective and the verb is frequently used: *xiangxi (De) chawen* 'inquiry in detail', *renzhen (De) yanjiu* 'research carefully', *chedi (De) jiejue* 'solve completely'.
> III When an adjectival adverbial is modified by a degree adverb, -*De* is necessary with few exceptions. *hen nan (*De) xiangxiang* 'very difficult to imagine', *hen reqing (*De) jiedai* 'welcome very enthusiastically', *hen kuai (De) jiejue* 'solve very promptly'.
> IV When reduplicated adjectives modify verbs, -*De* is often necessary. Only for a small number of reduplicated adjectives, -*De* is optional: *haohao (De) gongzuo* 'work hard', *gaogaoxingxing De zoule* 'leave happily'.

The observations of the distribution of -*De* in Lyu (1965, 1980) are mainly about the VP-oriented AAs, which are the M2 adverbials in Liu (1983). Liu observes the distribution of -*De* in a wider range. He observes the distribution of -*De* in three kind of descriptive adverbials:

subject-oriented adverbials (M1), VP-oriented adverbials (M2), and object-oriented adverbials (M3). His conclusions are given in (12):

(12) The distribution of -*De* (based on semantic orientation)
I -*De* is indispensible after M1 adverbial. Otherwise, the structure of the sentence will alter and the adjectival adverbial will become a predicate parallel with the primary predicate.
II M2 is so closely related to verb that M2+verb usually form a constituent. Except for monosyllabic adjectival adverbial, -*De* is optional for M2.
III M3 adverbials describe the objects of verbs and -*De* is necessary for M3 adverbials.

Liu (1983) describes the general tendency of the distribution of -*De*, and his observation on the distribution of -*De* in VP-oriented AAs is in agreement with the conclusions of Lyu (1965, 1980).

The distribution of -*De* has been described in great details and some accurate statistics have been provided, which deepens the understanding of function and distribution of the structural subordinator -*De*. Based on these data, some grammarians are trying to provide explanations for the distribution of -*De*.

2.3.3 Explanations for the Presence and Absence of -*De*

Based on the careful observations on the distribution of -*De*, the motivation for the presence or absence of -*De* is explained from various aspects. The nature of -*De* and the differences resulted from the presence and absence of -*De* are explained from syntactic, semantic, pragmatic, prosodic, and stylistic perspectives.

2.3.3.1 Syntactic Explanation

-*De* is a very important marker of the syntactic relation between the adverbial and the primary predicate. The presence/absence of -*De* after some adjectival adverbials will result in the change of the syntactic structure of the sentence, or make the sentence unacceptable. Liu (1983) states that *De* is indispensible after some AAs. If *-De* is removed, the structure of the sentence will be altered and the adjectival adverbial will become a predicate that is parallel with the verbal predicate. Once *-De* is absent and the sentence is uttered with a comma intonation, the original AA is not a part of the clause with regard to the accentuation and the information structure of the clause, and semantically, we get two clauses instead.

(13) a. Laoren wukenaihe -De hui jia qu le.
old man have no alternation De return home go Perf.
'The old man, who had no alternation, went home.'
b. Laoren wukenaihe (,) huijia qu le.
old man have no alternation return home go Perf.
'The old man had no alternation, and went home.'
(14) a. Li Si hen keqi -De yaoqingle Xiaoli.
p.n very courteous De invite Perf p.n
'Li Si courteously invited Xiaoli.'
b. Li Si hen keqi (,) yaoqing le Xiaoli.
p.n very courteous invite Perf p.n
'Li Si was very courteous and he invited Xiaoli.'

If *-De* in (13a) is absent, the adjectival adverbial will become a primary predicate and the sentence will become a verb-serial clause which can be decomposed into two clauses as in (13b). The adjective *keqi* 'courteous' in (14a) indicates the manner of the action *yaoqing* 'invite'; it means that 'the action of inviting is conducted in a courteous manner. In (14b), the adjective *keqi* is the primary predicate of the subject, expressing the property of the subject.

Xing (1996) also states that many adverbials are potential predicates. Once *-De* is absent, the adverbial will be promoted and become the primary predicate of the subject. The same adjective expresses the property or the state of the subject when it occurs as primary predicate, but modifies the event when it acts as adverbial.

2.3.3.2 Semantic Explanation
The presence/absence contrast of *-De* not only influences the syntactic

structure of a sentence, but also brings about semantic difference.

Liu (1983) suggests that the presence of -*De* is to emphasize the descriptive function of the adverbial. However, it is difficult to provide a definition for the descriptive function.

Zhang (1998: 301), based on iconicity theory, suggests that a modifier that denotes property which can be used to form a plausible conventional subset of the denotations of the head is closer to the head than a modifier that only describes but does not classify the denotation of the head. Consequently, if an adjectival adverbial is used to restrict and classify the relevant events denoted by the primary predicate, -*De* is not compulsory between the adverbial and the primary predicate; On the contrary, if an adjectival adverbial just describes the event denoted by the primary predicate, -*De* is necessary.

The "Distance-Marking Correspondence Rule" proposed by Lu (2004) expresses the similar idea. He suggests that the further a modifier is away from its head, the more an overt marker is needed to indicate the semantic relation between the modifier and the head.

(15) a. Xiaoming zai tushuguan renzhen (De) kan shu.
      p.n   at library careful de read book
      'Xiaoming read books dedicatedly in the library.'
  b. Xiaoming renzhen *(De) zai tushuguan kanshu.
      p.n   careful at library de read book
      'Xiaoming read books dedicatedly in the library.'

Lu (2004: 4)

In (15a), the adjective *renzhen* 'dedicated' is adjacent to the verb, so -*De* is optional, but in (15b), the location adverbial is inserted between *renzhen* and the verb, so -*De* is necessary.

According to the presence or absence of –*De*, Wang (2006) classifies adjectival adverbials into two groups: declarative AAs and descriptive AAs. The first class usually presents a fact, while the latter usually describes the state of the event. -*De* is absent after declarative AAs, but after descriptive AAs, -*De* is necessary.

(16) a. Li Si jianjue (De) fandui zhege jihua.

p.n resolute de oppose this plan.
'Li Si opposed this plan resolutely.'
b. Li Si jianjue *(De) yaoleyao tou.
p.n resolute de shake his head.
'Li Si shook his head resolutely.'

In (16a), the adjective *jianjue* 'resolute' expresses one's attitude in performing an action and it is used to classify the events denoted by the verb *fandui* 'oppose'. The adverbial and the verb are directly related and *-De* is optional. In (16b), the adjective *jianjue* 'resolute' is not a proper criterion to classify the events denoted by the verb *yao* 'shake', so the adjective is used to describe the situation in which the action is performed. The relation between the descriptive adverbial and the verb is not so close, so *-De* is necessary after the adjectival adverbial. Furthermore, he states that *-De* is optional after adverbials composed of event-related adjectives[①], whereas after object-related adjective adverbials, *-De* is usually necessary.

Xu (2003, 2011) proposes the principles of chunking and prominence, which is applicable in the analysis of both adnominal and adverbial modification, for he suggests that the two morphemes *-de* and *-De* should be unified (Xu 2004). The so-called chunks composed of adjectival adverbials and verbs are similar to the declarative AAs in Wang (2006). The function of highlighting the descriptive function of AAs is similar to the descriptive AAs in Liu (1983). Whether a modifier and the head can form a chunk depends on the relation between the adverbial and the verb. If the combination of the modifier and the head is considered to be a chunk, *-De* will be absent, but if the speaker intends to make the modifier prominent, *-De* can be used even if the whole modification phrase is a chunk. If the combination of the modifier and the head does not form a chunk, *-De* should be present.

2.3.3.3 Pragmatic and Prosodic influence

When *-De* is optional, the presence or absence of it will not result in structural and semantic ambiguity. Therefore, pragmatic factors will

---

[①] This classification is proposed by zhang Guoxian (2005).

influence whether-*De* appears or not. Tang(1979) states that in written Chinese, -*De* is usually present after disyllabic adjectival adverbial, and absent in oral.

Prosody is an important factor that influences the distribution of -*De* (Feng 1997; Xu 2003; Zheng 2005; Zhang 2006). Feng(1997) states that in Mandarin, two syllables constitute an independent disyllabic foot. A monosyllabic adjective and a monosyllabic verb will constitute a standard disyllabic foot, and the insertion of -*De* will destroy the foot. *kuai *(-De) pao* 'run fast', *wan *(-De) shui* 'sleep late'. Sometimes, the appearing of -*De* is decided by the rhythm of the sentence. When a multi-syllabic adjective modifies a monosyllabic verb, -*De* is often necessary to balance the rhythm: *renrenzhenzhen *(de) ting* 'listen carefully', *mantengteng *(-De) zou* 'walk slowly'.

It has been assumed that -*De* is the marker of adverbials, and the absence of -*De* is the omission of it. However, from the illustration in this part, it can be concluded that the absence or presence of -*De* will result in structural ambiguity or semantic difference. Whether -*De* appears or not is influenced by semantic, syntactic, pragmatic and prosodic factors.

In this work, -*De* will be analyzed in the framework of event semantics. We will analyze -*De* as the head of a depictive phrase. When -*De* is present, the relation between the modifier and the head is a kind of non-restrictive modification, whereas when -*De* is absent, the relation is a kind of restrictive modification provided that the modification relation is not destroyed by the absence of -*De*. Verbs denote events which have a number of properties. If an adjective happens to scale the value of certain property of the event, the adjective has the potential to form a restrictive modification with the verb. If not, the adjective can only modify the verb in a non-restrictive modification relation.

Restrictive modification is so called because the modifier "restricts" the denotation of the head they modify. By the same token, non-restrictive modification is probably so called because the modifiers fail to alter the denotation of the head --- they just provide additional information about an independently identifiable denotation. Whether a modifier is restrictive or not must depend on the actual extension of the modifier and of the head it modifies in a fixed situation. Therefore, restrictiveness is a context-sensitive property as illustrate in (16).

Whether AAs modify verbs in a restrictive or non-restrictive pattern is decided by the speaker's intention as well as whether the under adjective of the AA can scale the dimension of certain property of the event.

2.4 Reduplication of adjectives

As we can see, many under adjectives of AAs in the examples are in reduplicated forms. Adjectives in Mandarin are rich in morphological variations, and these morphological varieties are taken as a tangible classification criterion to classify adjectives. Zhu (1956) maintains a dichotomy of the adjectives: simple adjectives (SAs) and complex ones (CAs). His two criteria for such classification are: whether an adjective can be modified by the neutral degree intensifier *hen* 'very' and the reduplicated form of disyllabic adjectives are in AABB or ABAB pattern. Simple adjectives can be modified by the degree intensifier *hen* 'very', and disyllabic simple adjectives are reduplicated in AABB pattern, whereas complex adjectives cannot be modified by *hen* 'very', and disyllabic complex adjectives are reduplicated in ABAB pattern. This most influential adjective classification has been widely accepted among Chinese Grammarians.

(17) Simple adjectives (SAs):
　　including all the monosyllabic adjectives and most of the disyllabic ones:
　a. monosyllabic adjectives:
　　da 'big', *hong* 'red', *zang* 'dirty', *hao* 'good'
　b. disyllabic adjectives:
　　ganjing 'clean', *weida* 'great'

(18) Complex adjectives (CAs):
　　including all the derived forms and a few disyllabic adjectives:
　a. reduplicated forms:
　　A→AA　　　*xiaoxiaoer* 'really small'
　　AB→AABB　*ganganjingjing* 'really clean'

AB→A-li-AB   *hulihutu* 'muddled headed'
b. those with suffixes:
ABB   A + disyllabic suffixes: *chouhonghong* 'rampantly stinky'
A + trisyllabic suffixes: *huibuliuqiu* 'drab and grayish'
c. those with modifying prefix(the reduplicated pattern is ABAB):
bingliang 'ice cold',------*bingliangbinglaing*
tonghong 'very red' ------tonghongtonghong
d. phrases composed of degree adverb or adjective combinations:
henxiao 'very small'
yougaoyouda 'both tall and big'

Zhu (1956) states that all the members of SAs just express properties, whereas the members of CAs also express properties, but the property expressed by CA is related to the speaker's subjective evaluation or the concept of quantity. Monosyllabic adjectives are prototype members of SAs, and disyllabic adjectives are in the gradual process of assimilation towards CAs, so they share something in common with CAs. It is assumed that the morphological difference of adjectives is very important in deciding whether an adjective can occur as adverbial or not. According to Zhu (1982), similar dichotomy of adjectives is maintained, but under different terminologies: *xingzhi xingrongci* (property adjective) and *zhuangtai xingrongci* (state adjective). Besides the alternation of the terms, the forms of the adjectives also undergo some minor changes.

Shen (2011) doesn't think the criteria for classification are so indispensible, because some state adjectives combine with *hen* 'very' to strengthen depictive function, and the depictive function of state adjectives can also be further strengthened by a certain reduplication pattern (ABCC):

In a dynamic perspective, on one hand, state adjectives, whose depictive functions are faded away due to the high frequency of exposure in communication, tend to become property adjectives. On the other hand, the descriptive function of state adjectives are strengthened by a variety of methods, including increasing the number of syllables. These two counter processes are going on simultaneously in both archaic Chinese and Mandarin Chinese (Shi 2010, Shen 2011). As a result, Shen (2011) assumes that the function of reduplication or combination with *hen* 'very' is to strengthen the depictive function of adjectives, and can't be treated as the criteria to subcategorize adjectives.

Shen (2007, 2009) includes state adjectives as a subcategory of depictives, which is a hypernym term including all the complex forms derived from adjectives, nouns, and verbs. Shen (2011) assumes the number of syllables is a reliable and primary criterion to classify adjectives. Adjectives are first classified as monosyllabic adjectives and disyllabic adjectives. Monosyllabic adjectives are prototypical adjectives in Mandarin Chinese while all the non-monosyllabic adjectives have depictive function, strong or weak. The process of disyllabization of adjectives is a quasi-reduplication which makes adjectives depictives.

2.4.1 Restrictions on Reduplication of Adjectives

Not all simple adjectives have corresponding reduplicated forms. Many scholars are interested in finding out the factors that determine whether an adjective can be reduplicated or not (Tang 1988; Zhu 2003; Paul 2010; Liu 2013).

>(19) Restrictions on adjectival reduplication
>I Only gradable adjectives with a context-dependent standard are accessible to reduplication (Zhu 1956; Chao 1968; Lu et al 1980; Tang 1988; Zhu 2003; Liu 2013).
>II Adjectives denoting properties that can be perceived by human senses are more likely to have reduplicated forms (Tang 1988; Zhu 2003). It means the more concrete a property an adjective denotes, the easier it can be reduplicated.
>III Adjectives with commendatory meaning are more likely to have reduplicated form than those with derogatory meaning (Zhu 1956; Chao 1968).

However, the subject's intention or the speaker's subjectivity will permit the reduplicated forms of adjectives with derogatory meaning (Zhu 1956; Ding et. al. 1979; Lyu et al. 1980; Liu et al. 2004).
IV The coordinated disyllabic adjectives are more likely to be reduplicated (Tang 1988; Zhu 2003).

Adjectival adverbials usually express speakers' subjective observations of the event denoted by the primary predicate. Form these requirements on the reduplication of adjectives, we can notice that those adjectives can be reduplicated are more suitable to express speakers' subjective observation of an individual or an event, which is why adjectival adverbials are closely related to the reduplicated adjectives.

2.4.2 Consequences of Reduplication

Morphological difference certainly causes semantic variations. What differences does reduplication of adjectives cause? About the consequences of the reduplication of adjectives, scholars provide different explanations:

First, reduplication of adjective will alter the temporal feature of adjectives. It is commonly assumed that the reduplication of adjectives is closely related to the their aspectual features. According Zhu (1956, 1982), simple adjectives, which are renamed as property adjectives, denote permanent properties while complex adjectives, which are renamed as state adjectives, express transient states. Alexiadou (2010) also suggests that the function of reduplication of adjective is similar to an outer Aspect, which will result in the aspectual shift of the adjective. Liu (2013) states that reduplicated adjectives denote a perceptible state derived from the property denoted by the corresponding simple adjectives. This means the reduplication of adjective alters the temporal feature: from denoting permanent property by simple adjectives to denoting transitory state by complex adjectives.

Second, the reduplication of adjective can express the speakers' subjectivity. According to Zhu (1956), reduplicated adjectives introduce the speaker's subjective evaluation of the property expressed by the adjective rather than solely refer to the property. When the reduplicated adjectives appear at different syntactic positions, they convey different influence on the degree they denote, to intensify or weaken. Zhu (2003) points out that the degree denoted by the reduplicated adjectives is just right and lives up to the speaker's expectation. Liu (2013) states that the main function of reduplication is to denote states and the 'degree' conveyed by reduplicated adjective is just the by-product of the alternation from denoting property to denoting states.

Third, reduplicated adjective will make description more vivid. According to Chao (1968), Lyu et al. (1980), the reduplicated forms of adjectives are the life-like or vivid forms. Shen (2011) points out that the function of reduplication or combination with *hen* 'very' is to strengthen the depictive function of adjectives.

Forth, reduplicated adjectives describe a narrower scope of value relating to certain property. An adjective is relevant to a single property and scale the value of certain dimension relevant to the property. The phenomenon that reduplication of adjectives influences the scope that an adjective can scale has been studied intensively (Zhu 1956; Shen 1995; Li 1996; Zhang 2000). According to Shen (1995), Zhang (2000), a simple adjective expresses an extensive scope of the value of a certain dimension, whereas the scope expressed by reduplicated adjective is much narrower or even focuses on a very concrete point. Shen (1995) states that simple adjectives denote an unbounded scale, while reduplicated adjectives express a bounded scale.

Fifth, under certain circumstance, reduplicated adjectives can activate the agentivity of the subject. Zhu (2003) points out that when occurring as predicates, the reduplicated adjectives can express the agentivity of the subject. The agentivity is expressed clearer especially when the subject is in the second person or the sentence expresses an imperative mood.

2.4.3 Latest Research on Reduplication of Adjective

Sui (2014) studies the reduplicated adjectives within the framework of Generative Grammar, and she argues that the reduplication of adjectives takes place in L-syntax. She suggests that in L-syntax, adjectives have a nominal root N. When the reduplication mechanism applies, the nominal root N copies itself to form an NN complex. Then the complex merges with a functional Pred, which houses -*de*. The NN complex moves and adjoins to-*de*, forming NN-*de*. Before the merging of NN complex with the functional -*de*, NN complex is not a finished product, so it is not ready for syntactic computation. Take the reduplicated adjective *cuicui-de* 'crispy' as an example, and the derivation process of it is illustrated in (20):

(20) The syntactic structure of reduplicated adjectives:

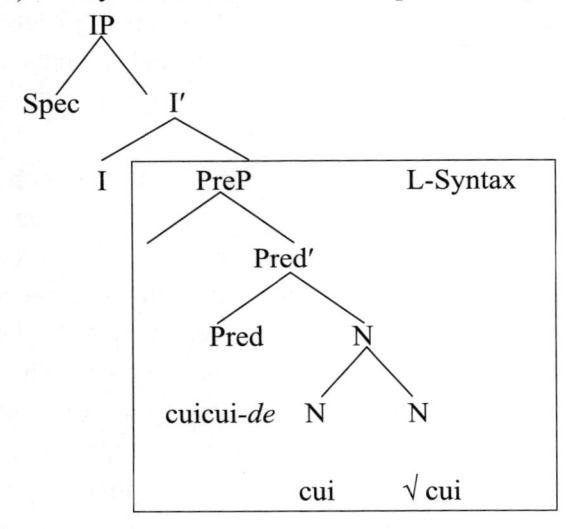

```
                IP
               /  \
           Spec    I'
                  /  \
                 I    PreP              L-Syntax
                     /    \
                   Pred'
                  /    \
                Pred     N
                         / \
              cuicui-de N   N

                        cui  √cui
```

Adapted from Sui (2014: 134)

Different from the syntactic structure of simple adjectives, the self-copied NN complex repels the projection of DegP above the PreP in the structure of the reduplicated adjective. This theory presents a dynamic and incremental process of the formation of the reduplicated adjectives from lexicon to the surface form of the adjective, and clearly explains the reason why the neutral degree adverb *hen* 'very' is repelled by the reduplicated adjectives and why -*de* is an indispensible part of the reduplicated adjectives. Her idea in analyzing the reduplicated adjectives and clitic -*de* is also applicable in the analysis of complex adjectives in other patterns.

Reduplication is highly relevant to whether an adjective can occur as AA or not. As we have reviewed, the motivations of reduplication are various, which one is the most prominent in permitting an adjective which originally cannot enter syntactic position of adverbial to occur as AA?

According to Zhu (1956, 1982) and Alexiadou (2010), reduplication changes the temporal features of the adjective. Therefore, the temporal feature of adjectives and that of verbs are in agreement. Li and Liu (2014) suggests that the stronger subjectivity and the relatively definite scope denoted by the reduplicated adjectives is the reason to permit AAs.

From the restrictions of reduplication of adjectives we notice that most of these adjectives conforming to the requirements for reduplication are very likely to occur as adverbials, because the adjectival adverbials are based on the speaker's perspective and evaluation of the property they can observe. That is one of the reasons why there are so many reduplicated adjectives occur as adverbials.

Up to now, the classification of AAs and the components of sentences with AAs have been discussed respectively. However, these researches relevant to AAs were not systematic enough, Zheng (2000) is a milestone of the research on adjectival adverbials, which represents the achievements of researches conduced in the framework of Chinese traditional descriptive grammar approach, and sets a new beginning for further research. In the following section, the researches in Zheng (2000) will be introduced briefly.

2.5 Researches on AAs in Zheng (2000)

It has been mentioned several times in this chapter that Zheng (2000), a milestone of the research on adjectival adverbials, is of great value for the further research on AAs. It has been the only monograph on adjectival adverbials in Mandarin. In this monograph, he advances the Relation Theory on the basis of Clause Center Theory. Relation is defined as a complex including the syntactic and semantic relationship between the adjectival adverbials and certain constituents of the main clause, such as the subject, object and the primary predicate. According to the relation, he classifies AAs into four categories:

> (21) Classification of AAs in Zheng (2000)
> a. AAs related to subject and predicate: *chidaidai* 'oafish'
> b. AAs related to object and predicate: *dada* 'big'
> c. AAs related to subject, object and predicate: *piaopiaoliangliang* 'beautiful'
> d. AAs related to predicate: *feikuai* 'rapid'

Based on such classification, he describes the features of each kind of AAs in great details. His contributions to the researches on AAs are listed as follows:

First, he emphasizes the relation between AAs and predicates, which accurately reflected the syntactic statues of AAs. It is indicated in his classification that all adjectival adverbials are at least related to the predicate. Sometimes, such relation between the AA and the predicate is a kind of pure syntactic relation, such as the relation between AA and predicate in (21a), and sometimes, the AA is semantically as well as syntactically related to predicate, such as the relation between AA and predicate in (21b). It is also possible for AAs to have relation with subject or object and such relation is a kind of potential but not necessary relation.

Second, he classifies AAs according to the temporal features, which is a very perspicacious observation. Zheng (2000: 23) classifies the states denoted by adjectival adverbials into two groups: primordial states and transitory states. Primordial states refer to the properties or states related to a participant of the matrix predicate before the happening of the event denoted by the matrix predicate as in (22a,b).

> (22) a. Houzi lingmin De tiao shang shu ya.
> monkey swift De jump up tree branch
> 'When the monkey jumped up to the branch, it was swift'

b. Zhubajie① benzhuo De taodong zhe shuang tui.
p.n   clumsy De jump Asp pair leg
'When Zhuabajie was jumping, he was clumsy.'

The transitory states are closely related to the event denoted by the primary predicate, and transitory states usually express the states in which a participant of the matrix verb is during or after the happening of the event denoted by the matrix predicate. Transitory states are further classified into accompanying states and anticipated states. The identification of these different states is closely dependent on some markers in the sentences.

(23) a. Ni yao de fancai mashang jiu xiangpenpen De zuohao.
you order meal soon will fregrent De get ready
'What you ordered will soon be ready and it will be goluptious.'
b. Nimen keyi gaogaoxingxing De huijia qu le.
you may happy happy De return home go Perf
'You will go home happy. '

Zheng classify the AAs in (23a,b) as anticipated states, because the markers such as *keyi* 'may', *mashang* 'soon', indicate that the state denoted by the adjectives have not appeared when the speaker uttered the sentences.

Third, he studies the relation between temporal features of AAs and syntactic and semantic constrains on the alternation between AAs and adnominal modifiers, as well as the alternation between AAs and *buyu*. Zheng argues that the primordial states are similar to the properties or states denoted by the adnominal adjectives, and the adjectives adverbials denote primordial states can alter with adnominal adjective modifiers. The alternation between AAs and *buyu* is affected by the morphological features and temporal features of the adjectives as well as the semantic of

---

① One of the chief characters in "Pilgrimage To The West", and it is usually described as clumsy and gluttonous.

the verb.

He points out that neglecting the function of verbs is the limitation of the research on AAs with the theory of semantic orientation analysis. In his research, the temporal feature of adjectives, the relation between AAs and primary predicates, constrains on the alternation between AAs and adnominal modifiers and AAs and *buyu* are all taken into consideration, which has greatly advanced the researches on AAs. The observation of the language facts and classification of AAs in Zheng (2000) have laid solid foundation for future research. Researches on the AAs get into a new stage with Zheng (2000) as the turning point.

2.6 Syntactic Research on AAs

After Zheng (2000), the researches on AAs are getting more and more diversified and specified. Scholars attempt to address this issue from different aspects with different theoretical assumptions, and more and more diversified theoretical frameworks are introduced to analyze adjective adverbials (Wang and Gu 2000; Lu 2003; Zhang 2005; He 2006/2010/2012; Tao 2009; Liu and Li 2011; Wang 2012; Xiong 2013; Cong 2013; Li 2014; Yang 2014; Su and Yang 2014).

Transformational-generative proposals assume an underlying structure, from which the surface structure is derived through various syntactic operations. The syntactic analysis of AAs in Mandarin mainly focuses on the relation between semantic orientations and different syntactic positions. Subject-oriented AAs are treated as adjunct phrases merged at the VP level, and some object-oriented AAs are analyzed as complement merged to the V layer (Liu and Li 2011; Xiong 2013)

Wang and Gu(2000) based on "IP splitting Hypothesis" proposed in Chomsky(1995), argues that object-oriented adverbials attach to AgroP (o means object) while subject-oriented adverbials attach to AgrsP (s means subject), and such difference in syntactic positions corresponds to the difference between object-oriented adverbials and subject-oriented adverbials.

Tao (2009) concludes that the participant-oriented adjective adverbials are subject to the following three syntactic constrains:

(24) Three syntactic rules constraining the semantic orientation of AAs
    I Participant-oriented AA can only semantically related to the constituent in front of it.
    II No other participant is permitted between the participant-oriented AA and its controller[①].
    III The controller of participant-oriented AAs should be overt.

Xiong (2013) comments that such constrains are applicable for subject-oriented adjectival adverbials, but, as for some object-oriented adverbials, her constrains do not work efficiently, so she has to resort to pragmatic factors to remedy the limitation of her explanation.

Based on VP-shell theory, Liu and Li (2011) suggests a hypothesis that some object-oriented adjective adverbials originate as the complement of the verb; then merge with the verb to form a complex verb and move up and merge with the causative light verb.

Xiong (2013) suggests that the object-oriented adjectival adverbials observe the control theory. The difference between resultative and depictive object-oriented adverbials is due to their different syntactic positions: resultative AA originates as the complement of the VP while depictive AA as the adjunct of the VP. Out of different motivations, they move to and merge with different functional categories, such as: Bec, Cau, Ex. This analysis explains the difference between two subcategories of object-oriented adverbials and also proves that such adverbials are not moved attributes. However, as Yang (2014) points out: Xiong (2013) sets too many functional categories which are ad hoc stipulations and against the economy principle of minimalist program.

Yang (2014) assumes that the original position of the adjectival adverbial is after the object, and these two elements constitute a complement clause. There is a null predicate (equals to be/become/feel) which connects the object and the adjective. This complement can be moved to the position between subject and verb, because manner adverbial marker *-De* can indicate the identity of the adjective.

[①] Controller refers to the participant that an AA is semantically related to.

A close examination of the above analysis of the adjectival adverbials exhibits the tenets of the transformational-generative grammar. The syntactic approach tends to refer to the paraphrase relation between two syntactic structures so long as they are truth-conditionally synonymous, and the subtle differences in meaning are overlooked. All these proposals assume that there is an original position for the adjective. Although the motivation of movement is different, the final position of the adjective is the result of movement and merging. At the same time, these scholars have realized that the meaning of adverbial is different from that of attribute, and they try to keep the meaning unchanged in the transformational process. However, based the "one form, one meaning" principle (Bolinger 1968; Haiman 1985; Wierabicka 1988), any change in form will result in the corresponding change in meaning. Different syntactic position will result in the meaning variation. As for the sentences with AAs, there is no exception.

The syntactic researches mainly focus on the syntactic features of object-oriented AAs, whereas the semantic research is relevantly less focused on. Object-oriented AAs, as a subcategory of AAs, have some specific features, so the researches on object-oriented AAs will reveal some general features of AAs. However, only through the comparison with other kinds of AAs, can we have an overall understanding of AAs.

2.7 Semantic Research on AAs

Semantic researches on AAs are mainly conducted in the framework of semantic orientation analysis. Semantic orientation analysis theory is widely and efficiently applied in the analyses of unnatural correlations between lexical terms. Lu and Shen (2004: 259-260) states that the formation of this theory is greatly influenced by the case grammar, valence grammar and argument structure theory. They point out that Chinese is a kind of typical isolating language, so parataxis is a dominant method to represent syntactic and semantic relationship in Chinese, for morphological inflections are too undeveloped to mark the semantic relationship clearly between constituents. Furthermore, the word order in Chinese is relatively flexible, so syntactic and semantic relations between constituents are often inconsistent. Consequently, semantic orientation analysis is badly needed to clarify the complex semantic relation.

2.7.1 Definition of Semantic Orientation

Semantic orientation analysis is widely applied; however, there is not a uniform definition for semantic orientation. Lu Yingshun (1995) suggests that semantic orientation is the possibility for a certain constituent to match semantically with other constituent(s). Shen Kaimu (1996) defines semantic orientation as the ability of certain constituent to pick out the meaning of other constituents as focus, and the focus is the semantic orientation of that constituent. Lu Jianming(1999) states that the semantic orientation is the semantic relevance between a certain constituent and other constituent. Take the sentences in (25) to exemplify the application of semantic orientation analysis:

(25) a. Ji   bu chi le.
       chick not eat Perf
       'The chicken does not eat food.'
       'We don't eat chicken any longer.'
    b. Xiaoming zhi xinhuan Li Si.
       p.n   only like p.n
       'Xiaoming only likes Li Si.'

(25a) is ambiguous, and the ambiguity is resulted from the thematic roles related to the verb. Semantic orientation analysis is very useful in disambiguation. Furthermore, semantic orientation analysis is also applied to identify the focus that is related to the quantifier. In (25b), the quantifier *zhi* 'only' is focus-sensitive, and it is semantically related to either the verb or the object.

From these definitions and examples in (25), we can find that this theory is not only applied in the analysis of AAs, but also applied in analyzing the relation between verbs and arguments; between *buyu* and its related constituent; between quantifier such as *quan* 'all', focus sensitive marker *zhi* 'only' and *jiu* 'just' and their relevant constituents; and even the relation between the pronoun and its antecedent is also included as the target of semantic orientation analysis.

2.7.2 The Shortcomings of Semantic Orientation Analysis

Although the theory of semantic orientation analysis is widely applied in analyzing various ambiguous relations between constituents, the identification of semantic orientation is mainly based on native speaker's intuition and description, and the scope of research of the theory is overly extensive. Generally speaking, semantic orientation is just a fairly loose and pre-theoretic concept although it is effective in analyzing abnormal semantic issues in Chinese (Chen 1999; Zhao 2008; Wang 2012).

First, semantic orientation and semantic relatedness is not distinguished. Semantic orientation is just one particular case of semantic relatedness (Valera 1996). Rothstein (2001, 2004) also states that semantic orientation is a kind of predicate relation, which is different from semantic relatedness. However, in the semantic orientation analysis in Mandarin, the semantic relation between the constituent and its controller is not uniform, the verb-argument relation, the predication relation, the co-referential relation, and the appositive relation are all exemplified as the semantic relevance.

Second, the identification of semantic orientation is mainly through the method of constituent substitution, structural transformations, structure decomposition, the movement of the constituents, and comparison. All such operation will cause the meaning variation.

Third, whether an adjectival adverbial can have more than one orientation is a controversial issue. Lu (1999) states that an AA is only semantically related to one constituent, while Zheng (2000) suggests that multi-semantic orientation is possible under proper circumstances.

Generally speaking, this theory mainly focuses on the description of the abnormal semantic relation between constituents. With the introduction of formal semantics into this theory, the explanatory power of this theory will be greatly improved.

2.7.3 Development of the Study on Semantic Orientation

In order to improve the semantic orientation research in Chinese, some new semantic theories are introduced.

Wu Ping (2009) analyzes some Chinese constructions from the event semantics perspective. Although he does not focus on semantic orientation analysis, his research provides valuable reference for this topic. Take the following sentence as an example to illustrate the ambiguity resulted from different semantic orientations between verbs and arguments:

(26) a. Liuqiang zhui   DE Wangwei zhi   chuanqi.
       p.n   chase DE p.n   continuously pant
       'Wangwei panted because Liuqiang chased him.'

There are two verbal predicates and two participants in this sentence. Different combinations between these predicates and participants will result in four different interpretations. Wu (2009) presents these four interpretations in the framework of neo-Davidsonian approach:

(27) a. $\exists e[\exists e_1[\exists e_2[e=^S(e_1 \cup e_2) \wedge zhui\ (e_1) \wedge Agt(e_1)=Liuqiang\ \wedge$
       Pant (e_2)
       $\wedge continuously(e_2)\ \wedge Agt(e_2)=Wangwei\ \wedge\ Cause\ (e_1, e_2)]]]$
   b. $\exists e[\exists e_1[\exists e_2[e=^S(e_1 \cup e_2) \wedge\ zhui\ (e_1) \wedge Agt(e_1)=Liuqiang\ \wedge$
       Pant (e_2)
       $\wedge continuously(e_2) \wedge Agt(e_2)=Wangwei$
       $\wedge\ TPCONNECT(Cul(e_1),\ e_2,\ Wangwei)]]]$
   c. $\exists e[\exists e_1[\exists e_2[e=^S(e_1 \cup e_2)\ \wedge\ Cause(e_1) \wedge Causer\ (e_1)=$
       Liuqiang
       $\wedge Th(e_1) = Wangwei \wedge chase\text{-}\ Pant\ (e_2)\ \wedge continuously(e_2)$
       $\wedge Agt(e_2)=Wangwei\ \wedge TPCONNECT(Cul(e1),\ e_2,$
       Wangwei)]]]
   d. $\exists e[\exists e_1[\exists e_2[e=^S(e_1 \cup e_2) \wedge\ zhui\ (e_1) \wedge Agt(e_1)=Liuqiang$
       $\wedge Th(e_1) = Wangwei \wedge\ Pant\ (e_2)\ \wedge continuously(e_2)$
       $\wedge Agt(e_2)=Liuqiang\ \wedge\ TPCONNECT(Cul(e1),\ e_2,$

Liuqiang)]]]

(Wu 2009: 111-112)

The semantic structure variations and the differences in semantic orientations of these interpretations are clearly and accurately indicated in these four logic forms in (27).

Wang (2012) analyzes the semantic orientation of adjective adverbials within the framework of context-free semantics. For any well-formulated formulas, the set of syntactic structures and that of semantic structures are isomorphic to each other, so she assumes that the issue of semantic orientation is transformed into searching for the correct path of grammatical combination which generates both the desired form and meaning of the concerned sentences.

From her analysis, we can find that setting the proper type for the adjectival adverbial indeed constrains the path of grammatical combination and results in the proper interpretation. However, where does the difference in type exist? In Wang (2012), the difference is a kind of pre-existence, so the burden of lexicon is greatly increased. Although she claims a dynamic perspective in her analysis, it is actually a kind of backward induction. However, her study of the semantic orientation of adverbials in a perspective of logical grammar indicates that it is very promising to study AAs in formal semantics.

With the aids of formal semantics, the semantic orientation is getting obvious and accurate, instead of just depending on description and native speaker's intuition. The introduction of formal semantics will certainly shed new lights on the semantic orientation analysis theory. Besides the syntactic and the semantic researches on AAs, some scholars study AAs from the pragmatic or cognitive perspectives.

Cong (2013) analyzes adjectival adverbial as mismatched adverbial modifiers and studies AAs under the framework of grammatical metaphor. He states that mismatched adverbials are most frequently used in literary writing, and the function of such mismatched modification is to make AA the focus and the most salient part of the clause in order to enhance the appraisal meaning and subjectivity of the clause. Li & Liu (2014) study AAs in the framework of Langacher's synchronic model of subjectivity, and claim that the states expressed by adjectival adverbials are subjective in that they designate prominent qualities concomitant with primary predicate and these states are bounded. The adverbial position is a more prominent cognitive position for speaker; therefore, adjective adverbials are more subjective than adjectives which appear at other positions.

Almost every proposition can be expressed in various roughly synonymous ways without altering the truth condition. Speakers, however, do not choose randomly from these options. As Birner and Ward (1998: 1) claim, "Speakers exploit their structural options to specific pragmatic ends." Zhang (2005) suggests that sometimes speakers destroy the unmarked relevance between constituents on purpose to form syntactic/semantic mismatch in order to convey speakers' specific communicational intension. Li (2007) emphasize that the attributive modifier and adverbial modifiers are more or less transformational, but they are not identical. The pragmatic motivation of using adjective as adverbial is to make the adjective prominent as a focus.

Higginbotham (1985) argues that modifiers have a thematic grid with an empty argument slot, which is subordinated to the thematic grid of the lexical category they modify and borrows arguments from it. The identification of the semantic orientation of the AAs is a process through which a predicational adverbial selects its subject from the possibilities provided by the primary predicate. When adjectives occur as adverbials, due to the semantic feature of adjectives, AAs are certainly different from other kind of adverbials. The semantic orientation of AAs is not a kind of loose semantic relevance. The semantic type of adjective is $<e, t>$, so it must be saturated by a constituent of type $<e>$. The semantic orientation of AA is the shared element between the AA and the primary predicate. In the event semantic perspective, the semantic orientation of an AA is just the shared element of two events denoted by these two predicates.

In this work, we focuses on the semantic features and semantic orientation of adjectival adverbials which is analyzed as a kind of predicate relation. The syntactic/semantic mismatch of AAs will be studied with reference to the event semantics and the predicate theory proposed by Rothstein (2001).

2.8 Summary

This chapter mainly sketches the researches relevant to adjectival adverbials in Mandarin. From this brief literature review, we can find that study on every subtopic related to AAs has produced a lot of elaborate descriptions as well as some theoretical generalizations. AAs have been studied intensively in traditional methods. All these fruitful researches will be helpful in exploring the semantic nature of AAs. The initial stage of identifying the status of AAs set a right starting point for the research on AAs; the classifications and statistical study on the various kinds of AAs provide a macro perspective of AAs; the study on distribution and functions of the structural subordinator *-De* as well as the study on the morphological variations of adjectives have established solid foundation for the formal analysis of AAs. Zheng (2000) presents one of the most overall and detailed researches on AAs with the traditional methodology in Chinese grammar reaserch. After that, researches are getting more and more specialized, mainly focusing on certain kind of AAs. These latest researches on AAs conducted within various theoretical frameworks have been deepening our understanding of the nature of adjectival adverbials from syntactic, semantic, cognitive and pragmatic aspects.

Generally speaking, due to the restrictions of theoretical methodology, most of the existing researches on AAs are based on the static analysing, and such static analyses are not adequate to provide satisfying answers to all these questions put forth in chapter 1. During the 15 years after Zheng (2000) conducted the overall research on AA, linguistic theory has been developing rapidly, so it is high time to reconsider AAs in Mandarin.

The under adjectives occurring as adverbials from lexicon to receiving the adverbial interpretation in sentences is an integrated process. In this process, semantically underspecified adjectives are getting saturated incrementally and finally the temporal features and semantic orientation of the under adjective are decided. The semantic of the adjectives per se, the morphological variation, the structural subordinator *-De*, the aspectual feature and the semantics of the primary predicate all contribute to the interpretation of the adjectival adverbials. How to integrate all these factors to analyze AA compositionally and dynamically is the main task in this work. Based on the previous analyses, contributions will probably be made to the researches on AAs in the following three aspects.

First, AAs will be studied from the perspective of formal semantic. A natural language like Chinese can be considered as an abstract system analogous to formal language of logic or mathematics. Both natural and formal languages are compositional in the sense that the meaning of any syntactically well-formed expressions is uniquely determined by the meaning of its constituent parts, as well as the operations that are used to combine these constituents together. These similarities between natural language and formal languages make it possible to analyze AAs with precise and well-understood tools from formal language theory. In addition, the isomorphism and interface between syntactic and semantic components can be reflected precisely. As is indicated in § 2.7.3, the formal semantic method will greatly improve the accuracy and efficiency of semantic orientation analysis.

Second, the research in this work treats the process of under adjective form lexicon to receiving the adverbial interpretation in the sentence as an integrated process. In this process, all these factors such as the semantic of the adjectives per se, the morphological variation of adjective, the structural subordinator *-De*, the aspectual feature and the semantics of the primary predicate, will be taken into consideration. Scholars have long realized that the analyses of AAs should not be conducted independently on AAs per se, but to take the relation between AA and the verb into consideration (Zheng 2000). In the syntax-semantics interface, the semantic derivations is superimpose on top of syntactic derivations. Each terminal node is labeled with a logical term that indicates the lexical semantics of the item and functional application is the motivation for the progressing of the derivation. In the derivation process, the semantic of the adjective is getting saturated.

Third, the research on AAs in this work will take nutrients from the research on secondary predicate and predicational adverbs in English, but at the same time, the special properties of AAs in Mandarin will not be neglected. Furthermore, the fruitful researches on adnominal modification will also shed light on the research of adverbial modification.

Chapter Three

Event Semantics and Aspectual Feature of Predicates

This chapter focuses on the theoretical framework that will be employed to analyze AAs, as well as the aspectual features of predicates. The organization of this chapter is as follows. Section 3.1 mainly focuses on modification relation. In this section, the attributive modification and adverbial modification are compared to explore the feasibility of applying the intersective pattern in the analysis of adverbial modification. In Section 3.2, Davidsonian and neo-Davidsonian approaches are sketched and compared briefly. Section 3.3 focuses on the aspectual classifications of eventuality: including Vendlerian four-way classification and the ILP/SLP distinction proposed by Carlson. In Section 3.4, the ontological properties of eventuality are made clearer and then the main elements of an event are introduced. In Section 3.5, the notion of coercion is introduced to explain the shift between different eventuality types. The compositionality and context-sensitivity of aspectual features of predicates are represented in the frame work of event semantics. Section 3.6 introduces the further development of event semantics: the theory of predication suggested by Rothstein (2001, 2004), and the FEO Calculus proposed by Ernst (2002). A summary is given in Section 3.6 to highlight the theoretical advantages of event semantics in presenting the compositionality and context-sensitivity of natural language.

3.1 Modification Relation

'Modification' and 'modifier' are terms we routinely use, but it is not easy to give a generally-accepted formally explicit theoretical definition. 'Modification' is only a cover term for a motley assortment of constructions and facts which may, in various combinations, have some features in common. 'Modifier' is simply a term for linguistic expressions (McNally to appear). A modifier can be any expression that maps a type to the same type: that is anything whose denotation is type <τ, τ>, where τ is a type (Marcin Morzycki, to appear). In Mandarin, the function of adjectives is multiple, but the main function of an adjective is to occur as a modifier, no matter it is an attributive or a predicate. An adverb is almost always a modifier, for the only function of adverb is to serve as adverbial. Adjectival adverbials are the adverbials that are composed of adjectives, so it looks like that AAs are hybrids of adjectives and adverbs. In the following sections, the modifications involve in adjectives and adverbs will be introduced respectively.

3.1.1 Combining Adjectives with Nouns

The relation between an adjective and a noun is not always the same. Siegel (1976) divides adjectives into two classes in her theory. The first class modifies nouns without taking the meaning of the noun into consideration. Such adjectives modify their targets in the intersective mode. In this mode, both the adjective and the target being modified denote a set with certain property, and the elements in these two sets can be individual, event, or anything, then the elements in the intersective set of these two sets are the denotations of the phrase composed of the adjective and the noun. One such case is in (1), in which both the adjective and the noun result in entailments:

(1) a. Mo Yan shi zhongguo-de zuojia.
     p.n   is a Chinese writer
     'Mo Yan is a Chinese writer.'
  b. Mo Yan shi zhongguoren,
     'Mo Yan is Chinese.'

a entails b
c. Mo Yan shi zuojia.
   'Mo Yan is a writer.'
a entails c

In (1a), adjective *zhongguo-de* 'Chinese' denotes a set of all elements that have the feature of being *zhongguo-de* 'Chinese', and *zuojia* 'writer' denotes a set of writers. Mo Yan belongs to the two sets simultaneously, which means that Mo Yan is an element of the intersection of these two sets. The intersection of two sets can be represented as in (2) and it can also be rewritten as conjunctive interpretation like (3):

(2) ⟦zhongguo zuojia⟧ = ⟦zhongguode⟧ ∩ ⟦zuojia⟧
(3) ⟦zhongguo zuojia⟧=λx. ⟦zhongguode⟧ (x)∧ ⟦zuojia⟧ (x)

Heim and Kratzer (1998) interprete such modification mode with the principle of Predicate Modification:

(4) Predication Modification
   If a branching node α has its daughter β and γ, and ⟦β⟧ and ⟦γ⟧ are both of type <e, t>, then ⟦a⟧ =λx. ⟦β⟧ (x)∧ ⟦γ⟧(x).

In terms of set theory, (4) can be rewritten as (5):

(5) If a branching node α has its daughter β and γ, and ⟦β⟧ and ⟦γ⟧ are both sets of individuals, then ⟦a⟧ = ⟦β⟧ ∩ ⟦γ⟧.

When an adjective combines intersectively with a noun, the adjective will keep the truth condition unchanged no matter what the noun denotes. That means no matter what the noun in (6b) is, as long as it denotes individuals, (6c) is true automatically.

(6) a. Mo Yan is a Chinese writer.
    b. Mo Yan is a celebrity.
    c. Mo Yan is a Chinese celebrity.

From (6a), it can be inferred that MoYan is a member of the set 〚zhongguo-de〛, (6b) indicates that he is also a member of the set of 〚celebrity〛, then, naturally, he is a member of the intersection of these two sets as indicated in (6c).

However, there are some adjectives do not modify in this manner, for example *an excellent student*, is not necessarily *an excellent cook*, maybe he/she is. Here we can't simply treat *excellent* as a set of things; we should get to know what kind of nouns is modified by *excellent*. One such case is in (7):

(7) a. Li Si is a good student.
  b. Li Si is a cook.
  =/=>Li Si is a good cook.

Even if (7a) and (7b) are both true, we still can't get 'Li Si is a good cook' automatically. That means adjectives like *good, excellent* can't not be interpreted intersectively. Although intersective interpretation is not available for these adjectives like *good* and *excellent*, the denotation of such combination is still a subset of the denotation of the noun:

(8) a. 〚excellent student〛 ⊆ 〚student〛
  b. 〚good cook〛 ⊆ 〚cook〛

Recently, some scholars attempt to interpret part of subsective adjectives in the pattern of intersective pattern. For example, Partee (2003, 2007, 2009) mentions Kamp's (1975) observation that apparently subsective adjectives like *tall* or *big* (tall/big for a boy =/= tall/big for a basketball player) may be considered intersectively after all, even though they are vague and context dependent. The reason is that we get the same effect even we keep the noun constant and change other aspects of the context.

There are still some other ways in which adjectives combine with nouns, such as non-subsective adjectives(former, alleged) and privative adjectives(fake, artificial). In this study, we mainly focus on intersective and subsective adjectives. It is indicated from the analyses of intersective adjectives that the modification can be represented on a conjunction-based semantics.

Adjectives are interesting and there are a lot of semanticists contribute their wisdom into the researches on adjectives. By contrast, adverbs constitute a difficult semantic territory, but they haven't been able to attract the same attention as adjectives do.

3.1.2 Adverbial Modification

Adverbials are a notoriously heterogeneous set, and the question of how adverbials are combined with the targets they modify constitutes a long-standing puzzle. In this section, we mainly focus on the analysis of typical VP-oriented adverbials.

It has been stated in previous section that both adjectives and adverbs are modifiers, and many adjectives can be analyzed intersectively. (9) will be taken as an example to test whether the same pattern is applicable in the analysis of VP-oriented adverbials:

(9) a. ⟦*kuaikuai –De xie zuoye*⟧ .
fast fast De write homework
=*λx. ⟦*kuaikuai-De*⟧ (x)∧ ⟦*xie zuoye*⟧ (x).
b. ⟦Xiaoming *kuaikuai –De xie zuoye* ⟧ .
p.n   fast fast De write homework
=* ⟦*kuaikuai-De*⟧(Xiaoming)∧⟦*xie zuoye*⟧(Xiaoming).

It is indicated that if the intersective pattern is applied in the analysis of VP-oriented adverbial, the resulted logic form will be against speaker's intuition, for the logic form requires *Xiaoming* intead of *xie zuoye* to be *kuaikuai-de*. The analysis in (9) clearly shows that the VP-oriented adverbial modification is different from attributive modification.

However, as far as the entailment relation is concerned, VP-oriented adverbial and attributive share a lot in common:

(10) a. Mo Yan shi zhuming -de zhongguo zuojia.
p.n is well-known de Chinese writer
'Mo Yan is a well-known Chinese writer.'
b. Mo Yan shi zhuming -de zuojia.

       p.n is well-known de writer
       'Mo Yan is a well-known writer.'
    c. Mo Yan shi zhongguo zuojia.
       p.n is Chinese writer
       'Mo Yan is a Chinese writer.'
    d. Mo Yan shi zuojia.
       p.n is writer
       'Mo Yan is a writer.'
(11) a. Xiaoming zaozao –De kuaikuai –De xie le zuoye.
       p.n   early De fast   De write Perf homework
       'Xiaoming finished his homework fast early'
    b. Xiaoming kuaikuai –De xie le zuoye.
       p.n   fast   De write Perf homework
       'Xiaoming finished his homework fast'
    c. Xiaoming zaozao –De xie le zuoye.
       p.n   early De write Perf homework
       'Xiaoming finished his homework early'
    d. Xiaoming xie le zuoye.
       p.n   write Perf homework
       'Xiaoming finished his homework'

All the sentences in (10) and (11) give rise to the Diamond Entailment Pattern illustrated in (12):

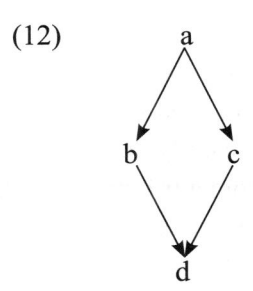

(12)
```
        a
       / \
      b   c
       \ /
        d
```

It seems that the analysis of VP-oriented adverbial is a contradiction: on one hand, the intersective pattern is not applicable; on the other hand, they present the same entailment pattern as adjectives.

An innovative solution to all this emerges from Davidson (1967).

He shows that in fact, VP-oriented adverbials and many other adverbials could in fact be analyzed intersectively. The great innovation of his theory is that the compositionality principle is still adhered to, but with the introducing of a new ontology. His theory is strikingly elegant and simple, for it perfectly parallels the denotation of the adjective.

In the following part, the Davidsonian way of analyzing adverbials and its further development will be introduced.

3.2 Event Semantics

Davidson (1967) introduces an underlying event argument into the logical form of action sentences. From then on, this underlying event argument as an ontology has been taking on an important role in linguistic theorizing.

Before the introduction of the underlying event argument, the intransitive verb *to dance* in (13a) and the transitive one *to butter* in (14a) would be represented in first-order predicate logic as (13b) and (14b).

(13) a. Mary dances
b. DANCE (mary).
(14) a. John buttered the toast
b. BUTTER (john, the toast)

After introducing adverbial modifiers, the logic formulae of sentences in (15) will look like those in (16) respectively:

(15) a. John buttered the toast.
b. John buttered the toast in the bathroom.
c. John buttered the toast in the bathroom with a knife.
d. John buttered the toast in the bathroom with a knife at midnight.
(16) a. butter (j, the toast)
b. butter(j, the toast, the bathroom)
c. butter(j, the toast, the bathroom, a knife)
d. butter(j, the toast, the bathroom, a knife, midnight)

From the logic forms in (16), it can be seen that all the terms except the predicate are analyzed in a parallel pattern. Adverbials are treated as argument of the verb, so the number of arguments that 'butter' takes is totally undecided. In (16a), the verb takes two arguments; in (16b), three; in (16c), four; and in (16d), the verb can take five arguments. Then some questions are waiting for answering. What is the relationship between these sentences? What is the lexical entry of 'butter' in lexicon? More exactly, how to determine the actual number of places for a given verb? (16d) can be set as the lexical entry of 'butter' in lexicon, and all the other three are the elliptical forms of it. However, it shouldn't be forgotten that if necessary, the number of the arguments that a verb can take still can be increased. As long as adverbials are treated as arguments of the verb, it is impossible to get a fixed number of arguments that a verb can take, thus it is not possible to set the lexical entry for the verb in the lexicon.

3.2.1 Davidson's Analysis of action Sentences

To provide a proper way to get out of the dilemma when facing adverbial modifiers such as *deliberately, slowly, in the bathroom, with a knife, at midnight*, Davidson (1967) proposes that certain predicates take an implicit variable over event as an argument and these adverbial modifiers are treated as predicates of the hidden event variable. Actually, the idea of increasing an event argument does not come without foundation. Philosophers, such as Plato and Russell, put forward the proposal that verbs should be related to events or states in some way. Both Ramsey(1924), and Hans Reichenbach (1947) once mentioned the concept of event in their works. In Davidson's original proposal, a predicate should have one more argument than is assumed in the traditional predicate logic. This newly-added argument is an event variable which is existentially bounded. According to such a proposal, the logical structures of sentences in (13a) and (14a) will be altered into (17) respectively:

(17) a. $\exists e$ dance(mary, e)

b. ∃e butter (john, the toast, e)

A traditional one-place predicate is analyzed as expressing a two-place relation between an individual who dances, and a dancing event, while traditional two-place predicate is expressed as a three-place relation between an individual who butters, an entity what is buttered, and a buttering event. With the introducing of the underlying event argument, some puzzles in traditional predicate logic are solved. The Davidsonian logical structures of the sentences in (15) are listed in (18):

(18) a. ∃e [butter(John, the toast, e)]
b. ∃e [butter(John, the toast, e) ∧in(e, the bathroom)]
c. ∃e [butter(John, the toast, e) ∧in(e, the bathroom)∧ with(e, a knife)]
d. ∃e [butter(John, the toast, e) ∧in(e, the bathroom) ∧with(e, a knife) ∧at(e, midnight)]

According to (18d), the sentence (15d) expresses that there was an event of John buttering the toast, and this event took place in the bathroom, in addition, this event was performed with a knife; and it happened at midnight. By introducing the underlying event variable, every adverbial modifier gets a suitable target to exert its influence on.

The underlying event account is a refinement of the standard predicate logic. The Davidsonian event argument easily resolved the confusion and conflict we have met in analyzing adverbials. An elegant intersective pattern of interpreting adverbials is provided, which is in analogous to the interpretation of adjectives. Firstly, it is indicated obviously that all the sentences (18b), (18c) and (18d) entail (18a). Secondly, the verb 'butter' is consistently treated as a three-place predicate and adverbial modifiers are interpreted conjunctively. Davidson distinguishes indispensible places of the verbal predicate from those optional ones. All the indispensible ones are included in the parenthesis following the verb and all others are treated as independent conjuncts. Thirdly, the event variable enables a logically parallel treatment of adverbial modifiers and adnominal modifiers. Both of these two kinds of modifiers target at the referential argument: the adverbial modifiers modify the event introduced by the verb and adnominal modifiers modify the individual denoted by the noun (Davidson 1969/1980: 167).

Donald Davidson once claimed that *"there is a lot of language we can make systematic sense of if we suppose events exist."* 'Armed with the theory, we can always answer the question, 'What are these familiar words doing here?' by saying how they contribute to the truth conditionals of the sentence". (Davison 2001 (1968: 94)) However, this innovative theory, out of three reasons, just as Parsons (1990) commented, caused less influence in philosophical semantics than it should deserve:

> 'First, some saw the proposal as a mere detail in Davidson's attempt to show how to formulate a Tarski truth-definition for English.... Second, others saw the proposal not so much as an account of the semantics of natural language but as a clause in Davidson's metaphysics of event and actions.... Third, the theory failed to impress many workers in the semantics of natural language (including me) because we saw its only virtue as yielding an account of the semantics and logic of adverbial modifiers. And here, the theory fails to provide a general account....'
>
> Parsons (1990: 5)

3.2.2 Neo-Davidsonian Approach

Davidson confines the underlying event variable to the action sentences. However, Vendler (1967) classifies situation types into four groups: states, activities, accomplishments and achievements. So it is quite natural to explore the feasibility of extending the event variable to cover all the four groups in Vendler's classification. Davidson's approach of introducing an underlying event variable and analyzing adverbial modifiers as separate propositions adjoining to the logic form through conjunctive operation is to establish the entailments in case of adjunct-dropping. While Davidson increases an event variable in the logical form, he maintains the consistent theta-grid of the verb and keeps the traditional arguments of the verb inside the parenthesis following it. It is quite natural to wonder whether the similar idea could be applied to separate the arguments in the parenthesis after the verb in (18). Although Davidson himself rejects such extension, such extension both in the categories of predicates introducing event variables and the practice of separating the necessary argument from the predicate is well-motivated and promising.

Higginbotham (1985, 2000), Parsons (1980, 1985, 1990) support that the predicates that are capable of introducing underlying event variable should not be confined to action sentences, and they argue that any verbal predicate includes an underlying Davidsonian event argument.

> *"The position E corresponds to the 'hidden' argument place for event, originally suggested by Donald Davidson (1967). There seem to be strong arguments in favor it, and little to be said against, extending Davidson's ideas to verbs other than verbs of changes or action. Under this extension, statives will also have E-position".*
>
> Higginbotham (1985: 10)

Nowadays, scholars working in what has been called the neo-Davidsonian paradigm, following Higginbotham(1985, 2000) and Parsons (1990, 2000), assume that any predicate may introduce such a hidden event argument. That is, not only verbs, no matter dynamic or static, but also adjectives, nouns, and prepositions are able to introduce Davidsonian eventuality arguments.[①] Motivation for this move comes from the observation that all predicative categories provide basically the same kind of empirical evidence that motivated Davison's proposal and thus call for a broader application of the Davidsonian analysis. Some

---

[①] Parsons doesn't support that noun predicate also has an underlying event argument.

scholars (Higginbotham and Ramchand 1997)[1] are for this trend while some against (Krifka 1988, 1995; Maienborn 2005).

Besides including more categories of predicates that can introduce the event variable, another concern of neo-Davidsonian paradigm is to extend the practice of treating the adverbial modifier as a separate conjunct to the regular argument of the predicate.

If all the participants of the predicate are included as the necessary arguments of the predicate, Davidsonian approach will run into the same dilemma as the traditional predicate logic when facing passive voice. When sentences in (15) are transformed into passive voice, Davidsonian approach would be in the same awkward situation just as traditional first-order logic faces in dealing with adverbials.

(19) a. The toast was buttered by John.
b. $\exists e$ [butter(John, the toast, e)]
c. $\exists e$ [butter(the toast, e)$\land$by(e, John)]
(20) a. The toast was buttered by John in the bathroom.
b. $\exists e$ [butter(the toast, e) $\land$by(e, John)$\land$in(e, the bathroom)]

(19a) should be interpreted as (19b) or (19c)? If the logic structure of (19a) is (19b), what is the difference between an active form and a passive one? If the (19c) is the choice, the uniform of the lexical entry of 'butter' cannot be maintained.

In order to get out of such a dilemma, neo-Davidsonian approach treats the participants of event analogously as the adverbial modifiers. In this pattern, verbs are uniformly analyzed as one-place predicates of eventualities, which means the event variable *e* is the only argument that the verb directly predicates of, while the other arguments such as,

---

[1] Higginbotham & Ramchand (1997: 54) support the idea that all predicates introduce an event variable: *"Once we assume that predicates (or their verbal, etc. heads) have a position for events, taking the many consequences that stem there from, as outlined in publications originating with Donald Davidson (1967), and further applied in Higginbotham (1985, 1989), and Terence Parsons (1990), we are not in a position to deny an event-position for any predicate; for the evidence for, and applications of, the assumption are the same for all predicates."*

subject, direct object, are mapped respectively to the event variable *e* through their thematic roles. Each adjunct gives rise to its own clause in logical structure, and they are combined with the clause corresponding to the verb and its arguments by ordinary propositional conjunction. The existential binding of the event variable takes scope over the whole structure. In neo-Davidsonian paradigm, the distinction between arguments and modifiers is blurred, and it is impossible to tell arguments from adverbial modifiers from the logical form. Neo-Davidsonian logic forms of the sentences in (15) are given in (21) respectively:

(21) a. $\exists e$ [butter(e) $\wedge$Ag(John,e) $\wedge$Th(the toast, e)]
b. $\exists e$ [butter(e) $\wedge$Ag(John,e) $\wedge$Th(the toast, e) $\wedge$in(e, the bathroom)]
c. $\exists e$ [butter(e) $\wedge$Ag(John,e) $\wedge$Th(the toast, e) $\wedge$in(e, the bathroom) $\wedge$with(e, a knife)]
d. $\exists e$ [butter(e) $\wedge$Ag(John,e) $\wedge$Th(the toast, e) $\wedge$in(e, the bathroom) $\wedge$with(e, a knife) $\wedge$at(e, midnight)]

'Ag' is the abbreviation of 'agent' and 'Th' is abbreviated from 'theme'. Out of personal style, some semanticists (Chierchia & McConnell-Ginet1990; Landman 2000, 2004; Rothestin1998, 2001, 2004) express the logic forms in (21a,b) as (22a.b):

(22) a. $\exists e$ [butter(e) $\wedge$Ag(e)=j$\wedge$Th(e)= t]
b. $\exists e$ [butter(e) $\wedge$Ag(e)=j$\wedge$Th(e)= t$\wedge$in(e)= b]

'j', 't', and 'b' means 'John', 'the toast', and 'the bathroom' respectively. Such logical forms appear different from those in (20). However, actually, there is no much difference.

Terence Parsons is one of the most representative figures of neo-Davidsonian approach, so, in the following section, his subatomic semantics will be introduced briefly.

3.2.2.1 Parsons' Subatomic Semantics

Terence Parsons, as one of the leading figures advocating the neo-Davidsonian approach, divides formal logic formulas into two sorts:

atomic formulas and non-atomic formulas. Subatomic structures are the inputs of atomic formulas. Phrases such as 'x is tall' and 'x stabbed y' are atomic formulas. Parsons (1990: 6) claims that "*Further, plenty of linguistic constructions in addition to adverbial modification can be well accounted for by positing underlying quantification over events.*" He applies the underlying event analysis extensively in the English language research, including, modifiers, causatives-inchoatives, and tenses.

a. Modifiers

The initial motivation of Davidson (1967) in introducing an implicit variable over event is to provide a proper way to analyze adverbial modifiers. Landman (2000: 1) states that the treatment of verbal modification is considered a very powerful argument in favor of event semantics. Parsons (1990) extends the range of adverbial modifiers and provides tentative analysis for some types of modifiers. Partially based on Jackendoff (1972) and Bellert (1977), Parsons divides modifiers into five categories:

(23) Parsons' classification of modifiers
   a. Speech-act modifiers
   b. Sentence modifiers
   c. Subject-oriented modifiers
   d. VP modifiers
   e. Other

Davidson (1967) suggests that "attributives" derived from attributive adjectives + ly, such as 'slowly', 'gently', 'softly', might not be treated properly with the theory of underlying event. However, Parsons (1990) argues that the theory of underlying event can be effectively applied to analyze such "attributes" by introducing a contextual parameter.

(24) a. Brutus walked slowly
   b. ($\exists$e) [walking(e) $\wedge$Subject(e, Brutus) $\wedge$Slow(e, F)

"F"is the contextual parameter, which limits the comparing classes for the underlying event. In Ernst (2002), this parameter is analyzed as an important feature to tell the manner reading adverbs from agent-oriented reading adverbs.

(25) a. Brutus walked slowly on the tightrope.
b. Brutus walked slowly-for-a-walk-on-the-tightrope on the tightrope.

(25b) means that, comparing with a walk on the tightrope, the event of Brutus' walking on the tightrope is slow. Such a contextual parameter is usually suppressed for simplicity in Parsons (1990).

VP modifiers, such as, 'gently', 'quietly', 'smoothly', 'with a knife', 'in the back' and VP-oriented reading of 'rudely', 'wisely', 'carefully' etc., are the focus of Parsons' research. VP modifiers express properties of the underlying events or states and they have some features that tell them from other kinds of modifiers:

(26) a. They are all factive. A sentence with VP modifiers entails the corresponding one without such modifiers.
b. If a VP modifier appears in a simple negative sentence, then the scope of negation is the whole sentence, including the VP modifier.
c. Some subject-oriented modifiers are homonymous between VP modifiers and subject-oriented modifiers due to different syntactic positions.

b. Thematic roles

Thematic role or thematic relation refers to the role that an argument plays in relation to the state or event described by a verb. It is often regarded as a term which is important in syntax. Semanticists are usually not fond of thematic roles because the number of thematic roles and the criterion to identify them is still a controversial issue (Fang 2000: 316-327); Furthermore, thematic roles are regarded as redundant, because the function application is enough to relate predicates to their arguments and the role of an NP has been included in the meaning of the verb. However, for the sake of clearness, thematic roles are helpful in the logic forms. Dowty (1991: 572) lists the following proto-agent properties:

(27) Contributing properties for the Agent Proto-Role:
a. volitional involvement in the event or state
b. sentience and/or perception
c. causing an event or state in another participant
d. movement (relative to the position of another participant)
(e. exists independently of the event named by the verb)

(28) lists the contributing properties for Proto-Patient-Role:
a. under change of state
b. incremental theme
c. causally affected by another participant
d. stationary relative to movement of another participant
(e. does not exist independently of the event, or not at all)

Dowty (1991: 572)

Before introducing thematic roles into the logic form, Parsons does use the relational symbols as predicate to relate NP to the underlying event.

(29) a. Brutus stabs Caesar.
b. $(\exists e)[stabbing(e)\&Cul(e)\&Subj(e,b) \wedge Obj(e,c)]$

Parsons (1990: 72) claims that 'Subj' and 'Obj' are just dummy placeholders for more specific "deep" thematic relations such as Agent and Theme. From the following chart, we can find that there is no one-to-one correspondence between the thematic role and its syntactic function. So Parsons advocates that thematic roles could be treated as predicates to relate participants to the underlying event argument, which is a prominent trait of neo-Davidsonian approach. He assumes there are six possible thematic roles for DPs in English.

(30) The relationship between thematic roles and syntactic positions:

Role	Typical Position in Active Sentence
agent	subject
theme	direct object; subject of 'is'
goal	indirect object, or with 'to'
benefactive	indirect object, or with 'for'
instrument(=performer)	subject; object of 'with'
experiencer	subject

(Parsons 1990: 73-74)

Besides these thematic roles, Parsons (1990: 78-80) proposes that in certain cases an NP can have more than one thematic role and investigates the possibility that a participant might be classified as both Agent and Theme at the same time. Take the subjects in the sentences in (31) as examples: all these subjects take more than one thematic role:

(31) a. Sam will swim to Catalina. (Agent-Theme)
    b. Bill will run behind the house. (Agent-Theme)
    c. The cup rolled under the sofa (Performer-Theme)

Adapt from Parsons (1990: 78-80)

There are two reasons for introducing thematic role into the underlying event analysis. First, it provides a more convenient way to describe verb extensions in purely semantic terms. The terms such as subject, object, are rigidly stipulated names for the syntactic position, and the functions of the NPs under such umbrella terms are heterogeneous. Second, thematic roles provide a flexible and direct identification of the individuals that involved in the verbs' denotation to replace the practice of depending on the order of NPs to determine their function in traditional predicate logic and Davidsonian approach. In fact, one of the major reasons for the popularity of neo-Davidsonian analyses is that it explicitly indicates the relationship between eventualities and their participants via thematic roles or by some kinds of event-decomposition.

c. Decomposition of event

David Dowty (1979) gives an analysis of causative and inchoative structure within the symbolism of Montague Grammar. His logic form of (32a) is (32b):

(32) a. Mary closes the door.
b. $(\exists P)[(P(Mary))CAUSE(BECOME(The\ door\ is\ closed))]$

In (32b), 'CAUSE' connects two propositions: $(\exists P)$ [(P(Mary))] and (BECOME (The door is closed)), and indicates the causal relation between these two propositions. 'BECOME' maps the proposition (the door is closed) into the proposition (the door became closed). Parsons took over the idea behind this proposed analysis, and incorporated this idea into a framework with underlying events.

(33) a. Mary closes the door.
b. $(\exists e)[Closing(e) \wedge Cul(e) \wedge Theme(e, door) \wedge Agent(e, Mary)]$
$$\text{Parsons}(1990: 117)$$
c. $(\exists e)[Cul(e) \wedge Agent(e, Mary) \wedge (\exists e') [Cul(e') \wedge Theme(e', door) \wedge CAUSE(e, e') \wedge \exists s[Being\text{-}closed(s) \wedge Theme(s, door) \wedge Hold(s) \wedge BECOME(e', s)]]]$
$$\text{Parsons}(1990: 120)$$

Parsons(1990) argues that the (33b) is an incorrect analysis of (33a), because it leaves out the notion of causality and does not explain the ambiguities caused by causative verbs. He thinks that causative-inchoatives are transitive verbs that are derived from a related adjective with meaning "cause to become ADJ", so the analysis he prefers is given in (33c), in which the causative-inchoative verb *to close* denotes an action *e* performed by agent *Mary* on the theme *the door*, and this action causes an event e' of *the door* entering a holding state *s* of being closed. From this analysis, we can find that the causative-inchoative verb is decomposed into three underlying event variables. The advantages of event decomposition are:

Firstly, the nature of causative verbs is explained more accurately. The relation between these extra sub-events or states derived from event decomposition can reflect the nature of the causative verbs more directly and disambiguate the causative verbs and common transitive verbs.

Secondly, a more explicit explanation is provided for modification. These extra underlying events and states are subject to modification introduced by different modifiers, and such event decomposition is applied in the analysis in the resultative secondary predicates.

3.2.3 Davidsonian Spproach and Neo-Davidsonian Approach

Neo-Davidsonian approach is regarded as a new stage of Davidsonian approach out of the following reasons:

Firstly, the category of predicate that can introduce event argument is different. Davidson just applies his underlying event analysis on action sentences, and he does not support that states should be treated as Davidsonian individuals. Katz (2003, 2008) also expresses similar idea about the distribution of the e-argument. In the neo-Davidsonian stage, the event variable has been applied to all four groups of situation types in Vendler's classification. Later on, all predicates, including adjectives, nouns and even prepositions, introduce the event variable. However, Parsons (1990) states clearly that noun predicate should not take an underlying argument event. Now, whether all predicates introduce an underlying event argument is the main controversial issue in the development of event semantics.

Secondly, these two approaches account the participants of the event in different patterns (Bayer, Samuel Louis 1996). Just like the traditional predicate logic, Davidsonian approach still depends on the order of the participants in the logic form to indicate their functions. However, Neo-Davidsonian approach adopts a radically innovative strategy. Verbal predicate just denotes a set of events, and every participant forms a relatively independent formula with the event variable e, then all these formulas are combined as conjuncts to form the logic form of a sentence. The combination of all the formulas in terms of intersection with an existential quantifier at the end is a compositional process represented in (34), and the entailment relation is directly exhibited in the classical diamond entailment pattern in (35).

(34) a. [(agent)]= $\lambda x \lambda e[Ag(e)=x]$
   b. [(theme)]= $\lambda y \lambda e[Th(e)=y]$
   c. [kiss]= $\lambda e[stab(e)]$
   d. [(Ag)Sam]= $\lambda e[Ag(e)=sam]$
   e. [(Th)Cindy]= $\lambda e[Th(e)=cindy]$
   f. [Sam kiss Cindy]=(34c) $\wedge$ (34d)$\wedge$ (34e)
   g. [Sam kissed Cindy]= $\exists e[(34c) \wedge (34d)\wedge (34e)]$

(35)   Sam kissed Cindy passionately in the classroom.

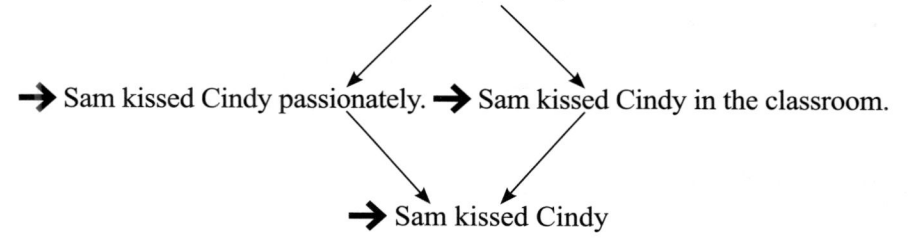

➔ Sam kissed Cindy passionately. ➔ Sam kissed Cindy in the classroom.

➔ Sam kissed Cindy

Thirdly, thematic roles are introduced into the logic form in neo-Davidsonian approach, and thematic roles appear as separate relational conjuncts relating event variable e to their participants (Parsons1980, 1985, 1990; Landman 2000, 2004; Rothstein 2001, 2004). In Davidsonian approach, the verb contributes a multi-place predicate to logical form, with a place for the event, and others for NPs, and all the thematic roles appear in the theta grid of the verb.

Fourthly, the explanatory ability is getting stronger. Davidson (1967) just treats some of the prepositional phrases as the predicates of underlying events, and doubts the feasibility of analyzing "attributives"[1] in the same way, which means that the theory just has a very narrow application. Parsons (1990) extents the application of the theory into the

---

[1] Attributes here refer to predicational adverb, mainly derived from gradable adjective + ly.

analysis of "attributes", such as 'slowly', 'violently', 'gently', which greatly increases the language data that can be included in the target of event semantic research.

3.3 Classification of Predicates

In Section 3.2, a general introduction of event semantics and a brief process of development of this theory have been provided. We notice that an innovation of neo-Davidsonian approach is that not only action verbs, but all kinds of predicates introduce the Davidsonian argument. Such an innovation is accepted by some researchers (Chierchia 1995; Parsons 1990; Rothstein 2004), and they maintain a consistent treatment of the predicates by assuming that all predicates have a Davidsonian argument, whereas some scholars try to prove that such an innovation is too radical (Milsark 1974; Kratzer 1995; Rapoport 1990, 1991; Carlson 1977; Maienborn 2003, 2005), and they maintain a clear dichotomy of the predicates between these have Davidsonian arguments and these don't.

What are the differences between these predicates? Considering different features of predicates, there are different classifications. Vendler (1967) maintains a four-way classification of verbal predicates, Dowty (1979) includes almost all kinds of predicates into the pattern of Vendler's classification. Carlson (1977) maintains an ILP/SLP contrast in his classification.

3.3.1 Vendlerian Classification of Verbal Predicates

It is a well-known semantic fact that verbs, exactly VPs, can be classified into different groups considering the aspectual features of the eventualities they denote. Event semantics is closely related to the classification of eventualities. As far as this field is concerned, it is the work of Vendler (1967)[①] that has been highly influential, so that is where we will begin with.

---

① Before Vendler (1967), Ryle (1947), Kenny (1963) have put forward some different criterion of verb classification.

3.3.1.1 Vendler's Four-way Classification of Verbal Predicates

Vendler (1967), mainly depending on some features related to time schemata, such as [+/- compatibility with particular temporal adverbials], [+/- compatibility with Progressive], divides eventualities into states, activities, accomplishments, and achievements.

(36) Four-way Vendlerian classification

	±telic	±stage	examples
states	-	-	know, believe, have, desire, be happy
activities	-	+	run, walk, swim, drive a car
achievements	+	-	recognize, notice, find, lose, die
accomplishments	+	+	paint a picture, make a chair,

The first class, state, involves time instants in an indefinite and non-unique sense. "X loved Y from t_1 to t_2." means that in the time stretch between t_1 and t_2, for every instant in the time stretch, the state "X loved Y" holds true.

The concept of activities matches with periods of time that are not unique or definite, "x was running at time t" means that time instant t is on a time stretch throughout which x was running.

Accomplishments imply the notion of unique and definite time periods. "x was drawing a circle at t" means that t is on the time stretch in which x drew that circle.

Achievements only focus on the terminus and involve unique and definite time instants. "x won a race between t_1 and t_2," indicates that the time instant at which x won the race is between t_1 and t_2.

3.3.1.2 Dowty's Development of Vendlerian Classification

Lexical aspect has traditionally concentrated on the study of verbal predicates, such that other grammatical categories, like adjectives, can also occur as primary predicate, have not received the attention they deserve. As early as in 1979, Dowty pointed out that the stative/non-stative distinction is also applicable in adjectives and nouns. In English, only copular be + adjectives can act as primary predicates freely, so Dowty classifies be + adjectives in the similar pattern of Vendler's verb classification:

> (37) Classification of adjectival predicates
> State: be tall, be big, be Chinese, be green, be true,
> Activity: be grave, be greedy, be rude/polite/ obnoxious to NP
> Achievement: become adj/adj-er
> Accomplishment: hammer NP flat, wipe NP clean, wiggle NP loose.
> (Dowty 1979: 68-70)

Vendler (1967) provides some methods to classify verbs, or more generally speaking, VPs. Dowty (1979) develops 14 diagnostic methods which make the features of each class clearer. Milada Walkova (2012) classifies these diagnostic tests into three categories: lexical co-occurrence tests; grammatical co-occurrence tests and logical entailment tests. Dowty's tests have been widely used in classifying eventuality types. Facing with so many diagnostic tests, it should be bear in mind that not all of these tests are applicable to all four situation types and sometimes, or even often, a combination of two or even more tests is required.

Dowty(1979) proposes three predicates, DO, CAUSE, BECOME, which are combined in different ways to get the four Vendlerian classes. The predicate DO is to symbolize agentivity involving volition and/or control. States are treated as simple predicate without involving anyone of these three predicates. Other aspectual classes are the combination of these three predicates in different patterns. In principle, the DO operator may take different scope. Dowty did not introduce the underlying event variable into his aspectual decomposition, but Rothstein (2001) reconstructs his verbal templates in neo-Davidsonian paradigm:

> (38) a. States: $\lambda P\lambda e.P(e)$
> b. Activities: $\lambda P\lambda e. (DO(P))(e)$
> c. Achievements: $\lambda P\lambda e. (BECOME(P))(e)$
> d. Accomplishments: $\lambda P\lambda e. \exists e_1 \exists e_2 [e=^S(e_1 \cup e_2) \wedge (DO(P))(e1) \wedge (BECOME(P'))$

$(e_2) \wedge Cul(e)=e_2]^{s}$ ①
Rothstein (2001: 321)

Such representations reflect the basic relationship between aspectual groups in a compositional pattern more explicitly.

3.3.2 Carlson's Individual-level Predicates and Stage-level Predicates

The distinction proposed by Carlson (1977) between SLPs and ILPs has interested grammarians as soon as it was proposed. Representative words of each category are listed in (39):

(39) a. stage-level adjectives:
sick, tired, hungry, drunk, open, naked, alert, awake, etc.
b. individual-level adjectives:
big, boring, intelligent, insane, orange, fat, smart, etc.
(Carlson 1980: 72)

Individual-level predicates (ILP) express quality of an individual with no reference to time and stage-level predicates (SLP) attributes temporary and transient properties to an individual at a particular time and space. According to this definition, many adjectives are individual-level predicates, for adjectives tend to denote time-stable and permanent properties. Adjectives relating to size, color, shape, etc., indeed denote fairly permanent properties. However, those adjectives relating to psychological states, emotions, and properties of events, denote less time-stable states. Sometimes, the syntactic positions in which adjectives appear will also cause them to lose some of their inherent temporal characteristics.

Carlson's idea is based on the distinction between state-descriptive predicates and property predicates made by Milsark(1974).

"Properties are those facts about entities which are assumed

---

① The superscript ^{s} indicates that the summing operation results in a singular event.

to be, even if they are not in fact permanent, unalterable, and in some sense possessed by the entity, while states are conditions which are, at least in principle, transitory, not possessed by the entity of which they are predicated, and the removal of which causes no change in the essential quantities of the entity."

Milsark(1974: 212)

Milsark (1974) states that all noun predicates, adjectives express shapes, colors, and other adjectives such as: *intelligent, beautiful, boring, crazy,* etc. are property predicates, whereas adjectives such as: *sick, hungry, tired, alert, clothed, naked, drunk, stoned, closed, opened,* etc. are state predicates. He notes that such a distinction also applies to verbal predicates: most verbal predicates are state predicates (e.g., *eat supper, think lovely thoughts*) while some are properties (e.g., *have long arms, own a bank, know how to fly an airplane*)

Carlson (1977) names the predicates, such as *tall, smart*, that express enduring or inherent property individual-level predicates, which express quality of an individual with no reference to time. The sates in Milsark (1974) are named stage-level predicates by Carlson. An ILP, denoting certain property of an individual, combines with an individual, and an SLP, is a description of the world, or more concretely, a spatiotemporal slice of the world, combines with a stage, which is roughly conceived of as a spatially and temporally bounded manifestation of something.

The ILP/SLP distinction, in some languages, shows up as a syntactic distinction in main clause predicates. Sera (1992) states that, in Spanish, the distinction is reflected in the form of the copula: *ser* selects individual-level predicates; *estar* selects stage-level predicates. The situation is similar in Portuguese with a slight difference in the boundary of division between ILPs and SLPs (Schmitt 1992). In Hebrew, the distinction is reflected by the absence or presence of the copular: overt copula selects individual-level predicates; null copular selects stage-level predicates (Greenberg 1994). Followings are the well-acknowledged diagnostics to tell ILPs from SLPs:

(40) Diagnostics to tell ILPs from SLPs.
    a. Only SLPs can be modified by spatio-temporal

modifiers.
b. Only SLPs can introduce a variable to be bounded by adverbs of quantification. (Kratzer 1989, 1996)
c. Only SLPs predicates can occur as secondary predicates.

(Rapoport 1991)

SLP/ILP distinction in Carlson (1977) is applicable to both verbs and adjectives, even all kinds of predicates. In this work, we mainly concern the ILP/SLP distinction in verbs and adjectives. ILPs are different from SLPs in their temporal features and temporal feature is also one of the important factors to classify aspectual classes. It is uncontroversial that all the achievements, accomplishments, some of the activities and some of states are SLPs, while some of activities and some states are ILPs. It is controversial in distinguishing ILP and SLP in statives, but at least it is safe to say that all ILPs are states and all non-statives are SLPs. Fernald (2000) states that the only reason to distinguish ILP/SLP is that there are some stative SLPs.

One of the most striking differences between the Davidsonian and neo-Davidsonian approaches is what kind of predicates can introduce the underlying event argument. Stative predicates is the most controversial category of predicates, and many scholars are trying to prove an ILP/SLP dichotomy of statives (Milsark 1974; Carlson 1977; Rapoport 1990, 1991; Kratzer 1995; Maienborn 2003, 2005).

3.3.2.1 Kratzer's Spatiotemporal Location Analysis

Kratzer (1995) tries to establish the relation between ILP and SLP contrast and the argument structure. She, following Carlson (1977), notices that SLPs fundamentally need to be anchored in time and location, while ILPs do not. For Kratzer (1995), the crucial semantic difference between ILPs and SLPs lies in their association with space and time. Compared with ILPs, SLPs tends to be modified more easily by temporal and locative modification. She proposes that the difference in tolerance of temporal and locative modification is due to the difference in the argument structures of ILPs and SLPs. SLPs have a logical argument that ILPs lack, and this logical argument is accessible for temporal and locative modifiers. As for the nature of the logical argument, she doesn't give an exact definition. Kratzer (1995) writes, "*At this point, I don't want to commit myself to a particular view with respect to the precise nature of the Davidsonian argument. It may not be an event argument. It may simple be an argument for spatiotemporal location*". She, following Barwise and Perry (1983), uses *l* to represent the logical argument modified by temporal and locative modifiers. The need for temporal and locative anchor causes a spatiotemporal variable to appear in the logical form of SLP in (41), For an SLP, the spatiotemporal argument has the same status as other thematic role, whereas in the theta-grid of ILP as (42), there is no such an argument:

(41) The argument structure of Stage-level predicates:
   a. hit < *l*, agent, theme>
   b. dance < *l*, agent>
   c. die < *l*, theme>
   d. fall < *l*, theme>

(42) The argument structure of Individual-level predicate:
   a. belong <theme, goal>
   b. be known to <experience, theme>

(43) a. *Mary is a dancer on the lawn.
   b. Mary is dancing on the lawn.
   c. [dancing (Mary, *l*) & on the lawn (*l*)]

The nominal predicate *a dancer* in (43a) is an ILP, so it repels a locative modifier, while in (43b), the predicate is an SLP, so it is needed to be anchored in time and space, which causes that a variable *l* to appear in the logical form, and the variable *l* can be the target of locative modification, as illustrated in (43c).

Although Kratzer doesn't define the logical argument *l* clearly, according to the three features of event concluded by Maiborn (2005), the logical argument in Kratzer (1995) can be definitely identified as an underlying Davidsonian event argument. So, for the simplicity and uniformity, I represent the logical argument in Kratzer (1995) as *e*.

As for the range of predicates that bearing an underlying variable, call it event variable or location variable, Kratzer goes between Davidson

(1967) and Parsons (1990). Kratzer suggests that only SLPs have an underlying location variable. The range of SLPs is bigger than actions in Davidsonian sense, because there are some static, non-action SLPs.

3.3.2.2 Chierchia's Generic Quantifier

Chierchia (1995) explains the ILP/SLP contrast in a different way from that of Kratzer (1995). In chierchia' account, all predicates have a Davidsonian argument. The crutial difference between ILP and SLP is that ILPs must stay in the scope of a generic quantifier, so ILPs are interpreted as involving a generic quantification over situation in which the subject appears. Take (44a) as an example:

(44) a. Tom is intelligent.
   b. Gen s [in(t, s)][intelligent(t,s)]

In (44b), Gen is the generic quantifier; s is the underlying Davidsonian variable. The logic is interpreted as; in a general situation involving Tom, it will be a situation in which Tom is intelligent. Such an explanation reflects the feature of an ILP. It denotes certain property of an individual and the property holds of that individual for a relatively long period of time and in that period, the predication relation between the individual and the property is always true. From the following examples, we can notice that an ILP can't be modified by other adverb of quantification except for generic quantification, but an SLP is compatible with other adverb of quantification.

(45) a. That is ?(always) a tree.
   b. Thomas is ?(often) a man.
(46) a. John (often) smokes.
   b. John (always) smokes.

The different degree of compatibility with adverb of quantification lies in that the ILP has been quantified by an invisible generic quantifier.

3.3.2.3 Parsons' State and Event

In Kratzer's analysis, only SLPs have an underlying event variable, while ILPs don't have. However, in Parsons (1990)'study, all predicates, including adjective, prepositional phrase, and states, have an underlying event variable. He doesn't discuss the ILP /SLP distinction, but focuses on the difference between states, processes, and events by assuming that aspectual predicates Hold (atelic) and Cul (telic) bind the underlying event variable. Parsons states that the only difference between state sentences and event sentences is that the underlying state variable of state sentence always has the property [+Hold].

(47) a. Brutus is clever.
  b. ($\exists$s)[s is a state of being clever & Subj(s, Brutus) &Hold (s, now)]
(48) a. Brutus has a dog.
  b. ($\exists$x)[x is a dog&($\exists$s)[s is a having & Subj(s, Brutus) & Obj(s,x) & Hold(s,now)]
(49) a. Brutus is under the tree.
  b. ($\exists$s)[Under (s, the tree)&Subj(s, Brutus)& Hold (s, now)]

Parsons (1990: 187)

As for attribute constructions, Parsons also treats the attributive modifiers in the same pattern as predicates, which is in agreement with the analysis of downgraded predicate proposed in Leech (1983).

(50) a. X is a red book.
  b. Red(x) & Book(x)
  c. ($\exists$s)[s is a state of being red & theme(s, x) & Hold (s, now)][1]

Parsons (1990: 194)

It is generally assumed that Parsons is one of the most typical neo-Davidsonists in that he assumes that all kinds of predicates have the underlying event argument. However, nominal predicate is an exception

---

[1] The Conjunction and Hold (s, now) is not included in Parsons (1990). We add it here for the consistency.

in Parsons (1990), he notices that copular + NP predicate is different form verbal predicate in that the former one repels adverbial modification, and NP predicate cannot occur as the complement of a small clause in perception sentence. So the logic form of 'Agatha is a doctor.' is (51c):

(51) a. Agatha is a doctor * through the house/cleverly/on the roof
b. *She felt him a doctor.
c. Doctor(Agatha)

Parsons suggests that all kinds of predicates except for copular + NP ones have an underlying event variable, and he concludes that there is no evidence based on the logic of modifier to favor the hypothesis that noun predicates stand for the underlying states. He writes:

Perhaps it is a major difference in our language between verbs and nouns that verbs automatically pick out kinds of events or states, and nouns (except for special cases) do not.
Parsons (1990: 202)

In Carlson's classification, nominal predicates are typical individual-level predicates, and Parsons agrees that nominal predicates don't have an underlying argument, which means that the ILP/SLP distinction is also valid in parsons' subatomic event semantics. The only difference is that the boundary between them is different. According to this statement, adjectives should stay between verbs and nouns, so, it is worth of reconsideration whether it is reasonable to issue an underlying state variable for all adjective predicates without taking the semantic difference of these adjectives into consideration just for theoretical consistency, because just like the noun predicate, some adjective predicates and some verbal states also repel adverbial modification and cannot act as complement of small clause of perceptive verbs.

3.3.2.4 Maienborn's Kimian States

About the applicable scope of the underlying event variable, there is no agreement. The most controversial issue is the non-dynamic predicates.

Maienborn (2003, 2005) proposes a dichotomy of the states: Davidsonian states and Kimian states. Davidsonian states refer to the states denoted by verbs like *sit, stand, sleep, wait, gleam*. Kimian states include the states denoted by other stative verbs such as *know, weigh, own, resemble,* and all the states denoted by the combination of copular and predicate.

Maienborn includes all the states denoted by the copular constructions into Kimian states, no matter the predicate in the copular construction is an individual-level predicate or an stage-level one. Kimian states do not have a real underlying eventuality argument, but they introduce an abstract object, which exemplifies a property at an individual holder x and a time t. The difference between the abstract object introduced by Kimian states and the event argument introduced by verbs is that the abstract object can be individuated, can be located in time, and can be referred to via anaphors, while the event argument can be perceived, can be located in space and can vary in its representation[①].

Maienborn separates Kimian states from Davidsonian eventuality mainly because the grammatical performance of Kimian states is radically different from that of Davidsonian eventuality in tempo-spatial location, perceptive verb report, and adverbial modification. If keep the Kimian states in the Davidsonian eventuality, a radical redefinition of the category of eventualities would be required. So, in Maienborn's opinion, the benefit of introducing a new ontology outweighs its cost.

Judged from the perspective of individual-level predicates and stage-level predicates distinction, it is uncontroversial that all activities, accomplishments and achievements are stage-level predicates and only some states are individual-level predicates. Researchers all agree that predicates are not homogeneous in their compatibility with time and spacial modification; some predicates being more easily associated with time, and/or space modifiers than others. Scholars have proposed different theories to explain the relation between ILP/SLP and neo-Davidsonian approach.

In the following part we will look into the relevant performance of ILP/SLP distinction in Mandarin Chinese, and we will follow the theory proposed by Kratzer and represent the ILP/SLP contrast by the hidden

---

[①] That means the event argument can be modified by manner and other adverbial modification.

argument which an SLP has but an ILP lacks. Different from Kratzer, we will follow Parsons (1990) and Rothstein (2001, 2004), and unify the underlying event variable of all SLPs as *e*.

3.3.3 Aspectual Features of Adjectives

Adjectives are considered to be different from nouns in that adjectives denote a single property (Jespersen 1924: 74), whereas nouns denote objects which have a large number of properties. Adjectives give prominence to the property per se while noun gives prominence to the object it denotes instead of the properties containing in its denotation. It is widely assumed in the formal semantics literature that gradable adjectives map objects onto abstract representations of measure which is formalized as sets of values. These values are ordered along certain dimension according to the degree these adjectives express. Creswell (1977), von Stechow (1984), Heim (1985), and Kennedy and McNally (2005) analyze a gradable adjective as a function between an object and a degree and its type is <d, <e, t>>. The core lexical entry of a gradable adjective includes at least three parts: a measure function, a domain in which the measurement is occurring, and an ordering relation on that domain. The representation of adjective *long* is like the following:

(52) $[\![\text{long}]\!] = \lambda d \, \lambda x. \, \text{long}(x) \geq d$

In (52) *long* represent a measure function which takes an individual and returns the value of the individual. This adjective is related to a degree on a certain scale, and the scale is the length of the object. Usually, the degree is highly context-sensitive. The degree of *long* in 'long hair' and 'long river' is extremely different. Kennedy (2007) explains this in explicit terms. The idea is that gradable adjectives take a contextually-supplied comparison class as an argument, which is marked as *C*. That means the comparison class is the average length of hair in the modification relation in 'long hair':

(53) $[\![\text{long hair}]\!] = \lambda x. \, [\![\text{long}]\!](x) \wedge [\![\text{hair}]\!](x)$
$= \lambda x. \, \text{long}(x)(C) \wedge \text{hair}(x)$

The object denoted by a noun exists fairly permanent, and the property denoted by adjective is also relatively permanent, for adjectives usually modify nouns to make the denotation of the noun more concrete. Therefore, adjectives are naturally related to nouns. Occurring as adnominal attributes to modify noun is the most prominent function of adjectives, for the temporal features of the adjectives and the targets that are modified are in agreement.

Adjectives differ from verbs in that verbs denote transient events which involve changes, whereas adjectives express fairly permanent and inherent properties. Event, like object, is a multidimensional conceptual structure, which also denotes a number of properties (Ernst 2002; Geuder 2005, 2012). Manner modification of an event involves one of the properties denoted by the event and a predicational adverbial that can scale the value of the dimension of certain property denoted by the event.

The above mentioned modification relation between gradable adjective and noun is also applicable in the modification relation between adverbials and verbs. Take *kuai* 'fast' and VP *kuaipao* 'run fast' as examples:

(54) $[\![kuai]\!] = \lambda d\, \lambda e.\, kuai\, (e) \geq d$
(55) $[\![kuai\, pao]\!] = \lambda e.\, [\![pao]\!]\, (e) \wedge [\![kuai]\!]\, (e)$
$= \lambda e.\, pao(e)(C) \wedge kuai\, (e)$

The difference between (52) and (54) consists in what is modified: in (52), an object is modified, while in (54), an event is modified. In (55), the adjective is related to the degree on a certain property, and the scale is the speed of the running event. Usually, the degree is highly context-sensitive. *C* is the comparison events denoted by the verb *run*. Such analysis will be introduced in great details in the following chapters.

In Chinese, lexical aspect of adjectives has been overlooked (Zhang 1995, 2006). The aspectual features of adjectives are assumed to be closely related to their morphological forms (Zhu 1956, 1982, Shen 2011). However, some scholars began to study the aspectual features without taking the morphological forms into consideration. Zhang (1995, 2006), based on the distinctive feature [±static], distinguishes adjectives into property adjectives, state adjectives[1] and adjectives expressing changes. The adjectives express changes should co-occur with aspect markers 'le', 'zhe'. As for such a classification of aspects of adjectives, some scholars have different ideas. Chao (1968) and Zhang Bojiang (2011) argue that the meaning of state change is not embedded in the adjective, but brought out by aspect markers.

In this work, we support the latter opinion. The default reading of an adjective is to denote a relatively permanent property or a state, and the aspectual features of adjectives are lexical-related as well as context-sensitive.

3.3.3.1 SA/CA & ILP/SLP

Zhu (1956) maintains a dichotomy of the adjectives: simple adjectives (SAs) and complex ones (CAs). Then he renames the two categories of adjectives: *xingzhi xingrognci* 'property adjectives' and *zhuangtai xingrongci* 'state adjectives'. Zhu (1982: 103) states that when property adjectives occur as predicate, they express permanent and static property of the subject, and when state adjectives occur as predicate, they express temporary and dynamic changes. The renaming of the categories of adjectives indicates obviously that Zhu (1982) roughly equals SAs to ILPs and CAs to SLPs. The state/property distinction made by Milsark (1974) is a semantic classification, whereas that in Zhu (1956, 1982) is mainly based on morphological difference of the adjectives.

Huang Shizhe[2] (2006: 2f) suggests that the difference between CAs and SAs mirrors the difference between individual-level predicates and stage-level predicates, but the correspondence is not perfect. She just makes a note of this analogy without further discussion in that article.

If the distinction of SA/CA is equal to ILP/SLP distinction, we can expect that the diagnostics in (40) are applicable in the sentences in (56) and (57):

---

[1] State adjectives in Zhang (1995, 2006) mainly concern whether there involve changes along the time axis. which is different from the state adjectives in Zhu Dexi (1956, 1982)

[2] Huang (2006) is, as far as I have read, among the few scholars who equal the distinction between CAs and SAs to that between ILP and SLP.

(56) a. Li Si zai feijishang henjinzhang/hen xingfen.   (SLP)
   p.n in plane on very nervous/very excited
   'On the plane, Li Si is very nervous/very excited'
 b. *Li Si zai fenjishang hen gao/hen congming.   (ILP)
   p.n in plane   very tall/ very intelligent
   'On the plane, Li Si is very tall/very intelligent.'
(57) a. Li Si hen jinzhang/hen xingfen De zuo zai feijishang.
                                                    (SLP)
   p.n very nervous/very excited De sit in plane on
   'Li Si nervously/excitedly sat on the plane.'
 b. *Li Si hen gao/hen congming De zuo zai fenjishang.
                                                    (ILP)
   p.n very tall/ very intelligent De sit in plane on
   'Li Si sat on the plane and he is very tall/very intelligent.'

The adjectives in (56) and (57) are complex adjectives composed of degree adverb *hen* 'very' and simple adjectives. When these adjectives act as primary predicate or adverbials, they exhibit different degree of tolerance to the modification of the locatives. If they denote transitory states as traditionally assumed, they should be uniformly acceptable when modified by spacio-temporal adverbials.

The classification in Zhu (1956, 1982) is very influential and widely accepted. However, it is difficult to imagine that the number of syllables corresponds to the contrast between properties and states so rigidly.

Lyu (1980) does not relate morphological forms of adjectives to the distinction between properties and states. He names the reduplicated forms of adjectives as life-like or vivid forms. The vivid form of an adjective just presents a property or a state in a more life-like or vivid style, but does not change its denotation from a permanent property into a transitory state:

(58) a. Yi ben hou shu
     one CL thick book
     'a thick book'
  b. Yiben hou de shu
     one CL thick de book

'a thick book'
c. Yi ben houhou de shu
  one CL thick$_{REDUPL}$ de book
  'a thick book'
d. Houhou de yibenshu.
  thick$_{REDUPL}$ de one CL book'
  'a thick book'
e. Nabenshu *(gangcai)houhou de.
  that CL book (just now) thick$_{REDUPL}$ de
  'That book is thick *(just now).'
f. Nabenshu shi houde.
  'that CL book is thick de'
  'That book is thick.'
g. Nabenshu *(zai shujia shang) henhou.
  that CL book (on book shelf)very thick
  'That book is very thick *(on the book shelf).'

(59) a. Yi bei re shui
  one glass hot water
  'a glass of hot water'
b. Yibei rere de shui.
  one glass hot hot de water.
  'a glass of hot water.'
c. Na bei shui (gangcai)henren
  that glass water (just now)very hot
  'That glass of water is very hot (just now).'
d. Na bei shui rere de.
  that glass water hot hot de
  'That glass of water is hot.'

From these examples in (58), we can find the property *hou* 'thick' is always the permanent and intrinsic physical property possessed by the book, no matter what form and what syntactic positions the adjective *hou* 'thick' appears in, although, in some degree, different forms and syntactic positions indicates the speaker's subjectivity. Similarly, *being hot* is not a permanent property of that glass of water, for it is easily to change with time passing by. As a result, (59c) can be modified by temporal modifiers.

However, the property 'thick' is permanent, so (58e, 58g) cannot be modified by temporal and spacial adverbial modifiers. If reduplicated forms of adjectives denote transitory states, the unacceptability resulted from adverbial modification of (58e, 58g) is difficult to explain.

Zhang (2000: 447) points out that morphological forms of adjectives are not completely in agreement with their semantic features. Sheng (2011) also disagrees with the opinion that reduplicated form or the degree verb intensifier can change property adjective into state adjective. He assumes that the function of reduplication or combination with *hen* 'very' is to strengthen the depictive capability of adjectives, and can't be treated as the criteria to classify adjectives into state and property adjectives. We assume that the depictive function in Sheng (2011) is roughly equal to the life-like or vivid form in Lyu (1980).

If the degree intensifier *hen* 'very' and reduplication cannot alter property adjectives into state adjectives, does this mean there is no property/state distinction in Chinese. The answer is certainly no. If the external morphological features of adjectives are not directly related to the property and state distinction; naturally, we can only assume that the property/state distinction is related to the meaning of the adjectives.

a ILP/SLP distinction in SAs

In Chinese, simple adjectives are restricted in occurring as predicates. However, as Liao (1985) states that when small clauses act as predicate, SAs can be the predicates of the small clauses. Such constructions provide a very good sally port to test whether there is ILP/SLP distinction among bare SA predicates. The simplest diagnostic for distinguishing a stage-level predicate from an individual-level predicate is its tolerance of spatio-temporal modifiers. SLPs are compatible with such modifiers, while ILPs are not.

(60) a. Li Si *(zuotian) yanjing da.
      p.n (yesterday) eye big
      'Li Si's eyes are big(yesterday).'
  b. Zhang San (gangcai) toufa shi.
      p.n   (just now)hair wet

'Zhang San's hair was wet(just now).'
c. Nabenshu *(zuotian) neirong nan.
   that book (yesterday)content difficult
   'That book is difficult (yesterday).'
d. Xiaoming (zuotian) tou tong.
   p.n (yesterday) head ache
   'Xiaoming had a headache (yesterday).'

It has long been assumed, that simple adjectives in Chinese express permanent property. If it is true, we can suppose that when simple adjectives occur as predicates, temporal and locative expressions will result in unacceptable sentences, for a permanent property will not change even time and location change. However, from the sentences in (60), we notice that simple adjective predicates exhibit different degree of tolerance to temporal adverbials. (60b) and (60d) are compatible with time adverbial, which indicates that at least they can express non-permanent property.

Disyllabic adjectives have similar performance[①]:

(61) a. Zhang San bu congming.
         p.n   not intelligent
         'Zhang San is not intelligent.'
     b. Li Si mei pibei.
         p.n not tired
         'Li Si is not tired.'
(62) a. *Zhang San jintianxiawu bu congming.
         p.n   this morning not intelligent
         'Zhang San is not intelligent this morning.'
     b. Li Si jintianxiawu mei pibei.
         p.n this afternoon not tired
         'Li Si is not tired this afternoon.'
(63) a. *Zhang San zai jiaoshili bu congming.
         p.n   in classroom not intelligent

---

① Negation is added to make the sentences complete, for bare simple adjective occur as primary predicate alone, has a comparative reading instead of a positive reading.

'Zhang San is not intelligent in classroom.'
b. Zhang San zai jiaoshili mei pibei.
   p.n   in classroom not tired
   'Zhang San is not tired in classroom.'

Normally speaking, if a person is *congming* 'intelligent', he is intelligent anytime and anywhere as long as there is no serious injury to his or her brain, whereas if somebody is *pibei* 'exhausted', it usually indicates that sometime and somewhere a person is exhausted. The contrast of acceptability of these sentences when the temporal and locative adverbials are added indicates that not all disyllabic adjectives are ILPs.

Negation in Chinese also reflects ILP/SLP contrast in SAs. There are two negation morphemes in Mandarin, *bu* and *mei*. These two negation morphemes combine with different predicates. Many explanations on the difference of *bu* and *mei* have been proposed (Li & Thompson 1981: 421-440; Huang 1988; Ernst 1995; Lin 2003). It is clear that *bu* can be used to negate both relatively permanent properties and transitory states, whereas *mei* can only negate transitory states:

(64) a. Na zuo shan bu gao.
        that CL mountain NEG high
        'That mountain is not high.'
     b. *Na zuo shan mei gao.
        that CL mountain NEG high
        'That mountain does not get high.'
(65) a. Wode chenyi bu zang.
        my shirt   NEG dirty
        'My shirt is not dirty.'
     b. wo de chenyi meizhang.
        my shirt   NEG dirty
        'My shirt doesn't get dirty.'
(66) a. Zhang San bu congming.
        p.n   NEG intelligent
        'Zhang San is not intelligent.'
     b. *Zhang San mei congming.

p.n   NEG intelligent
'Zhang San does not get intelligent.'
(67) a. Xiaoli bu xingfen.
p.n   NEG excited
'Xiaoli is not excited.'
b. Xiaoli mei xingfen.
p.n   NEG excited
'Xiaoli does not get excited.'

Human dispositions, such as *congming* 'intelligent', the height of a mountain, *gao* 'high' are ILPs denoting permanent properties of the modified entities, while psychological-emotional states such as *xingfen* 'excited', and some external states such as *zang* 'dirty' are SLPs, denoting transitory states of the relevant entities. The variation in acceptability reflects that not all simple adjectives denote permanent properties.

b. ILP/SLP distinction of CAs

In last section, we have made it clear that not all simple adjectives denote permanent properties. In this part, we will check whether such a contrast exist in complex adjectives.

Zhu (1956, 1982) suggests that all the CAs express transitory and dynamic states. If what he said is true, we should expect that when complex adjectives occur as predicates, they are compatible with temporal and/or special adverbial modification.

In the following sentences, the predicates are composed of *hen* 'very' + monosyllabic adjective, which is a subcategory of CAs.

(68) a. Zhang San de yanjing hen da.
p.n   of eyes very big
'Zhang San's eyes are big.'
b. Zhang san de yanjing hen hong.
p.n   of eyes very red
'Zhang San's eyes are red.'
(69) a. *Zhang San de yanjing zuotian hen da.

p.n   of eyes yesterday very big
'Zhang San's eyes are big yesterday.'
b. Zhang san de yanjing zuotian   hen hong.
p.n   of eyes yesterday very red
'Zhang San's eyes were red yesterday.'
(70) a. *Zhang San de yanjing zai xuexiao hen da.
p.n   of eyes   at school   very big
'Zhang San's eyes are big at school.'
b. Zhang San de yanjing zai xuexiao hen hong.
p.n   of eyes   at school very red
'Zhang San's eyes are red at school.'

Generally speaking, the bigness of eyes is a relatively permanent physical property without taking the plastic surgery into consideration. Eyes only get red after crying, catching Flu, or pinkeye, which is a transitory stage of the eyes. Form these minimal pairs we notice that permanent property repels the modification of time and space adverbials. We also get to the conclusion that the degree adverb changes a simple adjective to a complex one, but it cannot change the temporal features of the adjective.

The AABB pattern reduplicated adjectives are another category of complex adjectives. We will check whether AABB pattern complex adjectives uniformly denote transitory states.

(71) a. Zhang San zhuangzhuangshishi de
p.n   stocky   de
'Zhang San is stocky.'
b. Zhang San gaogaoxingxing de.
p.n   happy de
'Zhang San is happy.'
(72) a. *Zhang San jintian zaoshang zhuangzhuangshishi de
p.n   today morning stocky   de
'Zhang San is stocky this morning.'
b. Zhang San jintian zaoshang gaogaoxingxing de.
p.n   today morning happy   de
'Zhang San is happy this moring.'

(73) a. *Zhang San zhuangzhuangshishi De zuo zai cheli.
   p.n   stocky   DE sit at car in
   'Zhang San was stocky while he sat in the car.'
b. Zhang San gaogaoxingxing De zuo zai che li.
   p.n   happy   De sit at car in.
   'Zhang San was happy while he sat in the car.'

As exhibited from the contrast of the minimal pairs, the AABB pattern reduplicated adjectives also exhibit the ILP/SLP contrast in the same way as the complex adjectives composed of *hen* 'very' and simple adjectives. The reduplicated adjective *zhaungzhuangshishi* 'stocky' expresses a relatively stable physical condition, which is the same as other ILPs, repels the spatio-tempo modification and can't occur as adverbial. The reduplicated adjective *gaogaoxingxing* 'happy' is a stage-level predicate denoting the psychological state of the individual. This state is transitory and can be altered easily, so it is compatible with time and space location and can act as adverbials.

Carlson(1977) also tests the stage-level predicates at the predicate position following the post-verbal NP complement of perception verb *see*:

(74) a. Mary saw the policemen drunk.
    b. *Mary saw the policeman tall.

It has been commonly argued that the predicational complements of perception verbs are syntactically small clauses (Chomsky 1981, 1986; Stowell 1981, 1989). A small clause is composed of a subject and a predicate, but with no tense inflection on the predicate. Chinese does not have overt tense marking in morphology (Hu, Pan and Xu 2001). However, when different adjectives occur as predicates, the degree of acceptability is different. Only SLP can appear as the complement of perception verb:

(75) a. Zhang San kanjianguo Li Si guangguang de.
   p.n   see   Pas p,n naked naked de
   'Zhang San saw Li Si naked'

b. *Zhang San kanjianguo Li Si gaogao de.①
　　p.n　see　Pas p.n tall tall de
　　'Zhang San saw Li Si tall'
(76) a. Zhang San jianguo Xiaoli jinzhang.
　　p.n　see Past p.n　nervous
　　'Zhang San saw Xiaoli being nervous.'
　　b. Zhang San jianguo Xiaoli piaoliang.
　　p.n　see Past p.n　beautiful
　　'Zhang San saw Xiaoli being beautiful'

guangguang de 'naked', *jinzhang* 'nervous' both are stage-level predicates, denoting transitory, and alterable state, so they can act as the complement of perception verb *kanjian* 'see' as in (75a) and (76a). *gaogao de* 'tall', *piaoliang* 'beautiful' are both individual-level predicates, denoting permanent properties. When ILP occurs as the complement of perception verb, the sentence will be unacceptable as (75b) and (76b). The semantic function of the complement small clauses is just like a when-clause, and (75a) and (76a) can be paraphrased as following:

　　(77) a. When Li Si was naked, Zhang San saw him.
　　　　b. When Xiaoli was nervous, Zhang San saw her.

We have explained that only SLPs can occur in when-clauses, which is why (75b) and (76b) are unacceptable.

The analysis in this section shows that the morphological difference of adjectives does not reflect the temporal feature of the adjectives. About what kind of adjectives can occur as adverbials and what cannot, scholars try to explain the difference from other aspects.

3.3.3.2 Object-adjectives and Event-adjectives and ILP/SLP Distinction

The adjective in (78) is ambiguous, and can be paraphrased as (79a) and (79b) respectively:

---

① There is no pause before the predicate complement 'gaogaode' and 'guangguangde' otherwise, 'gaogaode' and 'guangguangde' will become an after-thought insertion.

(78) Olga is a beautiful dancer
(79) a. 'Olga is a dancer and Olga is beautiful'
　　b. 'Olga is beautiful as a dancer'/ 'Olga dances beautifully'

(Larson 1995: 1)

　　Muffy Siegel (1976) proposes that such ambiguous adjectives in English reflect a fundamental dichotomy between basic attributive interpretation and basic predicative one. Larson (1995) distinguishes such ambiguity as subject-modifying interpretation and VP-modifying interpretation. Geuder (2000: 2) notices that many adjectives function as predicates of individuals while their corresponding derived adverbs modify events:

(80) a. to open the package carefully　　Manner adverb: careful(e)
　　 b. a careful person　　Attributive adjective: careful(x)

　　He refers to such variants as "e-predicates" and "x-predicates"[①]. Some adjectives like *fast* only apply to event, and some others like *tired* only apply to non-event individuals. A lot of adjectives like *careful, intelligent, and beautiful* are ambiguous, for they can be applied naturally to either events or individuals.

　　Such ambiguity of adjectives is also reflected in Chinese, so Zheng (2000: 241) distinguishes two main functions of adjectives: participant-related function and predicate-related function. When an adjective occur as adnominal modifier or as predicate, it is a participant-related adjective. The participant-related function is the prominent function of adjectives. All adjectives in Chinese exhibit the participant-related function. Predicate-related function means that the adjective functions as adverbial of VP or the *buyu* of VP. Some adjectives in Chinese have no predicate-related function. Usually, if a word just exhibits predicate-related function, it will be categorized as an adverb, instead of being an adjective.

[①] In Gender's study, e means event, and x means entity.

Zhang (2005) proposes a similar classification based on the semantic contents of adjectives and targets they modify: object adjectives and event adjectives. Such a classification is highly relevant to the research in this paper.

(81) The distribution of entity-related and event-related adjectives:
object/event-related adjective

$\longleftrightarrow$

object-related adjectives　　　　event-related adjectives

Adapted from Zhang (2000: 454)

However, there are still a lot of adjectives can alternate between object-related interpretation and event-related interpretation. So, it is a continuum with typical object-related adjectives and event-related adjectives at two ends, and adjectives that are ambiguous between object-related and event-related stay in the middle, and this is one of the reasons why it is possible for an adjective to have both participant-oriented and VP-oriented readings.

a. Object-related adjectives and ILPs[①]

Object-related adjectives naturally function as attributives. That is to say, there is a natural relevance between object-related adjectives and attributives. A noun denotes an object with a number of properties, and an adjective is only related to certain dimension of one property. Object-related adjectives are subcategorized into seven groups according to the properties they are related to:

(82) a. space: *da* 'big', *xiao* 'small', *gao* 'tall', *ai* 'low', *kuan* 'wide',

　　b. measurement: *qing* 'light', *zhong* 'heavy', *yuan* 'far', *jin* 'near', *shen* 'deep', *qian* 'shallow', *song* 'loose', *jin* 'tight'

[①] Object, in this sense, equals to the denotations of nouns, including human being and entities except for events.

c. color: *hei* 'black', *xuebai* 'snow-white', *heihuhu* 'dark'
d. age: *lao* 'old', *nianqing* 'young',
e. property:, *jiu* 'used', *zang* 'dirty', *leng* 'cold', *shilulu* 'wet'.
f. evaluation: *hao* 'good', *congming* 'clever', *ehenhen* 'ferocious'.
g. physical and psychological state: *reqing* 'enthusiasm', *fanzao* 'restless', *fennu* 'angry', *xiaomimi* 'smiling',

In these seven groups, we can find that (82a, 82b, 82c, 82d) denote fairly permanent properties of the modified object, while (82 e,f,g) describe the states the object stays in. All the adjectives in (82a) denote physical properties of the modified object and usually these properties last permanently for the whole process of the existence of the modified object. The adjectives in (82e) describe a specific state of the modified object, and the state is not stable and will not last for the whole process of the existence of the modified object. From this analysis, we notice that not all object-related adjectives are individual-level predicates, such as (82g), so these adjectives denoting transitory states can be extended to the sentential function of adverbials easier than those denoting permanent properties.

b. Event-related adjectives and SLPs

Similar to object, an event also corresponds to a multi-dimensional concept with a number of properties, so event-related adjectives are divided into seven groups according to the properties these adjectives are related to (Zhang 2006; Wang 2006; Cong 2013):

(83) a. time: *zao* 'early', *wan* 'late'
b. speed: *kuai* 'fast', *man* 'slow', *xunsu* 'rapid',
c. manner: *wen* 'stable', *guai* 'abnormal', *caosuai* 'rash'
d. domain: *guangfan* 'wide range', *quanmian* 'comprehensive'
e. degree: *guofen* 'excessive', *shidang* 'proper', *jianyao*

'brief',
f. state: *congmang* 'hurried', *menglie* 'violently', *shunli* 'smooth'
g. frequency: *qin* 'frequent', *pinfan* 'often',

    Generally speaking, adjectives are restricted in occurring as adverbial modifiers, but typical event-related adjectives naturally appear as adverbials. There is a natural relevance between event-related adjectives and adverbials. All these seven groups of event-related adjectives in (83) denote the time of happening, the speed of moving, the manner of event, the domain an event covers, the degree and state of an event, and the frequency of an event takes place. The criteria of classification are not so clearly defined, and there are some overlaps between different groups, but it is helpful to explore the features of these event-related adjectives. All these adjectives are stage-level predicates denoting transitory states and modifying a certain property of a given event. However, whether all these event-related adjectives will introduce an underlying Davidsonian argument is also context-sensitive.

    When these event-related adjectives act as attributes or primary predicates of noun, they don't modify one of the properties denoted by the noun. A relevant event is involved in the interpretation of such adjectives:

(84) a. Zhe liang che hen kuai.
      this CL car very fast
      'This car is very fast.'
  b. Zheliangche kuaikuai de.
      this CL car fast$_{REDUPL}$ de
      'This car is very fast.'

(85) a. kuai che.
      fast car
  b. kuaikuai de yi liang che.
      fast$_{REDUPL}$ de one CL car
      'a fast car'

According to Qualia Theory proposed by Pustejovshy (1995), the lexical entry of nouns does not just name its referent flatly, but include a list of so-called qualia, which may provide additional information that can play a role in the semantic composition. He suggests a fixed list of types of qualia information:

(86) a. CONSTITUTIVE QUALIA: the relation between an object and its constituent parts
b. TELIC QUALIA: its purpose and function
c. AGENTIVE QUALIA: factors involved in its origin or the way it comes into being
d. FORMAL QUALIA: what distinguishes it within a larger domain

In (84) and (85), the adjective chooses to modify the telic qualia of the noun *che* 'car'. Roughly speaking, the telic qualia of the car is that a car can run, and the event-related adjective *kuai* 'fast' modify an event instead of the denotation of the noun.

(87) a. che: FORMAL QUALIA: x
TELIC QUALIA: run (e, x)
b. kuai: kuai(e)
c. kuaiche: FORMAL:x
TELIC QUALIA: run (e, x)& kuai(e)
$\lambda x. \lambda e. \exists e$ run (e, x) & kuai (e)

When event-related adjectives modify nouns, an underlying event is introduced because the property *kuai* 'fast' can only be elucidated on the basis of an event of moving. Following this line of thinking, we can suppose the interpretation of AAs all involve an event.

According to Croft (1984), event-adjectives have a natural correlation with the sentential function of adverbials. Typical event-related adjectives are stage-level predicates and they naturally appear as adverbials. Consequently, they occur as adverbials in the zero-derived form, and the structural subordinator *-De* is optional.

It is true that the morphological character of adjectives in Chinese has a strong influence on their grammatical functions and prosodic distributions; whereas it is also undeniable that the morphological character cannot so rigidly reflect the distinction between ILP/SLP.

From the previous analyses, we can draw a conclusion that the SA/CA contrast does not correspond to ILP/SLP distinction, in that the ILP/SLP distinction exists in both SAs and CAs. We can infer that morphological alternation cannot change the temporal feature of adjectives. This conclusion is in disagreement with the traditional opinion that SAs express permanent properties and all members CAs express transitory and dynamic states.

The ILP/SLP distinction is a semantic classification, which is reflected in both SAs and CAs. Separating ILPs from SLPs in both SAs and CAs can reflect language intuition more accurately and will be helpful in explaining some language facts.

The contrast between object-adjectives and event-adjectives proposed in Zhang (2005) steps over the boundary between simple and complex adjectives. Such a classification is closely related to the ILP/SLP distinction, although there are a lot of object-related adjectives are ambiguous between individual-level reading and stage-level reading. We can see that all the typical event-related adjectival are stage-level predicates, so they occur as adverbials freely. Object-related adjectives do not completely correspond to individual-level predicates. The contrast of object-related adjectives and event-related adjectives does accurately reflect the fact that event adjectives occur as adverbials freely, however, there are still a lot of object-related adjectives occur as adverbials. This classification fails to give an explanation for these AAs. The contrast between object-adjectives and event-adjectives does have its theoretical and practical merits: it provides another perspective to enrich and deepen the grammatical perception of adjectives in Mandarin Chinese. Zhang himself states that such a classification of adjectives presents more psychological reality than the SA/CA classification.

The ILP/SLP distinction is not only a static classification of predicates, because the context in which the predicate appears will greatly influence the interpretation of the predicate, just as Kratzer (1995) writes, "*If a distinction between stage-level and individual-level predicates is operative in nature language, it cannot be a distinction that is made in the lexicon of a language once and for all."*

The ILP/SLP distinction is very important for the analysis of AAs in Chinese, for we have found that only when an adjectives have SLP interpretation, can it occur as AA, whereas only when a primary predicate have a SLP interpretation, can it be modified by AAs. However, the number of syllables and morphological forms of adjectives cannot decide the ILP/SLP distinction of adjectives in Chinese once for all. It has been pointed out that the ILP/SLP contrast and the classification of eventuality are highly context-sensitive. The contexts can coerce the shift between ILPs and SLPs and the eventuality types (Verkuyl 1972; Dowty 1979, 1991; Rothstein 2004).

3.4 The Nature and Basic Elements of Event

In Section 3.3, we have reviewed the classification of predicates, including verbal and adjectival predicates. It has been stated that the Davidsonian argument is very important for the ILP/SLP contrast. However, as for the nature of the underlying event argument, there is no a uniform definition.

3.4.1 Ontological Properties of Event

Concerning the ontological properties of underlying event argument, Maienborn (2005) put forth such questions: What does it mean for a predicate to have a Davidsonian eventuality argument? What linguistic properties follow from its presence? And what means are available to detect these hidden arguments? Of course, Davidsonian approach has proposed many versions of answers to these questions, but none of these questions has so far received anything like a defin, it, ive answer.

As LePore (1985: 151) puts it, *"Davidson's central claim is that events are concrete particulars---that is, unrepeatable entities with a location in space and time."* However, such a highly abstract philosophical definition is not very workable for the semantics of natural language. Maienborn (2005: 297) provides a working definition of Davidsonian notion of eventualities:

(88) Eventualities are particular spatiotemporal entities with functionally integrated participants.

Following this working definition, three ontological properties that are generally accepted are summarized in (89):

(89) Ontological properties of event

I. They are perceptible.
——Event expressions can be infinitival complements of perception verbs.

II. They can be located in space and time.
——It is possible for event expressions to combine with locative and temporal modifiers.

III. They can vary in the way they take place.
——Event expressions are capable of combining with manner adverbials, instrumentals, comitatives, etc.

(Maienborn 2005: 280):

From the definition of eventuality given by Maienborn, it can be concluded that spatiotemporal feature and participant are the basic elements of eventuality. In the following sections, these two elements will be studied in detail.

3.4.2 Temporal Feature

From the classification of the predicates in Section 3.3, we can find that the temporal feature is the most important factor deciding the classification of predicates. Telicity is about whether an event has a natural stopping point. If an event has a natural ending, it is telic; otherwise, it is atelic. Stage is about whether we can analyze the event as progressing or developing.

Another feature we will take into consideration is the homogeneity.

The default reading of an adjectival predicate is always homogeneous. Roughly speaking, both state and activity in Vendler's classification are homogeneous. Rothstein (2004: 11) further distinguishes homogeneity down to instants and homogeneity down to small part: the former corresponds to state and the latter corresponds to activity. In this sense, the default reading of adjective is always homogeneity down to instants. The definition is expressed formally as in (90):

(90) a. P is homogeneous iff P is cumulative and divisive.
  i. P is divisive
     iff $\forall x[P(x) \rightarrow \exists y(P(y) \wedge y < x)] \wedge \forall x,y[P(x) \wedge P(y) \wedge y < x \rightarrow P(x-y)]$
  ii. P is cumulative
     iff $\forall x[P(x) \wedge P(y) \rightarrow P(x \cup y)]$
b. P is quantity iff P is not homogeneous

Adapted from (Borer 2005: 192)

In a sentence containing an AA, there are two stage-level predicates, which means that there are two events. Following Krifka (1989, 1998), Rothstein (2004) adopts a temporal trace funciton τ_E to define temporal realtion between two events, which maps an event to its running time such that "$\tau(e_1 \cup e_2) = \tau(e_1) \cup \tau(e_2)$, and $\tau(e_1) \subseteq \tau(e_2)$".

(91) Part-of (e', e) iff
  (i) $\tau(e) \subseteq \tau(e')$ (the run time of e is temporally contained in e') and (ii) e' and e share a participant.

Adapted from (Rothstein 1999: 10)

In the analysis of the temporal relation between events, we will revise the definition of Part-whole relation to represent the temporal relation between the two events denoted by the two predicates in a sentence containing an AA.

3.4.3 Participant(s)

Parsons (1990) and Maienborn (2005) treat participant as basic element of event. The relation between event and its participant(s) is one of the focuses that reflect the theoretical development from classical Davidsonian approach to neo-Davidsonian approach. In different grammatical theories, linguists attempt to define and derive the notion of argument, especially the notion of subject in various methods; consequently, the logic forms of event semantics also reflect these varieties.

(92) Logic forms of different periods:

	Verbal denotation	e.g: Mary kissed John
traditional	$\lambda y \lambda x[kiss(x,y)]$	$kiss(m,j)$
Davidsonian	$\lambda y \lambda x \lambda e[kiss(e,x,y)]$	$\exists e[kiss(e,m,j)]$
Neo-Davidsonian	$\lambda e[kiss(e)]$	$\exists e[kiss(e) \wedge Ag(e,m) \wedge Th(e,j)]$
Landman(1996)	$\lambda y \lambda x \lambda e[kiss(e) \wedge Ag(e,x) \wedge Th(e,y)]$	$\exists e[kiss(e,m,j)]$
Kratzer(2000)	$\lambda y \lambda e[kiss(e,y)]$	$\exists e[Ag(e,m) \wedge kiss(e,j)]$

In classical work of formal semantics, the verb *kiss* is a two-place verb, and both the subject and object are the bounded variables of the verb. After Davidson introduces the underlying event argument into the logic forms, the verb *kiss* became a three-place predicate, and all these three arguments are bounded variables. In neo-Davidsonian approach, all predicates are one-place predicate, and event argument is the only variable bounded by the verb. Other arguments are combined with the event via thematic roles. Landman (1996) includes all the information of the thematic roles in the lexical entry of a verb, and all the arguments and event argument are bounded variables of the verb. Krazar (1996, 2000, 2002) proposes a semi neo-Davidsonian approach in that she claims all the arguments except for the agent are introduced in neo-Davidsonian style. In her proposal, the agent is introduced indirectly via a syntactic node, Voice, written as *v*, pronounced as 'little *v*', which heads a functional head above VP.

In this part, we have studied the basic elements of event. These elements are closely related to each other. Rothstein argues that verbs can be classified into verb classes, and this classification reflects the properties of the event in their denotation; verbs from particular class can interact with participant and modifiers to form different predications.

Verkuyl (1972) states that aspectual features come from two aspects: verbal predicates and nominal arguments. Participant and modifiers will cause the shift of the type of event.

3.5 Aspectual Shift

Verkuyl (1972) states that situation aspect is compositional, determined not only by the verb but also the verb's argument. Verbs have a certain lexical aspect, but it is context-sensitive. He suggests that the classification of eventualities should take the whole VP into consideration instead of just the verb. Dowty (1979) provides some examples to support that the idea that the number feature of the subject of the verb is capable of alternating the eventuality type of the verb in the classification. The eventuality type of a sentence need not be the eventuality of the main verb, and there are several types of syntactic constituents that directly affect the eventuality type of the entire clause, for example, the types of complements, PP attachment, verb particles, and resultative secondary predicates. Such phenomenon of aspectual changes is known as aspect shift (de Swart 1998; Rothstein 2004).

The temporal feature of adjective is lexical related but highly context-sensitive. As a result, under the contextual pressure, adjectives can be shifted into other aspectual classes corresponding to these of verbs. We will explain this phenomenon in terms of 'aspectual coercion' (Pustejovsky1995; Fernald 2000) Coercion is a reinterpretation process set up to eliminate the conflicts between the semantic content of a constituent and the requirements of the elements in the same construction. The predicate is coerced to reflect the aspectual features which are typical in the new context. In other words, coercion is a way out of ungrammaticality, if possible. Coercion in this work is not only relevant to the alternations between the four aspectual classes but also the alternation between ILP and SLP.

3.5.1 Coercion of Verbal Predicates

Whether a primary predicate can be modified by AAs is very

sensitive to the ILP/SLP contrast. In this paper, static verbal predicates will be further divided into ILPs and SLPs, and we hold that stage-level verbal predicates have an underlying Davidsonian event argument that the individual-level verbal predicates lack.

The ILP/SLP distinction and the eventuality types are compositional, instead of being exclusively lexicon-based. Sometimes, ILPs don't always express the property of individual, for the adding of adverbial modifiers will cause the verbal predicate shift from an ILP to an SLP.

(93) a. They know the answer.
   b. Her parents know Italian.
(94) a. Suddenly, Tom knew the answer.
   b. After six years of hard work, Alice knew Italian.

In (93) the verb *know*, as a typical ILP, denotes the relative permanent property of the subjects, but in (94), the same verb denotes transitory and dynamic progresses which have a definitive beginning. When the property denoted by an ILP doesn't belong to the subject for a considerable length of time, it is reasonable to imagine that the predicate has become a stage-level one, or that the speaker intends to use it as an SLP. Similarly, such alternation is common in Chinese:

(95) a. Zhang San renshi Li Si.
    p.n   know p.n
    'Zhang San knows Li Si.'
   b. Zhang San zai Beijing renshi le Li Si.
    p.n   at Peking know Perf p.n
    'Zhang San got to know Li Si in Peking.'
(96) a. Li Si xiang baba.
    p.n resemble father
    'Li Si resembles his father.'
   b. *Li Si xiang le baba.
    p.n resemble Perf father
    'Li Si resembles his father.'

In (95a), *renshi* 'know' is an ILP indicating a stable and relatively intrinsic property of a person, *le* is inappropriate here. However, (95b) is a good sentence in Mandarin. In (96a), *xiang* 'resemble' is a typical individual-level verbal predicate, expressing the relatively permanent property of Li Si, and the perfective marker *le* is not permitted. Such contrasts indicate that the stative verbal predicates are not a homogeneous set.

In Chinese, according to the syntactic position at which it appears, "*-le*" is divided into le_1 and le_2. le_1 is also known as verbal *le*, for it appear right after a verb, and le_2 appears at the end of a sentence, so is also called sentential *le*. We mainly focus on le_1 in our research. Sometimes, there is no constituent following the verb, so it is difficult to tell le_1 from le_2. When the verbal le_1 goes with different kind of predicate, it will have different semantic behaviors. Why does the verbal le_1 make the ILP reinterpreted as an SLP?

Smith (1997) suggests that when *-le* comes with a stative predicate, the static predicate is shifted into a dynamic one. The shifted situation is inchoative, which indicates the coming about of a new state. Lin (2003) also agrees that *le* indicates inchoative meaning when it goes with atelic predicates.

Pan (1993: 13) points out that *-le,* as a perfective marker, is an operator which has clausal scope, so it must bind some variable; otherwise the Prohibition against Vacuous Quantification will be violated:

> (97) Prohibition against Vacuous Quantification:
> For every quantifier Q, there must be a variable x such that Q binds an occurrence of x in both its restrictive clause and its nuclear scope.

In (95) and (96), all the constituents are constants, which cannot be bound by the operator, since *–le* requires an underlying event argument. As a result, the verbal predicate in (95b) is reinterpreted as an SLP which has an underlying event argument that can be bound by the perfective operator, whereas the stative predicate in (96b) failed to be re-interpreted as SLP, so *–le* ends up binding nothing. The prohibition in (97) is violated, thus (96b) is not acceptable. The logic forms of (95b) and (96b) are represented as (98a) and (98b):

(98) a. ∃e [renshi (e) & Exp (e)=Zhang San & Th(e) =Li Si&In (e, Peking)]
　　b. xiang (Li Si, baba)

Moens and Steedman (1988) state that when a stative predicate appears in a position where a non-stative predicate is required, the stative predicate is often coerced to receive a change-of-state reading. A change of state is a telic event and denoted by an SLP. The inchoative coercion will coerce an ILP into SLP. The logic form in (98a) doesn't reflect the inchoative meaning, but at least, we can detect the difference between the individual-level verbal predicate and stage-level verbal predicate from the contrast between (98a) and (98b).

The coercion between ILP and SLP as well as between different aspectual classes is out of various reasons. I just take the aspectual operator *–le* as a sample to illustrate the principle of coercion. Such abnormal usage of ILP is not peculiar to verbal predicates. In the following section, the coercion of the adjectival predicates will be explained.

3.5.2 Coercion of Adjectival Primary Predicates

Individual-level adjectives usually denote relatively permanent property. However, the interpretation of adjective is highly context-sensitive.

(99) a. Zhang San de lian hen yuan
　　　　p.n　of face very round
　　　'Zhang San's face is round.'
　　b. Zhang San de lian yuan le.
　　　　p.n　of face round Perf
　　　'Zhang San's face become round.'

In general, when the adjective *yuan* 'round' indicates the shape of one's face as in (99a), it is an ILP, denoting stable and permanent property, so it should not be compatible with *-le*, for *-le* usually goes after stage-level predicates. The difference between (99a) and (99b) consists in the presence and absence of the particle *-le*.

Chao (1968) and Zhang (2011) suggest that -*le* makes the difference between (99a) and (99b). Different from this opinion, Zhang (2006) treats these adjectives compatible with -*le* to indicate a change of state as a group of special adjectives and names them as changing adjectives, but this explanation is not very influential. A lot of simple adjectives in Mandarin, ILP or SLP, are compatible with -*le*. If we set up a separate subcategory of adjectives just because they are compatible with -*le* to denote the change of state, the value of such a classification is questionable. Chao (1968), Zhang (2011) argue that the meaning of state change is not embedded in the ILP, but brought out by -*le*. In other words, individual-level adjective is coerced into having a stage-level interpretation by the perfective operator –*le*.

Not only individual-level adjectives can be coerced to have stage-level interpretation, but stage-level adjectives can be coerced to have different aspectual readings.

(100) a. Gaoxing dian.
   happy little
   'Be happy!'
  b. Xiaoming jintian hen gaoxing.
   p.n   today very happy
   'Xiaoming is happy today.'
  c. Xiaoming gaoxingle.
   p.n   happy Perf
   'Xiaoming got happy.'

In (100), *gaoxing* 'happy', as a stage-level adjective, in different context, can be coerced to have different aspectual readings corresponding to those of verbs. For example, (100a) is roughly equivalent to an activity, (100b) is roughly equivalent to a state, (100c) is reinterpreted as an achievement.

Kratzer (1989, 1995) suggests that SLPs have an underlying event variable that ILPs lack. Pan (1993) points out that –*le* is a perfective operator and should bind an event variable. (100c) is an acceptable sentence, which indicates that there is an event variable is bound by the perfective operator –*le*. However, what is the event argument in

(100c) like? The difference between (99a) and (99b) is reflected in the logic forms in (101), and the logical forms of the sentences in (100) are represented in (101):

> (101) a. yuan (Zhang San de lian)
> b. $\exists e\ [yuan\ (e)\ \wedge Th(e)=Zhang\ San\ de\ lian]$
> (102) a. $\exists e\ [gaoxing\ (e)\ \wedge Th(e)=x]$
> b. $\exists e\ [gaoxing\ (e)\ \wedge Th(e)=Xiaoming\ \wedge jintian(e)]$
> c. $\exists e\ [gaoxing\ (e)\ \wedge Th(e)=x]$

(101a) expresses that Zhang San's face has the property of being round. However, the logic form (101b) is inadequate to express the native speaker's intuition about (99b). (99b) intends to express a dynamic process in which Zhang San's face manifested the property of being round or Zhang San's face became round. The logic forms in (102) are also far from being accurate reflections of the meanings of the corresponding sentences.

Rothstein (2004: 16) states that if stative predicates are coerced out of their natural stativity, they are coerced into an inchoative or achievement reading. Following this line of thinking, we can analyze the adjectives in (99) and (100) in the same pattern as Rothstein analyzes different verbal aspectual classes in (38) (repeated here for clearness):

> (38) a. States: $\lambda P\lambda e.P(e)$
> b. Activities: $\lambda P\lambda e.\ (DO(P))(e)$
> c. Achievenments: $\lambda P\lambda e.\ (BECOME(P))(e)$
> d. Accomplishments: $\lambda P\lambda e.\ \exists e_1 \exists e_2 [e=^S(e_1 \cup e_2)\ \wedge\ (DO(P))(e_1)$
> $\wedge(BECOME(P'))(e_2)\ \wedge Cul(e)=e_2]$
>
> Rothstein (1999: 404)

(101b) will be revised as in (103):

> (103) $\lambda P\lambda e.\ (BECOME(P))(e)\ \wedge Arg(e)=Zhang\ San\ de\ lian])$
> (yuan)

=∃e. [(BECOME(yuan))(e) ∧Arg(e)=Zhang San de lian]

The logic forms in (100) are revised as those in (104):

(104) a. λP ∃e [(DO(P)) (e) ∧Arg(e)=x](gaoxing)
=∃e [(DO(gaoxing)) (e) ∧Arg(e)=x]
b. ∃e [gaoxing (e) ∧Arg(e)=Xiaoming ∧jintian(e)]
c. λP ∃e [(BECOME(P))(e) ∧Arg(e)=Xiaoming](gaoxing)
=∃e [(BECOME(gaoxing))(e) ∧Arg(e)=Xiaoming]

The logic forms in (103) and (104) are much better than these in (101) and (102) in that the introduction of the predicates DO, BECOME expresses the dynamic process denoted by these adjectives. When adjectives occur as primary predicate, the coercion of the predicate is caused by the aspectual marker in (99b) and (100c), by the imperative mood in (100a), by the adverbial in (100b).

With the introduction of the notion of coercion, we can account for some apparent anomalies in the distribution of linguistic elements without being compelled to abandon independently justified classifications.

Generally speaking, predicates are not inherently ILP or SLP. When adjectives are independent predicates, it is relatively easier to decide whether it is an ILP or SLP. However, in a particular context, some of the adjectives are alterable between ILP and SLP. The logic forms in (103) and (104) indicate that the aspectual features of predicate are compositional and context-sensitive. With the introducing of the notion of coercion, the temporal feature mismatch between the adjective and the context is settled down.

3.6 Further Development of Neo-Davidsonian Approach

No matter in classical Davidsonian or neo-Davidsonian approach, the semantic analyses is still conduced in a static pattern and the logic forms espress the final interpretation of a sentence. However, the interpretation of a sentence is a dynamic and incremental process. How to reflect such a dynamic and incremental process? In another respect, classical Davidsonian approach just analyzes some prepositional phrases as the predicate of the underlying event argument, and neo-Davidsonian approach includes some attributive adverbs as the predicates of the underlying event. Generally speaking, the adverbials that can be analyzed as predicates if underlying event argument are still restrained to VP-oriented modifiers. Whether other predicational adverbials can be analyzed analogously?

In this part, development of event semantic in these two directions will be briefly sketched for they are closely related to the research in this work.

3.6.1 Theory of Predication (Rothstein 2001, 2004)

A sentence is a binary structure including two different kinds of constituents which are traditionally known as subject and predicate. The VP-internal subject hypothesis supposes that the original position of the subject is within VP (Koopman and Sportiche 1991; Pollock 1989; and Fukui & Speas 1986).

(105) a. Tom hit John.
　　　b. [$_{IP}$Tom$_i$ [$_{I'}$[$_{VP}$ t$_i$[$_{V'}$[$_V$ hit] John]]]]

Syntactically, all arguments of the verb appear within the VP; the subject appears in the Spec of VP and moves to the surface subject position, with a trace left there at the original position. The VP-internal hypothesis assumes a different model of combination of elements, so the semantic representation will be changed accordingly. After the VP-internal subject hypothesis has been put forth, attempts have been made to give the corresponding semantic representation (Chierchia 1989; Wyner 1994).

(106) a. Tom hit John
　　　b. [$_{IP}$(Tom) [$_{I'}$ λz[$_{VP}$ (z)[$_{V'}$[$_V$ λy λx Hit(x.y)](John)]]]]
　　　c. [$_{IP}$(Tom) [$_{I'}$ λz[$_{VP}$ (z)[$_{V'}$ λx Hit(x.John)]]]]
　　　d. [$_{IP}$(Tom) [$_{I'}$ λz[$_{VP}$ Hit(z, John)]]]
　　　e. hit (Tom, John)

In the semantic translation of the sentence in (106b), the verb takes two bounded variables as its arguments. With the introduction of the internal argument *john* and the λ-reduction operation, the verb is a relation which takes as its arguments *john* and a trace of the moved argument which is translated into a variable. As we can see in (106d), before the subject *tom* entering into the semantic representation, the θ-grid of the verb has been saturated. In order to get the subject *tom* into the relation, the saturated VP will be reopened by an operation of λ-abstraction. Finally, the semantic representation (106e) is derived.

In the neo-Davidsonian version of underlying event theory, as argued for in Higginbothan (1985), Parsons(1990), and Landman (1995, 2000), the verb *kiss* in (107b) binds an event variable e, and these two participants are bound variables bounded by lambda operators. (107a) has the representation in (107c):

(107) a. Mary kissed John.
b. $\lambda y[\ \lambda x[\lambda e\ KISS(e) \wedge Ag(e)= x \wedge Th(e)= y]]$
c. $\exists e[Kiss(e) \wedge Ag(e)= Mary \wedge Th(e)= John \wedge PAST(e)]$

Rothstein (2001, 2004) doesn't assume the VP-internal subject hypothesis. She assumes that the subject is base-generated in [Spec, IP] position, instead of being generated in [Spec, VP] and then moved to [Spec, IP]. She writes:

"The grammatical theory of predication assumes that a predicate is a structurally open syntactic constituent; predication is relation between a predicate and a structurally closed constituent in which the latter closes the former by filling the open position in it. The element which closes a predicate is its subject".

Rothstein (2001: 42)

She agrees that a set of thematic roles of a lexical head can be empty, and keeps the neo-Davidsonian underlying event variable e in the semantic formula. In Rothstein's predication theory, (108a) is represented as (108b):

(108) a. Mary kissed John.
   b. λy λe. [Kiss(e) ∧ Ag(e)= x ∧ Th(e)= y](John)

In (108b), the subject is a free variable, which means that a constituent of type <e, t> will form after applying the verb to all the arguments inside its VP①. However, there is a typal mismatch, for VPs should be unsaturated and functional, while the expression which resulted from combing the verb with its internal argument is saturated. In order to absorb the subject, Rothstein introduces the predicate formation rule, which is equal to the operation of lambda abstraction.

(109) Predicate Formation:
   If α is the translation of a syntactic predicate then
   α→λx.α
                                            (Rothstein 2001: 138)

Such a lambda abstraction operation which introduces bounded variable is an operation which occurs automatically at the XP predicate level, and it occurs independently of whether the expression α contains a free variable x or not. That means it permits vacuous λ-abstraction operation. The predicate formation rule is triggered by the category of the node and not by any thematic properties of the lexical head. Different from the expressions in type theory, in the event semantic analysis, the type of individual is marked as *d*; *e* is for the type of event; and t is truth value. Based on the predicate theory of Rothstein, (110) will be taken as a sample to illustrate the event semantic derivation process:

(110) The derivation process of 'Mary kissed John'

   a. [kiss]$_V$ → λyλe.kiss(e) ∧Ag(e)=x∧Th(e)=y
   b. [kiss John] $_{V'}$→[λyλe.kiss(e) ∧Ag(e)=x∧Th(e)= y](John)
      =λe.kiss(e) ∧Ag(e)=x∧Th(e)= John
   c. [Kissed John]$_{VP}$→λx[λe.[kiss(e) ∧Ag (e)=x

---

① Here e stands for event.

$\wedge$Th(e)= John $\wedge$ PAST(e)] (by predicate formation)
d. [Kissed John]$_{I'}$ →λx[λe.[kiss(e) $\wedge$Ag (e)=x$\wedge$Th(e)= John $\wedge$PAST(e)]
e. [Mary kissed John]IP→ λx[λe.[kiss(e) $\wedge$Ag (e)=x $\wedge$Th(e)= John $\wedge$PAST(e)](Mary)
=λe[kiss(e) $\wedge$Ag (e)=Mary$\wedge$Th(e)= John $\wedge$ PAST(e)]
f. Existential quantification leads to: ∃e [kiss(e) $\wedge$Ag (e)=Mary
$\wedge$Th(e)= John$\wedge$PAST(e)]

(111) The derivation tree:

∃e [kiss(e) $\wedge$Ag (e)=Mary$\wedge$Th(e)= John$\wedge$PAST(e)]
| **(existential quantification)**
IP. λe.[kiss(e) $\wedge$Ag(e)=Mary$\wedge$Th(e)=John$\wedge$PAST(e)]

DP. Mary   VP. λx[λe.[kiss(e) $\wedge$Ag (e)=x$\wedge$Th(e)=John]
             | **(predicate formation)**
             V'. [λyλe.kiss(e) $\wedge$Ag(e)=x$\wedge$Th(e)=John]

      V. λye.kiss(e) $\wedge$Ag(e)=x$\wedge$Th(e)=y   DP. John

Mary kiss < θ_{Ag}, θ_{Th}>   John

It is usually assumed that the syntactic rules by which constituents are combined together are what syntacticians should care about. Semanticists should care more about the process of interpretation. However, in any meaningful structures, there is a systematic correspondence between syntax and semantics, or the set of syntactic structures and that of semantic structures are isomorphic to each other, which is obviously presented in the derivation process proposed by Rothstein. Such a dynamic and incremental derivation process is very valuable for the analysis of AAs, for that the semantic orientation of AA is unspecified and context-sensitive. It will get specified incrementally with the derivation process going on.

3.6.2 Scope-based Analysis of Predicational Adverbs by Ernst (2002)

A difference between Davidsonian approach and neo-Davidsonian approach is that more kinds of adverbials can be analyzed as the predicate of the underlying event argument. Davidson (1967) just treats some VP-oriented prepositional phrases as the predicates of underlying events, and he doubts the feasibility of analyzing "attributives" in the same way. Parsons (1990) extents the application of the theory into the analysis of "attributes", such as 'slowly', 'violently', 'gently', which greatly increases the amount of language data that can be included as the targets of event semantic research. However, these adverbials just constitute a very small subset of the predicational adverbials. Cross-linguistically, predicational adverbials are generally subcategorized and ordered according to the template in (112):

(112) Discourse-Oriented > Evaluative > Epistemic >
Subject-Oriented
> Manner

(Ernst 2007: 1009)

From (112), we can find that manner (VP-oriented) adverbs are only a subcategory of predicational adverbs. Ernst (2002) attempts to apply the pattern of analyzing adverbials in neo-Davidsonian approach to the other groups of predicational adverbials, and he proposes the FEO (*Fact-Event Object*) Calculus, which consists of rules for building events and propositions. More complex FEOs are constructed from simpler ones in a compositional and stepwise way by adding layers of adverbials, quantificational operators, aspectual operators, modality, etc. He states that semantics plays a substantial and direct role in deciding the distribution of predicational adverbials. Take (113) as an example to illustrate how the FEO Calculus operates and the relationship between predicational adverbial and its argument:

(113) a. Obviously, Mark wisely did not kick the ball for an hour.
b. [$_{PROP}$ OBVIOUS[$_{PROP}$ [$_{STATE}$ WISE[$_{STATE}$ PAST[$_{STATE}$ ¬

[PROC for-an-hour[Q-EVENT KICK(E) ∧Agt(e)=MARK
∧Th(e)=BALL]]]]]]

Adapted from (Ernst 2002: 52)

From (113b), we can notice that all the predicational adverbials are analyzed in the same pattern as the predicate of the relevant argument. However, the argument is not always the event argument, but different categories of FEOs. Central concepts of Ernst's theory are expressed in (114):

> (114) Essential Points of the Scope-based analysis of predicational adverbs:
> a. The adjectival base of the predicational adverb semantically selects for certain properties of its FEO (including it type, controllability).
> b. Predicational adverbs only select FEO as arguments, and the FEOs are composed in agreement with the order of the FEO Hierarchy:
> Speech-Act >Fact > Proposition>Event >Specified Event
> c. Failure in satisfying the requirement of predicational adverbs on FEO will result in ill-formed or ungrammatical sentences.

The scope-based analysis of predicational adverbs proposed by Ernst (2002) is highly relevant to the analysis of AAs in Mandarin, for AAs in Mandarin, different from secondary predicates in English, are not only semantically related to participants of the verb. There are VP-oriented AAs, clause-oriented AAs, so the FEO calculus is very helpful for the analyses of non-participant related AAs.

The latest development of the theories related to the underlying event argument has greatly improved the explanatory power of this theory. The theory of predication proposed by Rothstein provides a dynamic perspective for the analyses of AAs and the FEO calculus proposed by Ernst enlarges the application of the idea of neo-Davidsonian approach to various predicational adverbs besides the VP-oriented adverbs.

Combining these two theories, we can get more inspirations for the analyses of adjectival adverbials in Mandarin. The unspecified argument of the adjective occurring as adverbial is a free variable, and the value of the variable is not restricted to the participants of the verb, it can also be any FEO in Ernst's sense. As we get to know in Chapter 2, the adjectival adverbials are not always participant-oriented.

In recent years, the means of psycholinguistic experiments are employed in testing the hypotheses on theoretical linguistic assumptions about the event structure. Such new methods are highly relevant to the processing of underlying event structure and of event coercion. These new developments indicate that Davidsonian events are going to develop into a subject of psychological research on natural language.

3.7 Summary

Compositionality and context-dependency are two theoretical issues that any linguistic theory must take into consideration. Compositionality of language means that words can be combined to form sentences with arbitrary degrees of complexity. The principle of compositionality is also known as Frege's principle. It states that the meaning of a complex expression is a function of the meanings of its parts and of the syntactic rules by which they are combined (Partee, B.H., ter Meulen, A.and Wall, R.E. 1990: 316).

Context-dependency means that linguistic expressions can be utilized to express different interpretations in different contexts. The concept of context not only refers to the inter-relationships among sentences but also the intra-relationship between the constituents in a sentence. The context-dependent property is embodied in the interaction between the interpretation of a constituent and those neighboring it.

The adjectival adverbials in Chinese reflect the mismatch between syntactic positions and semantic orientations, as well as the temporal feature mismatch between adjective and verb. From this perspective, any attempt to provide a pure syntactic analysis or a pure semantic analysis will fail to catch the characteristics of AAs in Chinese.

In order to resolve these problems concerning AAs, we have to find a methodology that is suitable to represent these features of AAs. The Davidsonian event argument has become an important linguistic instrument to reveal fresh insights into the compositionality of natural language meaning. With the event argument as a particular ontology introduced into the logic form, event semantics provides a ready platform to analyze the compositionality and context-sensitivity of the meaning of natural language. The predicate theory based on event proposed by Rothstein provides a dynamic and incremental perspective to analyze predicates. This approach is attractive because of its simplicity and because it naturally accounts for the fact that a clause with a manner adverb entails the corresponding clause without a manner adverb. At the same time the temporal feature mismatch and the syntactic-semantic mismatch will be explained in a simple and direct style.

Although Rothstein provides a dynamic prospective to present the derivation process of logic form, and the TPCONNECT is very effective in indicating the temporal relation and the shared participant between events, it is not completely suitable to analyze AAs in her pattern. The AAs in Chinese have some features that make them different form that of secondary predicates and predicational predicates in English. So in the following parts, we will try to adapt the existing theories to make it suitable for AAs in Chinese.

AAs in Mandarin are usually composed of under adjectives and structural subordinator *-De,* and sometimes, the under adjectives are complex adjectives derived from simple adjective. How these under adjectives and the structural subordinator *–De* are composed to get different AAs with different semantic orientation is one of the major concerns in this work. In the following chapters, the main task is to focus on revealing the compositionality and context-sensitivity of adjectival adverbials and representing the dynamic and incremental derivation process of under adjective from lexicon to the adverbial interpretation.

Chapter Four

Clarification and Reclassification of AAs

This chapter mainly focuses on confirming the nature and the reclassification of adjectival adverbials in Mandarin. The confirmation of the nature of the AA is conducted through comparing AAs with other kinds of downgraded predicates. The classification of AAs in this chapter is not based on the morphological features of the under adjectives but on the function of the under adjectives as adverbials. The organization of this chapter is as follows. In Section 4.1, AAs are identified as a kind of downgraded predicates, and to clarify the nature of it, AAs are first compared with attributes, primary adjectival predicates, and *buyu* in Chinese, and then with predicational adverbs and secondary predicates in English. Section 4.2 mainly focuses on the criterion of classification of AAs based on three factors: temporal relation between events denoted by the two predicates in the sentence, the aspectual feature of the event denoted by the adjective and its semantic orientation. AAs are separated into seven kinds. Section 4.3 mainly analyzes three kinds of subject-oriented AAs. Two kinds of object-oriented AAs are discussed in Section 4.4. Section 4.5 is about VP-oriented AAs. Clause-oriented AAs are analyzed in Section 4.6. The summary of this chapter is presented in Section 4.7.

4.1 The Nature of Adjectival Adverbials

Adjectives in Chinese can occur as subjects, objects, predicates, attributes, adverbials, and *buyu*①. Except for occurring as subjects and objects, all the other functions of adjective express a kind of predication relation, and when the predication relation expressed by the adjective is focused by the speaker, the adjective occurs as the primary predicate.

Croft (1984) distinguishes 'natural' and 'unnatural' correlations of lexical items and their sentential functions. In a natural correlation, the lexical items have the zero-derived form which is no more complex than any other form in less natural correlations. In unnatural correlations, lexical items will lose many of their own typical characteristics and would be taking on the characteristics of other categories depending on what function they take in the unnatural correlations.

According to croft, the correlation between adjective and the sentential function of adnominal modifier is a natural relation, whereas the correlation between adjective and sentential function of adverbial is an 'unnatural' one. The unnaturalness is reflected in two mismatches.

Firstly, the temporal feature mismatch. Adjectives denote a single relatively permanent property, and verbs denote transitory events or actions involving change. Naturally, it is not appropriate to modify a transitory event with a permanent property. However, there are a lot adjectival adverbials in Chinese, which seems to constitute a contradictory. Because of the mismatch between the temporal features of the denotations of adjective and verb, adjectives are not so free to occur as adverbials as they do when they modify nouns.

When adjectives are extended to the sentential function of adverbials, adjectives will take on the temporal characteristics of verbs. Verbs, especially these denoting actions, are not time-stable, which means that the adjectives occurring as adverbials also share this property. Only these adjectives that can be interpreted as having transitory features can occur as adverbials.

(1) a. *Xiaoli dada De you yishuang yanjing.
　　　p.n big big De have one CL eye
　　　'Xiaoli has big eyes.'

---

① Here, the complement is *buyu* in Chinese, usually appear after verb. It is different from the concept of complement in syntax.

b. Xiaoqiang rere De he   le yi bei cha.
   p.n   hot De drimk Perf one cup tea
   'Xiaoqiang drank a cup of tea hot.'
c. *Li Si pangpang De zhan zai zhuozi shang.
   p.n fat fat   De stand at desk on
   'Li Si is standing on the desk and he is fat.'
d. Xiaoming jidong De tiao shang le zhuozi.
   p.n   excited De jump on Perf desk
   'Xiaoming excitedly jumped onto the desk.'

The adjective *da* 'big' denotes the physical property of one's eyes, and *pang* 'fat' describes one's figure. They denote relatively permanent properties. Furthermore, the event denoted by the main verb in each sentence cannot coerce these adjectives to have transitory features, so the sentences in (1a, c) are not acceptable. In (1b, d) the under adjectives *rere-de* 'hot' and *jidong* 'excited' denote transitory states, so they can occur as adverbials. The contrast of acceptability among these sentences initially supports the hypothesis that adjectives denoting transitory states can occur as adverbials.

Secondly, syntactic position and semantic orientation mismatch. Adverbials are typically the modifiers of verbs. However, as indicated in (1), not all AAs are semantically related to the verb. In (1b), *rere-De* "hot" is semantically related to the object *yibeicha* 'a cup of tea', while in (1d), *jidong-De* is semantically related to the subject *Xiaoming*.

As a result of these two mismatches, adjectives are highly constrained for the adverbial sentential function, so the proportion of adjectives which may function as adverbials is not high. The correlation between adjective and the function of adverbial is an unnatural one in Croft's sense. Consequently, many adjectives are in the reduplicated forms when they occur as adverbials and the structural subordinator *-De* is often compulsory.

Among the researches on AAs in Chinese, AAs are often compared with the other relevant constituents. In this section, in order to reveal the nature of adjectival adverbial, Adjectival adverbials in Mandarin will be compared with adnominal modifiers, adjectival primary predicates and *buyu*. In addition, some researchers treat AAs that are semantically related to participants of the event denoted by the primary predicate as secondary predicates, so in this section, a comparison will also be made between AAs and secondary predicate as well as predicational adverbs in English. All these comparisons will be conducted from an event semantic perspective.

4.1.1 AAs Are Downgraded Predicates

The term 'predicate' was originally used in Greek logic for all the rest parts in a clause besides the subject. The grammatical theory of predication assumes that a predicate is a structurally open syntactic constituent; predication is a kind of relation between a predicate and a structurally closed constituent in which the latter closes the former by filling the open position in it. The constituent that closes a predicate is its subject. Rothstein (2001) states that a syntactic predicate is a monadic, unsaturated syntactic function and every syntactic predicate must be syntactically saturated. Adjectives and verbs naturally occur as predicates for they are inherently unsaturated.

As for the relation between a modifier and its head, scholars have noticed that the relationship between subject and its predicate can be utilized to paraphrase most kinds of modification relation (Jesperson 1929). Jin (2009) states that a clause should include at least one predicate and the more complex a clause is, the more predicates the clause includes. The primary predicate is just the one that is chosen and highlighted by the speaker from predicates in the clause. When a sentence includes more than one predication relation without any conjunction, these predication relations usually are distinguished as primary predication and non-primary predication. Non-primary predication is often called downgraded predication or secondary predication (in a broad sense)[①]. Even in a single language, downgraded predicates may be represented in various syntactic forms.

[①] The secondary predication here is different from the secondary predication in a narrow sense, which just includes depictives and resultatives. In order to avoid misunderstanding, we use the term downgraded predication for secondary predication in broad sense, and the secondary predicate in this work mainly refers to the secondary predicateion in a narrow sense.

Leech (1983: 142-146) classifies predications into subordinate predications and downgraded or 'featurized' predications. A matrix predicate may govern not only arguments, but also other predicates. The governed predicate is the subordinate predicate, which is a part of main predication in semantics. In this way, with the aid of predicates such as 'DO', 'CAUSE' and 'BECOME', a very complex sentence may be decomposed into smaller and simpler elements through the concept of subordinate predication.

Downgraded or 'featurized' predication is another way to include one predication relation into another. As for downgraded predication, the status of the predicate is reduced to a feature. The notion of downgraded predication can also be extended to predications which are features of predicates. Leech distinguishes two kinds of downgraded predications:

> (2) Two kinds of predication distinguished by Leech:
> I *A qualifying predication occurs within an argument. Adjective, relative clause, qualifying prepositional phrases all function as qualifying predication.*
> II *A modifying predication occurs within a predicate. Adverbs, adverbial clauses, adverbial prepositional phrases all function as modifying predication.*
> (Leech 1983: 142)

The concept of subordinate predication and downgraded predication is represented clearly in neo-Davidsonian paradigm. In this diagram, adverbial modifiers are analyzed as predicates of an underlying event variable:

> (3) a. Mary closes the door.
> b. $(\exists e)[Cul(e)$ & $Agent(e, Mary)$ & $(\exists e')$ $[Cul(e') \wedge Theme(e', door)$ & $CAUSE(e, e')$ & $\exists s[Being\text{-}closed(s)$ & $Theme(s, door)$ & $Hold(s)$ & $BECOME(e', s)]]]$
> Parsons(1990; 120)
> (4) a. Brutus walked slowly.
> b. $(\exists e)$ $[walking(e)$ & $Subject(e, Brutus)$ & $Slow(e)]$

The complex predicate in (3a) is decomposed into many sub-atomic propositions in (3b), and the adverbial modifier in (4a) is analyzed as a predicate over the underlying event argument in (4b).

According to the definition of downgraded predication by Leech, adjectives in Chinese can be properly analyzed as downgraded predicates when they occur as attributes, adverbials and *buyu* (Zhang 1998; Wu 2009; Pan 2010, 2012).

Various forms of downgraded predicates have something in common with the primary predication. That is they must be semantically saturated by a subject. The subject of primary predicate is usually clearly specified. However, it is not the case for downgraded predicate. That is why the semantic orientation analysis is necessary for AAs. In addition, not only primary predicates but also downgraded predicates are divided into stage-level and individual-level predicates and such a contrast is very important for the compatibility between primary predicates and downgraded predicates.

4.1.2 AAs and Adnominal Attributes

It is assumed that adnominal adjective modifier is altered from predicate of the NP (Vendler 1968; Jin 2009 among others). An NP including adjective adnominal modifier can be rewritten as a relative clause:

(5) a. a red rose
b. a rose which is red

It is indicated in (5), adverbial is also analyzed as predicate over the underlying event argument in neo-Davidsonian approach. So what is shared in common by adverbials and attributes is that both of them modify the reference of another lexical item. Zhu (1984) defines attributive as the modifier in a nominal phrase and the adverbial as the modifier in a predicate phrase. In this way, the contrast between attributives and adverbials is reflected by the contrast between the property of noun and verb. As the modifiers of nouns, attributes mainly express static, relatively permanent properties of nouns. Similarly, adverbials are related to event, so adverbials tend to have the temporal features of events. Taylor (2002: 455) states that predicative adjectives tend to denote more temporary, circumstantial properties, whereas attribute adjectives tend to characterize a thing in terms of a stable, inherent property. The event denoted by AA holds true when the eventuality denoted by the primary predicate takes place. However, attributive modifiers are not linked to the temporal frame established by the main verb. The main function of attributive modifier is to make the reference of the noun more restrictive.

Huang (2006, 2008) further illustrates this idea based on the property theory proposed by Chierchia (1984, 1985). Huang assumes that modification relation is in fact a kind of conjunction or intersection, so it is quite natural to require the head noun and the modifier share the same semantic types. Because bare noun in Chinese can occur as subject or object, Chierchia (1998) states that bare noun in Chinese is of type *e*. Correspondingly, the adjective attribute is also of semantic type *e*.

Different from nouns, verbs prototypically denote transitory events or actions. As Bolinger (1967) states that temporality is one of the characteristics of verbs. Zhu (1956, 1982)and Chierchia (1998) suggest temporality is also a prominent feature of AAs, for they are closely related to verbs. When an attributive adjective combines with N to form an NP, the attributive adjectives don't display the characteristic of temporality. The property expressed by the adjective is not temporally related to the matrix verb and will last independently from the event. However, the property or state denoted by the adjectival adverbial is closely temporally related to the event denoted by the main verb.

The difference between AAs and attributive adjectives is apparently exhibited though the interpretation of the universal quantifier. When the adnominal modifier appears before the subject or object, they have similar performance. In (6a), the adnominal attributive modifies the subject:

  (6) a. Suoyou fennu de xuesheng dou likai le jiaoshi.
     all angry de student all leave Perf classroom
     'All of the angry students left the classroom.'
   b. Suoyou de xuesheng fennu De likai le jiaoshi.

           all   de students angry De leave Perf classroom
           'All of the students left the classroom angry.'

   The main function of the attributive adjective in (6a) is to form a subset of students, and the property denoted by this adjective is not related to the action, so maybe there were still some students who were not angry still stayed in the classroom. Jin (2009) states that predication relation that exists before the action denoted by the main verb is usually expressed as adnominal attributive and the predication relation that is temporally concomitant with the primary predicate but is not focused by the speaker is expressed as the adverbial modifier or adnominal attributive modifier. The adjective *fennu* in (6b), serving as an adverbial modifier, does not separate a subset from these students. The sentence indicates that all the students left the classroom, and when they did that, they were angry. In (7a), the adnominal modifier modifies the object:

   (7) a. Chushi chi le suoyou de sheng   jidan.
          cook eat Perf all   de uncooked egg
          'The cook ate all the uncooked eggs.'
       b. Chushi sheng   chi le suoyou de jidan.
          cook uncooked eat Perf all   de egg
          'The cook ate all the eggs uncooked.'

   (7a) means that some of the eggs were uncooked and eaten by the cook and (7b) means that all the eggs were raw and eaten by the cook. That is to say, some AAs, denoting concomitant states, are not involved in the sub classification of the referents of the noun involved as certain participant of an event, whereas adnominal attributives usually form a plausible subset of the denotations of the noun.
   Besides the universal quantifiers, negation also indicates the difference between adverbial and attributive adjectives.

   (8) a. Fengnu de Zhang San meiyou likai fangjian
          angry de p.n   not leave room
          'Angry Zhang San didn't leave the room.'
       b. Zhang San meiyou fengnu De likaile fangjian

p.n not　angry De leave room
'Zhang San didn't leave the room angry.'

In (8a), the scope of negation is the verb, and at last, Zhang San was still in the room. In (8b), the AA is in the scope of negation, and the sentence can be understood as: 'When Zhang San left the room, he was not angry.'

It is very interesting that contradictory adjectives appear as adverbial and attribute respectively will not result in unacceptable sentences, although it sounds a little bit weird:

(9) a. Congming de Zhang San yuchun De huidale nage wenti.
intelligent de p.n　stupid De answer that question
'Intelligent John answered that question stupidly.'
b. Yuchun de Zhang San congming De huida le nage wenti.
stupid de p.n　clever De answer that question
'Stupid John answered that question cleverly'

The difference between attributive and adverbial modifiers is exhibited obviously in these examples. Adnominal modifiers usually denote permanent, stable property of the referent of the noun, and sometimes adjective denoting transitory and temporally limited state also occur as non-restrictive adnominal modifier. Generally speaking, adnominal adjectival attributes are not sensitive to the ILP/SLP contrast.

Adverbial modifiers mainly express transitory and temporally delimited states or dynamic eventualities which are temporally related to the event denoted by the verb. AAs in (9a, 9b) are ambiguous between agent-oriented reading and VP-oriented reading. Both readings should be interpreted as stage-level predicates regardless of the default ILP reading of the adjectives. That is the reason why it is observed that the meaning of many adjectives has changed when they occur as adverbials (Hu 1991). However, event usually has no coercing effects on adnominal modifiers, so the adnominal adjectival modifiers mostly keep the default ILP meaning of the adjectives.

Attributive adjectives are related to certain property of the head it modified, and they are compatible with various verbs. However, when the same adjective occurs as adverbials, it can only be compatible with certain verbs.

(10) a. Xiaoli hua/ na/ chi le yi ge honghong de pingguo.
p.n draw/take/eat Perf one CL red de apple.
'Xiaoli drew/took/ate a red apple.'
b. Xiaoli honghong De hua/ *na/*chi le yi ge pingguo.
p.n red De drew/held/ate Perf one CL apple.
'Xiaoli drew/*held/*ate an apple red.'

Generally speaking, adnominal adjectives put very loose requirements on the context in which they appear, while adjectival adverbials are much more particular about the semantic features of the verbs and the aspectual features of the eventuality denoted by the verb.

4.1.3 AAs and Primary Adjective Predicates

Both primary predication and downgraded predication are different forms of predication relations. The main difference between primary predicate and downgraded predicate is that the downgraded predicates do not need overt temporal anchor. In inflectional languages, a noticeable difference is that the primary predicates are accompanied by Infl, whereas downgraded predicates lack Infl. In English, the contrast is obvious:

(11) a. Mary *(is) drunk.
b. Mary drove the car (*is) drunk.

When an adjective occurs as primary predicate, the copular is needed as in (11a). However, when it acts as a downgraded predicate, the copular is repelled as in (11b).

Chinese does not have overt tense marker in morphology (Hu, Pan and Xu 2001). The anchor and reference of time can be realized by some other methods, including: time adverbial, modality, focus, etc, but all these are not compulsory (Tsai 2008). When simple adjectives occur as matrix predicate and downgraded predicate, there are indeed some differences.

First, in Mandarin Chinese, adjectives of simple forms, monosyllabic or disyllabic, cannot serve as primary predicates independently, for the bare adjectives cannot express the positive meaning.

(12) a. Zhang San ? (hen) gao.
    p.n   very tall
    'Zhang San is (very) careful.'
  b. Li Si ?(feichang) congming.
    p.n very   smart
    'Li Si is very smart.'

Without the degree intensifier *hen* 'very', the sentences in (12) express comparative meaning, indicating that 'Zhang San is taller than someone known from the context.' or 'Li Si is smarter than someone known from the context'. Why is the degree intensifier *hen* 'very' or *feichang* 'fairly' a necessary part of the predicate when SAs act as primary predicate? Scholars have different explanations.

Huang (2006) proposes that simple adjectives in Chinese are nominalized properties and its semantic type is *e*. The function of degree intensifier acts as a type lifter, which turns the nominalized property *e* into a predicate of type <e, t>.

Gu (2008) suggests that the degree intensifier is required to check the feature on Tense when adjectives occur as primary predicate. Gu states that a subject, a predicate, and a time anchor (tense) are the necessary components of a declarative clause in natural languages, and the neutral intensifier *hen* 'very' provides the time anchor for the clause. Although tense is not overtly encoded in Mandarin, it must be displayed in some other ways. The neutral degree intensifier *hen* is required to check the telicity feature on tense. She supports her theory with the following sentences:

(13) a. Women yizhi kua tamen congming.
      IPL   always praise 3PL smart.
      'We always praised them for being smart.'

b. Laoban ma ta lan.
   boss scold 3SG lazy
   'The boss scolded him for being lazy.'

(Gu 2008: 14)

In (13a) and (13b), the adjective is embedded in a small clause, which is tenseless, and the degree intensifier is not compulsory. It is an intriguing idea to establish the relation between the obligatory status of degree intensifier and Tense, and we can further support her theory with the following sentences:

(14) a. Zhang San zai jiaoshi renzhen De zuo jiatingzuoye.
        p.n   in classroom careful De do homework.
        'Zhang San is doing his homework carefully in the classroom.'
     b. Li Si congming De suan chu le na dao nanti.
        p.n clever   de solve out Perf that CL problem
        'Li Si solved that problem cleverly.'

In (14a) and (14b), the adjectives occur as adverbial modifiers, as a kind of downgraded predicate, tense is not obligatory, so the degree intensifier is not obligatory. Zhang Bojiang (2011) also states that the neutral degree intensifier functions like a copula.

Second, aspect markers can co-occur with the bare adjectives to form primary predicate, whereas AAs repel such aspect markers:

(15) a. Haizimen gaoxing le.
        kids   happy Perf
        'Kids got happy.'
     b. Haizimen gaoxing *(le) De jin le jiaoshi.
        Kids   happy (Perf) De enter Perf classroom
        'When these kids entered the classroom, they were happy.'

As for the nature of the SAs in front of the aspect marker, there are different opinions: Zhang Guoxian (2006) assumes that these adjectives are state-changing adjectives. Lyu(1980) treats such adjectives as verbs. Chao Yuanren (1968), Zhang Bojiang (2011) maintain that such adjectives are the same as other SAs, and the meaning of state changing is brought out by the aspect marker -*le*.

We agree that such adjectives have nothing special, compared with other adjectives. The default or unmarked reading of adjective is to denote permanent property or transitory state, and the whole predicate in (15a) has the state-changing meaning because of the coercion of the aspect marker.

Based on these explanations, we can conclude that the main difference between AAs and the adjectival primary predicate lies in the tense anchor, which is necessary for primary predicate adjectives. Tense anchor is not necessary for AAs, or more accurately speaking, overt and direct tense anchor is not necessary, for the run time of the event denoted by AA is completely dependent on the run time of event denoted by the primary predicate. The primary predicate is temporally anchored overly or covertly, and AAs are temporally anchored indirectly through the event argument of the primary predicate. Adjectival primary predicate is not particular about the ILP/SLP contrast of the adjectives, and the alternation between ILP and SLP can be realized through overt aspectual operators while all the AAs must have stage-level interpretation.

4.1.4 AAs and *buyu*:

An adverbial modifier in front of a verb is often compared with *buyu* behind the verb. Some adverbial modifiers can be altered as the *buyu*[1] *of the verb*, but some not:

> (16) a. *Li Si kuai De paole
>   p.n fast De run Perf
>   'Li Si run away fast.'

---

[1] The non-argument constituent following verb is called *buyu* in Chinese grammar, and be translated as complement, but it is oberviously different from the complement in Generative Grammar. We just mark it as *buyu*.

b. Li Si pao DE[①] kuai.
   p.n run DE fast
   'Li Si can run fast.'
(17) a. Zhansan zhengzai shangxin -De ku zhe.
   p.n ASP sad De cry ASP
   'Zhang San is crying sad.'
   b. *Zhang San zhengzai ku DE shangxin.
   p.n ASP cry DE sad
   'Zhang San got himself sad from crying.'

It is indicated in (16) and (17) that not all adverbials can be altered to be *buyu*, and these two kinds of constituents exhibit different preferences in morphological forms and aspect of the sentence. Such differences between adverbials and *buyu* have been clearly recognized.

It is generally assumed that the *buyu* following the verb is more closely related to the verb and acts more like a primary predicate. Wang(1943), Gao(1948: 287), Lyu(1966), Wang(1991) all agree that the *buyu* following the verb is the predicate of the verb. Sometimes, *buyu* is so prominent that the verb can be dropped, and *buyu* becomes the primary predicate. Ding(1961: 67-68) states that: "*adjectival adverbial modifiers are in front of the verb, whereas buyus are following the verb. More or less, the buyu is nore like predicate and are more important than the adverbials.*" Pan Guoying (2010) also states that *buyu* is a part of the predicate, and sometimes just *buyu* itself can be the primary predicate without the appearing of the verb.

Huang(1988), Jing(2009) treat some *buyu* following the verb as secondary predicates. Wu (2009) analyzes some constructions in Mandarin Chinese in the framework of underlying events, such as Shi-Construction, V-de construction, Ba-Construction, verb-copying construction. He analyzes the *buyu* following the verb in these constructions as a sub-event, which combines with the event denoted by the matrix verb through a summing operation. Take the V-de construction

---

[①] This structural subordinator is written as '得', to distinguish it from '的' de and '地' De, we mark it as DE, which is analyzed as a function head related to potential, resultative and descriptive constructions in Chinese (Wang 2014).

as an example:

(18) a. Liuqiang zou DE lei le.
     p.n walk de tired Perf
     'Liuqiang is tired as a result of walking.'
  b. $\exists e[\exists e_1[\exists e_2[e=^S(e_1 \cup e_2) \wedge zou(e_1) \wedge Ag(e_1)=Liuqiang \wedge lei(e_2)$
     $\wedge Arg(e_2)=Liuqiang \wedge TPCONNECT(Cul(e_1), e_2, Liuqiang)]]]$

It is indicated in the logic form (18b) that the *buyu* is a composing part of the matrix predicate, and it is temporally connected to the matrix predicate. The summing operation means that the event denoted by the *buyu* is a necessary part of the predication, and can't be dropped.

The difference between AAs and *buyu* is also reflected from the formation of some compound words. We can find that the relation between verbs and *buyu* is closer than that between verbs and adverbials, and the combinations of verbs and *buyu* are highly lexicalized.

(19) a. verb + *buyu*:
     dadao   'overthrow'   tuifan   'overturn'
     kuoda   'enlarge'   tigao   'improve'
     shuofu   'persuade'   yanchang 'prolong'
  b. AA + verb:
     qingfang 'put down gently'   gaohan   'shout loudly'
     manzou   'go slowly'   xixiang   'think carefully'

From the corresponding English interpretation, we can also find that the words in (19a) roughly correspond to verbs in English, and the adjectives somehow look like the focus of the combinations. The words in (19b) approximately correspond to phrases in English and the adjectives just function like a criterion to classify the events denoted by the verb. The status of *buyu* in these phases indicates that the relation between the verbs and *buyu* is closer than that between AAs and verbs, and the *buyu* somehow is more like the primary predicate.

The information structure also indicates the difference between adverbials and *buyu*. Ernst (1984: 240) states that the preverbal position is normally taken as holding back-grounded information, while VP-final position is associated with foregrounding information. Chinese grammarians generally acknowledge that *buyu* is the information focus of a clause. Xuan (2007) states that in the verb-complement configuration, the verb, according to the speaker's presupposition, is the given information, so the *buyu* usually bears more information than the verb, while, the adverbial, in adverbial-verb configuration, does not bear more information than the verb. So the verb is the natural focus or is embedded in the natural focus in adverbial-verb configuration. Adverbial or *buyu* are preferred in different contexts:

(20) a. Zhang San chiwan fan hui fangjian le. (given situation)
p.n   eat finish meal return room Perf
'Zhang San went back to his room after eating.'
b. Zhang San chang le san ge xiaoshi
p.n   sing Perf three CL hour
'Zhang San sang for three hours'
(21) a. Zhang San hen gaoxing De change. (adverbial-verb configuration)
p.n   very happy De sing song
'Zhang San was singing happily'
b. Zhang San chang DE hen gaoxing. (verb- *buyu* configuration)
p.n   sing DE very happy
'Zhang San got very happy from his singing.'

In the given situation (20a), (21a) is a natural utterance, while (21b) sounds abrupt, because (21b) usually presupposes the existence of the event denoted by the verb. However, such information is not provided in the context. As for the given situation (20b), (21b) would be the appropriate utterance, because the context has given the needed information about the presupposed event.

Pan (2012) also points out that the *buyu* has stronger capability of being predicate than adverbial. However, whether adjectival adverbial is the focus is a controversial issue. Liu and Xu(1998), Xuan(2007), Pan(2012) agree that AAs are not the information focus, but Yuan (2006) argues that AAs are the information focus.

Zheng (2000: 45) suggests that AA usually occurs between the subject and the main verb, and this position usually doesn't hold information focus. However, for the special semantic structure of the clause with an AA, the AA can be the contrastive focus. A clause with an AA which orients a participant of the verb states two propositions simultaneously, and the one composed of the adjectival adverbial is grammaticalized, but the adjectival adverbial consequently become the contrastive focus.

The differences between adjective adverbial and adjective *buyu* can be summarized as:

Firstly, adjective adverbials are optional. All the sentences with adjectival adverbials entail the corresponding sentences without adjectival adverbials, while the adjective *buyu* following the main verb cannot be dropped, for the *buyu* following the verb is usually the information focus, whereas the AA is the contrastive focus. Take sentences containing *buyu* in (22) as examples to illustrate the entailment relation:

(22) a. Tamen tiao * (DE hen lei).
　　　they jump (DE very tired)
　　　'They got tired from jumping.'
　　b. Ta *ba* yifu xi * (DE hen ganjing).
　　　he/she Ba cloth wash (DE very clean)
　　　'They washed the clothes clean.'
　　c. Zhang San zou # (kuai) –le.
　　　p.n walk (fast) Perf
　　　'Zhang san walked too fast.'
　　d. Li Si xie * (DE hen man).
　　　p.n write (DE very slow)
　　　'Li Si writes slowly.'

According to the criteria given by Jin (2009), the adjective in (22a) is subject-oriented secondary predicate and (22b) object-oriented secondary predicate. The adjective in (22c) and (22d) are post-positing adverbials. It is indicated that when the adjectives (22a), (22b) and (22d) are cancelled, the remains can't form complete sentences, or the sentence without the adjective expresses complete different meanin as (22c).

Secondly, the morphological constraint on the adjectival adverbial is more rigorous than that on the adjectives following the verb. Few monosyllabic adjectives can occur as adverbials preceding verbs except for *duo* 'more', *shao* 'less', *zao* 'early', *wan* 'late' etc (see Zhu 1956), while 91.07% of 168 monosyllabic adjectives can appear after verb to perform the function of *buyu* (Ma &Lu 1997).

Thirdly, adjective adverbials mainly focus on concomitant temporal relationship with the matrix predicate, while the resultative relationship is often what the *buyu* emphasizes. The sentence with AAs is compatible with progressive, but sentences with *buyu* are usually incompatible with progressive tense.

(23) a. Jingji zhengzai huanman De zengzhang.
Economy ASP slow   De grow
'Economy is growing slowly.'
b. *Jingji zhengzai zengzhang DE hen huanman.
Economy ASP grow   De very slow
'Economy is growing slowly.'

This also reflects that AAs are not the focus of the sentence, and AAs do not affect the event type denoted by the verb. However, in a sentence with *buyu*, the *buyu* is the focus of the sentence; it is usually an adjective. When adjectives occur as primary predicate, they denote states, so they are incompatible with progressive.

4.1.5 AAs & Secondary Predicates in English

Secondary predicate has been an increasingly attractive topic and some kinds of AAs in Mandarin are analyzed analogouly to secondary predicates in English (Zhang 2001, 2002; Lim, J.-H 2005). The examples in (24) and (25) illustrate classic cases of secondary predicates.

(24) a. John^i drove the car drunk^i.①
　　b. Mary drank the coffee^i hot^i.
(25) a. Mary painted the house^i red^i.
　　b. John sang the baby^j asleep^j.

These examples have been discussed at least since Halliday (1967: 63). He divides secondary predicates into two classes: depictive predication (as in (24)) and resultative predication (as in (25)). Dowty (1979) and Simpson (1983) follow the similar classification. Both depictive and resultative describe the relationship between the event denoted by the main verb and the event denoted by the adjuncts. The difference between depictive and resultative consists in the temporal characteristics between these two events.

In English, adjuncts with similar semantic features have two different forms: one is predicational adverbials and the other is secondary predicates. The comparison between secondary predicates and adverbial in English is an interesting topic. The most controversial issue is centered on the subject-oriented depictive secondary predicate and the transparent reading of the subject-oriented adverbs. Some scholars argue that secondary predicates and predicational adverbs are totally different (Rothstein 2001, 2004), while some hold that they are roughly the same (Geuder 2002, Ernst 2002). Geuder states that:

In fact, depictives have been found to carry an almost 'adverbial' reading: Their interpretation is linked to the event variable of the verb. The difference between depictives and transparent adverbs lies merely in the fact that depictives assert the independence of a concurrent state while the adverbial forms assert the existence of a closer connection to the event.
　　　　　　　　　　　　　　　　　　　　Geuder (2002: 201)

Depictives and resultatives differ in that a depictive predicate denote a state of the controller (usually is the subject) and the state holds during

---

① Conventionally, since Williams (1980), superscript indices are used to indicate the predication relation between subject and predicate.

the period that the event denoted by the main verb takes place, while the latter expresses the resultant state of the event denoted by the main verb.

Secondary predicate is a kind of downgraded predicate, but it has not been clearly defined yet. As soon as the concept of secondary predicate was put forth, the content of this concept began to enlarge rapidly. The simple cases of secondary predication involving various phrase types whose subjects are always dependent on primary predicates for the instantiation of their subjects, so Paul Kay terms secondary predication as co-instantiation construction, and he categories more than ten kinds of secondary predicates:

> (26) Different kinds of secondary predicates categorized by Paul Key:
> a. Joe sounds angry.
> b. You need to pick tomatoes green.
> c. I shouted myself hoarse.
> d. The soldiers reached the camp exhausted.
> e. I started this project quite enthusiastic.
> f. We kept them busy.
> g. They found my argument unconvincing.
> h. I like my steaks thick.
> i. I saw her naked.
> j. They left the money on the kitchen table.
> k. I regard Joe as quite hostile.
> l. He came towards me with his uniform unbuttoned.
> Adapted from (http://www1.icsi.berkeley.edu/~kay/bcg/II-Pred.html)

From these examples we can see that the secondary predicates constitute a heterogeneous set, and their dependency on the primary predicate is different. Generally, secondary predicates in English have the following characteristics:

> (27) The main characteristics of secondary predicates in English:
> a. Secondary predicates appear after the primary

predicators in linear order.
b. They semantically orient one argument of the primary predicates.
c. Most of the secondary predicates are not droppable.

Seen from the perspective of event semantics, both depictive and resultative denote events and the difference between depictive and resultative consists in the temporal relation between the event denoted by the primary predicate and the secondary predicate. Susan Rothstein (2001, 2003, 2004) argues that both depictive and resultative secondary predicates are aspectual modifiers in the sense that they introduce a new event and define a relation between it and the event introduced by the main predicate. She defines secondary predication as following:

(28) The definition of secondary predicate:
a. α is a secondary predicate of β iff α is predicated of β, and α and β c-command each other and β is theta-marked by a head not contained in α.
b. If α is a secondary predicate of β, then α and β form an instance of secondary predication.
Rothstein (1983, 2001)

Secondary predicates in Mandarin Chinese have been discussed as early as in Huang (1988). He holds the idea that the second verb in a ...V1...V2 sequence should be treated as secondary predicate and he doesn't consider the semantic orientation of the V2, so the adjective in (29a) is also treated as a subordinate verb (secondary predicate) (Huang 1988: 275):

(29) a. Wo pao DE[1] hen kuai.
　　　 I run DE very fast
　　　 'I run very fast'

---

[1] DE here corresponds to ' 得 ', which is analyzed as a functional head formed at the interface between syntax and morphological merger (Wang 2014). For the sake of clearness, ' 得 ' is written as DE.

b. Tamen tiao DE hen lei.
they jump DE very tired
'They jumped till they got very tired.'

Jin (2009) claims that *buyu* after the primary predication can be classified into two categories: secondary predication and post-positing adverbial. He stipulates three criteria to tell the secondary predicate from the post-posing adverbial:

(30) X is a secondary predicate if and only if:
   a. X is a predicate and
   b. X must be predicated of a participant of the event denoted by the main verb and
   c. X should appear after the primary predicate.
   (Jin 2009: 393)

According to these criteria, Jin (2009) treats the adjectives after the verbs in (31) as secondary predicates, while the adjectives in (32) after the verb are adverbials, because these adjectives are predicated of verbs instead of NP:

(31) a. Li Si gan DE hen lei
      p.n work DE very tired
      'Li Si got very tired from working.'
    b. Ta *ba* yifu xi *de* hen ganjing.
      he BA cloth –DE very clean.
      'He made the cloth clean by washing'
(32) a. Zhang San zou kuai -le
      p.n walk fast-Pef
      'Zhang San walked too fast.'
    b. Li Si xie DE hen man.
      p.n write DE very slow
      'Li Si writes slowly.'

Both Huang (1988) and Jin (2009) analyze the predicates following main verbs as secondary predicates, although they differ in the subcategory of predicates which semantically orients the main verbs. Zhang (2011) claims that the complement of object in English is similar to the adjective after verb in Chinese in that they both express the resulted state of the action denoted by the verb. From these researches, we conclude that some *buyu* in Mandarin share something more in common with secondary predicates in English. In English, the resultative secondary predicate will cause the shift of the aspectual feature of the event. A well-known example is given in (33), the activity denoted by *hammer the metal* is shifted to an accomplishment denoted by *hammer the metal flat*:

(33) a. Mary hammered the metal for hours/*in two hours.
   b. Mary hammered the metal flat * for hours/in two hours.

Rothstein (2004: 59)

So in sum, we have got a clearer understanding about the features of the adjective adverbials in Mandarin Chinese, which is different from the secondary predicate in that:

a. Adjective adverbials can be dropped without affecting the completeness of the sentence and entailment relation between sentence with an AA and the one with it dropped.
b. Adjective adverbials in Mandarin Chinese don't cause the event type shift.
c. The function of AAs are more various than that of secondary predicates in English. In the following section, we will notice that unlike the secondary predicates in English, some AAs in Mandarin are not semantically related to participants.

4.1.6 English Adverbs and AAs in Chinese

Predicational adverbs in English are usually adverbs derived from adjective bases, and adjectival adverbials in Mandarin refer to the adjectives that occur as adverbials. Naturally, these two kinds of constituents exhibit some similarities, for both are downgraded predicates in Leech's classification. Therefore, relevant research centered on adverbs in English certainly will shed light on the analysis of AAs in Mandarin Chinese. Ernst (2002) states that predicational adverbs represent gradable predicates taking events or propositions as their argument, and predicational adverbs in English are usually composed of an adjective plus *–ly*.

Jackendoff(1972) classifies predicational adverbs in English into three main classes and proposes sematic interpretation rules for each class.

(34) Jackendoff's classification of adverbs:
    a. manner: loudly
    b. subject-oriented: cleverly, reluctantly
    c. speaker-oriented: clearly, amazingly, frankly

Compared with the classification of AAs in Chinese, the function of AAs is not totally corresponding to that of adverbs in English.

First, the most striking difference is that the functions of adverb in English are much more various than those of AAs in Chinese.

Second, the object-oriented adverbs are missing in English. However, it doesn't mean object in English can't be modified by adjuncts. From Jackendoff's calssification of adverbs, we can notice that there is no a class of object-oriented adverbs in English, and the corresponding function of object-oriented AAs in Chinese is relaized through secondary predicates in English. However, Geuder (2004) notes that there are some adverbs that can be interpretated as being predicate of the object, especially when the adverb is between the object and PP complement of verbs:

(35) a. I watched how the police took a man reluctantly to the car.
                                                  (Geuder 2004: 156)
    b. Mary put Tom contentedly on the bed.

Such adverbs in English are marginal instances of object-oriented adverbs.

Third, the corresponding function of speaker-oriented adverbs in English is mainly realized by some less lexicalized clause-like phrases in Chinese. Only a few adjectives can occur as speaker-oriented adverbials.

Forth, adjectival adverbials in Chinese can only partly realize the function of manner adverbs in English, and some adverbs in Chinese also have the manner interpretation.

It is indicated from the comparison that AAs in Chinese can only realize part of the functions of adverbs in English, but AAs also have some function that adverbs in English lack, such as the object-oriented interpretation.

In this section, AAs are compared with the other kinds of downgraded predicates in order to explore the difference between these different kinds of downgraded predicates. AAs in Mandarin are also compared with secondary predicates and predicational adverbs in English. We find out that AAs share more in common with predicational adverbs in English than with secondary predicates. However, the functions of predicational adverbs in English are much more various than those of AAs in Mandarin. After getting a clearer picture on the AAs in Mandarin, AAs will be classified from the perspective of event semantics.

At the beginning of this chapter, it has been pointed out that there are two mismatches reflected by the adjectival adverbials: one is the mismatch between syntactic position and semantic orientation, the other mismatch is the temporal feature mismatch between the permanent temporal feature of adjective and the transient temporal feature of verb. If all the participant-oriented AAs are analyzed as the relocated attributes, the two mismatches disappear at once, for the correlation between adjectives and nouns are natural corelation in that their temporal features are in agreement and there is no mismatch between syntactic position and semantic orientation for adnominal modifiers are naturally related to their heads. However, by the comparison between AAs and adnominal modifiers in Section 4.1.2, there are some sharp differences between these two kinds of downgraded predicates, so there are a lot of AAs are not exchangeable between attributes and adverbials (Zheng 2000; Lu 2003; Zhang 2005). Furthermore, AAs have some specific requirements on the morphological forms of the under adjectives, whereas such requirements on adnominal modifier are much more relaxed.

Another attempt is to explain the temporal feature mismatch from the morphological forms of adjectives. If all reduplicated adjectives denoted transitory state, the temporal feature mismatch is explained. However, it has been verrified in Chapter 3 that the morphological form of adjectives does not correspond to the ILP/SLP distinction. There are a lot of simple adjectives occur as adverbials, which means that the morphological variations of adjectives are not enough to explain the temporal mismatch.

All the adjectives that occur as adverbials should receive stage-level reading. In Chapter 3, it has been stated that the operator 'BECOME' can coerce an individual-level adjective into denoting an achievement. This seems to be a promising solution for the puzzle brought about by the individual-level adjectives when they occur as adverbials.

4.2 Criteria for Classification of AAs

It has been pointed out that due to the temporal mismatch between adjectives and verbs, all the adjectives that occur as adverbials should receive stage-level reading. All the primary predicates that are compatible with adjectival adverbial modification should be stage-level predicates. All the stage-level predicates have Davidsonian event argument, so there are two events in a simple sentence with an AA. In this study, the event denoted by the adjectival adverbial is marked as e', and the event expressed by the primary predicate is marked as e. The following factors will be taken into consideration when classifying AAs: first, the temporal relation between e' and e; second, the aspectual feature of e'; third, the identity of the free variable of e'. All these three factors are the basic elements of an event. As we have stated in this chapter, there are two mismatches when adjectives occcur as adverbials: temporal mismatch and syntactic/semantic mismatch. Among the three creteria for classification of AAs, the first two are relevant to the tempotal mismatch between the adjective and the verb, while the last one is related to the syntactic/semantic mismatch.

4.2.1 The Temporal Relation between E and E'

The relation between the event denoted by the main verb and the event denoted by the AA should be taken into consideration when classifying AAs. Only when an adjective modifies a verb, it is termed as adjectival adverbial. Without the event denoted by the main verb, the adjective can occur as a primary predicate. The identity of adjectival adverbial and the primary predicate is based on the mutual relation between them. Thus the classification of AAs should not only be based on the meaning of adjectives. The classification of AAs without considering the relationship between e and e' could not reflect the nature of AAs in Mandarin accurately.

The most important relationship between events is the temporal order, and the temporal relation between e and e' is indicated by the feature [±concomitance]. All the other relations between e and e', such as causal relation, inchoative relation, are based on the temporal order. [+concomitance] means that the run time of these two events overlap, or the run time of e is a part of the run time of e'. Rothstein defines the part-of relation as:

(36) Part-of (e', e) iff
(i) $\tau(e) \subseteq \tau(e')$ (the run time of e is temporally contained in e') and (ii) e' and e share a participant.
Adapted from (Rothstein 1999: 10)

The feature [+concomitance] is not rigidly defined, and the initial points and the endings of these two events are not required to be exactly simultaneous. [−concomitance] means that the two events do not occur at the same time, and usually the run time of e' is after the culmination of e.

Based on the [±concomitance] feature, we can maintain a dichotomy of AAs. All the AAs with [+concomitance] features denote states or events involved certain participant of the event e. All the [+concomitance] AAs have transparent readings. This term comes from Geuder (2000). Such AAs express the state or a process which the participant is in and [+concomitance] AAs are the objective description of the participant of the event e, so most of the [+concomitance] AAs denote external and perceptible processes or states.

All the [−concomitance] AAs express evaluations towards different targets, including event, proposition and agent. When the target of evaluation is an event, AA will have manner reading. When the target is a proposition, the AA will get an evaluative reading. When the target is the agent, AAs will get agent-oriented reading. Evaluative adjective adverbials attribute a property to an individual, an event or a proposition, because of the culmination of the event denoted by the primary predicate. So although evaluative AAs denote properties of individuals, they are still stage-level predicates. Whether an individual or an event manifests the property denoted by the adjectival adverbial is mainly based on the speaker's judgment with the event denoted by the main verb as the background.

4.2.2 Aspectual Feature of E'

Another feature should be considered in classifying AAs is the feature [±homogeneity] of e', which mainly refers to whether the event denoted by the adjectival adverbial is homogeneous or not.

(37) a. P is homogeneous iff P is cumulative and divisive.
　　　　i. P is divisive
　　　　iff $\forall x[P(x) \rightarrow \exists y(P(y) \wedge y<x)] \wedge \forall x,y[P(x) \wedge P(y)$
　　　　$\wedge y< x \rightarrow P(x-y)]$
　　　　ii. P is cumulative
　　　　iff $\forall x[P(x) \wedge P(y) \rightarrow P(x \cup y)]$
　　b. P is quantity iff P is not homogeneous
　　　　　　　　　　　　　　　　　　　(Borer 2005: 192)

The default aspectual feature of the event denoted by an adjective is [+homogeneity], no matter it denotes a permanent property or a transient state. However, when the adjective occurs as adverbial, it is semantically underspecified and the interpretation of it is highly context-sensitive. As the result of the interaction between events, the event e' denoted by the adjective may be coerced out of its original event type into denoting a dynamic and culminating event. According to our initial observation, when stage-level adjective occurs as adverbial, it usually denotes an event with the aspectual feature [+homogeneity]. When individual-level adjectives occur as adverbials, the event denoted by the adjective would be coerced to be a dynamic and culminating event with [−homogeneity] feature.

The [−homogeneity] feature is usually related to telicity. Caudal and Nicolas propose an explicit scalar analysis of telicity, they defines telicity as:

>(38) A predication is telic if and only if:
>   a. It has an associated set of degrees with,
>   b. a specified standard value, and
>   c. its verbal predication satisfies axiom BECOME [---]
>   (Caudal and Nicolas 2005: 294)

Such a definition of telicity is somehow similar to the incremental process in Rothstein's sense. It is especially suitable to describe the aspectual features of the event e' with [−homogeneity]. This kind of telicity refers to a gradual change of state along the degree scaled by the under adjective. In the following sections, we will find that [−homogeneity] feature also can be realized in different eventualities.

4.2.3 Identity of the Participant of E'

The third feature we take into consideration when classfying AAs is [±participant]. An adjective is of type <d, t>,[1] which indicates that it is not semantically saturated, so it must be saturated by a certain element. In Rothstein's theory of predication, this element is a free variable before the application of predication formation rule. The value of the free variable can be a participant of the event denoted by the primary, or FEO in Ernst's sense. When the free variable is co-indexed with a participant of the event e, the AA is participant-oriented with [+participant] feature; when the free variable is co-indexed with a sepcified event, the AA gets manner reading; when the free variable is co-indexed with a fact or

---

[1] In this book, d refers to individual, while e refers to event.

proposition, the AA gets eveluative reading. When the free variable is co-indexed with FEOs, the AA has the [−participant] feature. Here, we should note that the free variable x is coindexed, i.e., co-referent with the participant of the event e, or FEOs, but not identical to it (Haider 1997).

When an adjective occur as primary predicate, the value of the free variable x is arbitrary. However, when the adjective occurs as adverbial, the value of the free variable of e' is relatively restricted in a set composed of members derived form e:{subject, object, VP, clause}. The free variable of the e' is co-indexed with certain element of this set.

4.2.4 Subcategories of AAs

In Chapter 2, the classification of AAs has been briefly reviewed, and we have got a very general picture about the existing classification. However, it is necessary to reconsider the classification of AAs out of the following reasons:

First, the criteria of classification are not clearly stated. It looks like that the existing classification of AAs rely too much on the semantic orientation and the semantic difference of adjectives per se, and the features of adjectival adverbials are not fully appreciated.

Second, the ambiguity of adjectival adverbials is not fully explained. Sometimes, some adjectival adverbials are ambiguous and have more than one potential interpretation, but the rigidly lexical semantic based classification can't reflect the flexibility of the interpretation of AAs.

Third, the features of different groups are not clearly stated, which makes the classification less meaningful.

In the classification system of AAs in this work, the nature of adverbials will play a more important role. Based on these three groups of features and different way of combination of these features, AAs can be classified into seven different kinds with different semantic orientation. Every kind of AA is the result of composition of different features. The tree type diagram (39) below provides a road map to the typology of adjectival adverbials in Mandarin:

(39)

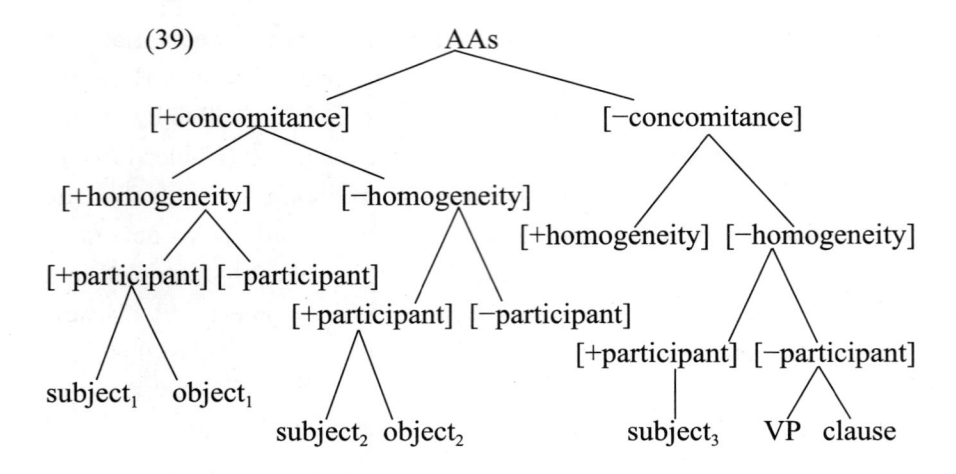

```
                              AAs
                   ╱                    ╲
         [+concomitance]            [-concomitance]
          ╱          ╲                ╱        ╲
[+homogeneity]  [-homogeneity]  [+homogeneity] [-homogeneity]
   ╱    ╲         ╱     ╲          ╱    ╲        ╱      ╲
[+part] [-part] [+part] [-part]  [+part] [-part]
  ╱  ╲    ╱  ╲   ╱   ╲            │       ╱  ╲
subj₁ obj₁  subj₂ obj₂          subj₃   VP  clause
```

From this diagram, we can notice that there are three different kinds of subject-oriented AAs: subject₁, subject₂ and subject₃. There are two different kinds of object-oriented AAs: object₁ and object₂. There is one kind of VP-oriented AAs and one kind of clause-oriented AAs. According to this chart, the features of these seven categories of AAs are listed in (40):

(40) Feature of seven kinds of AAs:

	semantic orientation	[±participant]	[±homogeneity]	[±concomitance]
a	subject₁	+	+	+
b	subject₂	+	−	+
c	subject₃	+	−	−
d	object₁	+	+	+
e	object₂	+	−	+
f	VP	−	−	−
g	clause	−	−	−

In form (40), these seven kinds of AAs form four groups: subject-oriented AAs(composed of 40 a, b, c), object-oriented AAs (composed of 40d, e), VP-oriented AAs (40f) and clause-oriented AAs (40g), and AAs with same semantic orientation are put together. From this table, we can compare clearly AAs with different semantic orientations and AAs with same semantic orientation but different features.

Such a classification of AAs is closely based on the function of the adjectival adverbials. At the same time, the lexical entry of the adjective is highly relevant to its performance at the syntactic position of adverbials. Each kind of AAs has different requirements on their under adjectives, including the semantic, morphological features. The demanding for structural subordinator *-De* is also different. For some kinds of AA, *-De* is compulsory, while for some other groups, *-De* is optional. The aspectual feature of the event denoted by the primary predicate is also influential in deciding what kind of AAs is compatible with it. Furthermore, some kinds of AAs have scope features and are focus-sensitive, and some not. Some kinds of AA can have more than one interpretation, so what is the difference caused by different interpretations? In the following section, the features of each kind of AAs will be explored in great details.

In the following section, great emphasis will be put on the study of the compositionality and context-sensitivity of these AAs. Section 4.3 is mainly about the analyzing of three kinds of subject-oriented AAs. The focus of Section 4.4 is the two kinds of object-oriented AAs. VP-oriented AAs will be analyzed in Section 4.5. Clause-oriented AAs are the focus of Section 4.6.

4.3 Subject-oriented AAs

Subject-oriented AAs are the most common adjectival adverbials. However, the relevant researches on this kind of AAs are not so fruitful, compared with those on object-oriented AAs. Jackendoff (1972) notices that, in English, the interpretation of some subject-oriented adverbs are dependent on surface structure. In the following examples, the semantic orientation of the adverbial changes with the alternation from passive to active voice, but they are always semantically related to the surface subject or the logical subject, it is the reason why such adverbials are called subject-oriented adverbials:

(41) a. The police$_i$ carelessly$_i$ have arrested Fred[①]
    b. Fred$_i$ carelessly$_i$ has been arrested by the police.
(42) a. John$_i$ intentionally$_i$ seduced Mary.
    b. John$_i$ was intentionally$_i$ seduced by Mary.

In these examples, the preferred interpretation attributes the carelessness or intention to the surface subject. The subject-orientated adjectival adverbials in Chinese exhibit the same features:

(43) a. Jingcha$_i$ hulihutu$_i$ De daibu le Li Si.
    policeman muddle-headed De arrest Perf p.n
    'Policemen muddle-headedly arrested Li Si.'
    b. Li Si$_i$ hulihutu$_i$ De Bei jingcha daibu le.
    p.n muddle-headed De Bei policeman arrest Perf.
    'Li Si was muddle-headedly arrested by policemen.'

No matter in active voice in (43a) or in passive voice in (43b), the state of being muddle-headed always orients the subject of the sentence. Jackendoff (1972) has provided some inspirations for the analysis of such adverbials. He proposes the following interpretation rule for subject-oriented adverbs:

(44) If Adv is a daughter of S, embed the reading of S (including any member of F to the right of Adv)[②] as one argument to Adv, and embed the derived subject of S as the second argument to Adv.
                                          (Jackendoff 1972: 107)

According to this interpretation rule, the Adv is analyzed as a two-place predicate and there are two propositions asserted in one sentence (Irena Bellert 1977). One proposition is the sentence without the Adv, and the other proposition is 'Subject is Adj' (Adj is the adjectival base of Adv). Our analysis of a sentence with an AA as two events is in

---

[①] The orientation of adverbial is indicated by the co-indexing.
[②] F designates Adv, PP, Modal, or parenthetical S.

agreement with this proposal.

Based on the criteria we set in §4.2, we get three different kinds of subject-oriented adjectival adverbials, and their features are listed in (45):

(45) Three kinds of subject-oriented AAs:

a	subject$_1$	+participant	+homogeneity	+concomitance
b	subject$_2$	+participant	−homogeneity	+concomitance
c	subject$_3$	+participant	−homogeneity	−concomitance

From (45), we notice that although these three kinds of AAs have the same semantic orientation, the features of each kind are different from those of other kinds. For example, subject$_1$ and subject$_2$ are different in the aspectual feature of the event e', while subject$_3$ is a more special kind, for the temporal relation between e and e' is different from these other two groups. In the following sections, these three kinds of subject-oriented AAs will be analyzed respectively.

4.3.1 Subject$_1$-oriented AAs

Subject-oriented AAs with [+concomitance] [+participant] [+homogeneity] features are just a subset of the subject-oriented AAs. The free variable x of the event e' is co-indexed with the subject of the event e, and its thematic role can be agent, theme or experiencer. (46) will be taken as an example to illustrate the features of this kind of AAs:

(46) a. Xiaoming shengqi De rengdiao le shouji.
      p.n   angry De throw Perf cellphone
      'Xiaoming angrily threw his cell phone away.'

In (46), the adjectival adverbial *shengqi-De* 'angry' is a subject-oriented [+concomitance] [+participant] [+homogeneity] AA. This kind of AA denotes a state of its own and predicates of the subject who is the holder of the state. [+concomitance] feature means that e and e' are concomitant. Usually the run time of e is a part of e'. In (45), *shengqi-De* 'angry' is a stage-level predicate, so it has a Davidsonian event argument, and the run time of e 'throw away' is a part of the run time of e'. The feature [+participant] means that the free variable of e' is a participant of event e. According to native speaker's intuition, the free variable x of e' should be co-indexed with Xiaoming, the agent of e. The event e' is not dynamic, so it has the feature of [+homogeneity].

4.3.1.1 Typical Adjectives for Subject$_1$-oriented AAs

Adjectives that can occur as subject$_1$-oriented AAs are required to be stage-level adjectives, for subject is usually the controller of the event and the event almost has no coercion effect on such kind of AAs. Adjectives can occur as this kind of AAs include following groups:

First, adjectives expressing mental state and attitude are the most common members of this group. In Chen (1987), these adjectives are categorized as uncontrollable adjectives, for the subject of sentence cannot control the metal state or attitude expressed by the adjectives. In Zhang (1990), he defines these adjectives as expressing subjects' perceivable states: In Zhao (2010/2011), these adjectives are categorized as emotional adjectives expressing subject's reactions towards certain stimulus and the reaction denoted by the adjective can't be controlled by the subject. Representative examples are listed in (47):

> (47) *beiai* 'sad', *cankui* 'guilty', *jinzhang* 'nervous', *manyi* 'satisfaied', *xingfen* 'excited', *zihao* 'proud', *jiaoji* 'anxiously', *xizizi* 'happy', *qichongchong* 'angry', *gaogaoxingxing* 'glad'...

This group of adjectives expresses subject's psychological-emotional states or attitudes during the time that the event denoted by the main verb occurs. These states or attitudes are externalized by some perceivable signs. Only a concrete and perceivable manifestation of some signs can make the speaker infer that the subject is in the state denoted by the adjective. When these adjectives occur as adverbials, they describe a state of mind experienced by the referent of the subject of the verb.

Second, adjective that describe the temporal appearance or physical state are also included into this kind of AAs. Representative lists are given in (48):

(48) *pibei* 'exhausted', *chenzhong* 'serious', *guangliuliu* 'naked', *zuixunxun* 'drunk', *gulingling* 'alone', *shilulu* 'wet', xiaomimi 'smiling' ...

This group of adjectives expresses the transient physical states of the referent of the subject is in, and the states are perceivable as indicated in (49):

(49) a. Li Si zuixunxun De kaizhe che.
      p.n drunk De drive ASP car
      'Li Si is driving the car drunk.'
   b. Haizimen guangliuliu De zai heli xixi.
      kids naked De in river play
      'Kinds are playing in the river naked.'

Adjectives for this kind of AAs are also stage-level adjectives, for that a subject is often the controller of an event and the state of the subject usually is not to be influenced by the event. When these adjectives occur as primary predicate, they denote a transitory state of the subject, and this state can exist anytime and anywhere. When they occur as adverbials, the state denoted by such adjective is anchored by the event denoted by primary predicate, and the event e takes place in the frame established by the state. In this sense, such AAs have dual nature: on one hand, these adjectives are predicates of their subjects; on the other hand, such AAs perform the function of adverbials for they establish a circumstance frame in which the event e takes place.

4.3.1.2 Aspectual Feature Match Between E and E' for Subject$_1$-oriented AAs

It has been stated that the adjectives for subject$_1$-oriented AAs should be stage-level adjectives. This kind of AAs put least restrictions on the aspectual features of the event denoted by the primary predicate. However, the primary predicate should not be an individual-level predicate, for the event denoted by the primary predicate is needed to provide the temporal anchor for event e'.

(50) a. Zhang san *(xingfu De) you yi er yi nv.
     p.n   (happy De) have one son one daughter.
     Zhang San happily has one son and one daughter.
  b. Zhang san xingfu De you le yi er yi nv.
     p.n   (happy De) have one son one daughter.
     Zhang San happily has one son and one daughter.

The primary predicate in (50a) is a typical individual-level predicate, so there is no a Davidsonian event argument. As a result, the event e' cannot be temporally anchored, so it is not compatible with subject-oriented AAs. In (50b), *you* 'have' is coerced by the aspectual operator *-le* to obtain an achievement reading, roughly equal to *get*, which is a stage-level predicate with a Davidsonian event argument, so (50b) is compatible with the modification of subject-oriented AAs.

The remaining question is that we have stated that reduplication of adjective cannot alter an ILP into SLP, why *gaogao De* 'tall', as an ILP is acceptable in (51b)?

(51) a. Zhang San *(gaogao De) zuozai cheli.
     p.n   (tall De) sit at car in
     'Tall Zhang San is seated in the car.'
  b. Zhang San gaogao De zuozai che ding shang.
     p.n   tall De   sit at car top on
     'Zhang San sat high on the top on the car.'

In (51a), the AA *gaogao-De* 'tall' refers to the height of Zhang San, which is a typical individual-level predicate, so it cannot occur as adverbial. In (51b), *gaogao-De* 'high' refers to the transitory state of Zhang San while he is sitting on the top of the car, so (51b) is a good sentence. Furthermore, the reduplicated form of the adjective makes it possible to express the subjectivity of the speaker.

Except for the stage-level requirement on the aspectual features of the event e, this kind of AAs has no more requirements on e.

(52) a. Li Si gaoxing -De chang zhe ge.
     p.n happy   De sing Asp song.

'Li Si is happily singing a song.'
b. Xiaoli shangxing -De likai le jia.
   p.n sad   De leave Perf home
   'Xiaoli sadly left home.'
c. Xiaoming xizizi-De   zha-le yi pan huashengmi.
   p.n   happy-DE fry-Perf one plate peanuts
   'Xiaoming fired a plate of peanuts and he was happy during that process.'
d. Laonainai huanghuangzhangzhang-De fangxia baofu.
   Granny flustered-de   De put   parcel.
   'Granny put down the parcel and she was flustered at that moment.'

In (52a), the event denoted by the main verb is an activity, in (52b) is an achievement, and in (52c) is an accomplishment. Only individual-level primary predicates are restricted from being modified by this group of AAs. Both simple adjectives and complex ones can occur as this kind of AAs. The adjectives in (52a) and (52b) are simple adjectives, and in (52c) and (52d), the adjectives are complex ones. During the holding of the event in (52a), the state denoted by the adjective *gaoxing* 'happy' holds simultaneously. All the events in (52b),(52c) and (52d) are telic, and the culmination of these events are concomitant with the holding of the states denoted by the adjectives *shangxin* 'sad' *xizizi* 'happy' and *huanghuangzhangzhang* 'flustered'. Furthermore, the event denoted by the adjective is homogeneous and distributive, which means any subpart of the event e must be accompanied by the same state of being 'adj'. Regardless of the variation of the aspectual features of e, e' is always homogeneous and occurs simultaneously.

A very special feature of this kind of AAs is that such AAs have temporal independency which means that they can be combined with the assertion of a prolonged existence of the mental state in question. That is to say, the event e' can still exist when then event e is over. According to the definition of temporal independency, this kind of AAs we are talking about in Chinese have the property of temporal independence. This is illustrated in (53):

(53) a. Xiaoli shangxin De likai le jia, daole xuexiao haishi
hen shangxin.
p.n   sad   De leave Perf home, get to school still very sad
'Xiaoli sadly left home, and she was still sad after getting to school.'

Geuder(2000) defines a group of trannsparent adjectives, which express the perceivable mental states of the subject. Adverbs derived from such transparent adjectives are called transparent adverbs. Only the transparent reading of subject-oriented AAs has the property of temporal independency as in (54), while the manner reading in (55) doesn't have this property.

(54) John sadly left, and he was still sad when he was walking down the street.
(55) John defended his thesis cleverly, and was still clever at the party.

(Geuder 2000: 22)

4.3.1.3 The Latest Researches Relevant to Subject$_1$-oriented AAs

In Mandarin Chinese, emotional adjectives constitute an important subset of subject-oriented [+concomitance] [+participant] [+homogeneity] AAs. All kinds of emotions are the psychological reactions to external stimuli, and such psychological reactions can be the motivations of other actions, so emotional adjectives can naturally serve as adverbials to indicate the emotional states of the subjects. Their semantic orientations are relatively easier to decide. Consequently, this class of AAs has not got the deserved attention. Actually, the relationship between the event denoted by the verb and the event expressed by the AA are much more complicated than it appears. (Lu 2002, Zhao 2011, 2012, Kong 2013)

Zhao and Shi (2011)'s research mainly focuses on the emotional adjectival adverbials in Chinese, and based on the relation between the adjective and the verb, they classify emotional adjectival adverbials into three groups:

> (56) Three kinds of emotional adjectives:
> I. adjectives expressing emotions which are caused by verb
> II. adjectives expressing emotions which are the cause of the verb
> III. adjectives expressing emotions which are parallel with the verb

(57) a. Li Si xinxi   De yujian le lao pengyou.   (I)
　　　p.n delighted De meet Perf old friends.
　　　'Li Si delightedly met with his close friend.'
　　b. Xiaoli xiukui De dixia le tou.   (II)
　　　p.n guilty De low Perf head
　　　'Xiaoli guiltily lowered her head'
　　c. Zhang San xingfen De jiangge bu ting   (III)
　　　p.n   excited De talk   no stop
　　　'Zhang San excitedly kept on talking'

　　The classification is similar to the analysis of psychological adverbs in Geuder (2000), the relation I is roughly equal to the ψ CAUSE, which means that the event is the cause of the emotional state. The relation II is equal to R_{motive}, which means that the emotional state is the motivation of the event. However, different fron Geuder, they argue that the temporal relation between the verb[①] and the adverbial is not concomitant besides III. In (57a), the adverbial is before the verb, in (57b), after the verb.
　　According to our analyses, all the emotional adjectival adverbials in (57) are AAs with [+concomitance] [+participant] [+homogeneity] features. In (57a) the event *e* is an achievement, the emotional state is a kind of strong and uncontrollable state of the referent of the subject, and this emotion is brought out simultaneously as the punctual event *e* takes place. In (57b), if the causal relation is focused, the structural

---

① Their research is not conducted in the framework of event semantics, so the part of speech is used to represent the event.

subordinator will be in another form DE. If not, we tend to treat the emotion state as a concomitant state which holds when the event e takes place.

4.3.1.4 Subject1-oriented AAs in Chinese and English Psychological Adverbs

In English, the mental-attitude adverbs are treated as an independent sub category of subject-oriented adverbs (Geuder 2000; Ernst 2002; Frey 2003). However, compare with the subject$_1$-oriented [+concomitance] [+participant] [+homogeneity] AAs in Chinese, there are some obvious differences.

First, most subject$_1$-oriented AAs in Chinese only have transparent reading, which means they always describe the real mental or physical state of the referent of the subject, and the subject actually is in the mental state satisfying the predicate.

(58) a. *Xiaoli shangxin De likai le jia, qishi ta yidian ye bu
p.n sad De leave Perf home actually she a little too not shangxin.
sad.
'Xiaoli left home sadly, but she was not sad at all.'
b. John sang the song sadly, but he is not sad at all.

In English, the corresponding psychological adverbs have manner reading as in (58b), which just requires the overt manifestation of the quality denoted by the adjective base, but the subject is not truly in the state denoted by the adjective. Rothstein (2004: 55) suggests that the manner reading of adverb is not equivalent to predication. Manner adverbs just say how the agent participated in the event, but not indicate the agent really had the property denoted by the adjective base, while predications attribute the property to the agent.

(59) John greeted Mary enthusiastically/ reluctantly.

These adverbs are manner adverbs, saying how the agent of the event

Chapter Four Clarification and Reclassification of AAs 157

participated in the event—enthusiastically or reluctantly—but do not entail that the agent had the property of being himself/herself enthusiastic or reluctant. Different from English, the manner reading of psychological adjectival adverbial in Chinese can only be derived with the aid of lexical method:

>(60) Xiaoli jiazhuang shangxing De likai le jia, qishi ta yidian ye bu.
>p.n pretend sad De leave Perf home,but she a little too not shangxin.
>sad
>'Xiaoli pretended to be sad when she left home, but she was not sad at all.'

In English, the difference between transparent reading and manner reading is often indicated by the different syntactic position of the adverb: the adverb with transparent reading is placed between the subject and the primary predicate, while adverb with the manner reading is after the verb. In Romanian, the difference between transparent reading and manner reading is sometimes clearly indicated by inflectional suffix:

>(61) a. Copiii merg linistiti la scoalâ.(transparent reading)
>children-THE walk calm-ADJ masc,pl. to school
>'The children walk to school calm.'
>b. Copiii merg linistit la scoalâ. (manner reading)
>children-THE walk calm-ADV to school
>'The children walk to school calmly.'
>   (Daria Protopopescu2007: 188)

When the subject is plural or feminine, the morphological agreement on the adjective will indicate the transparent reading as in (61a), while the ADV form indicates the manner reading in (61b).

Second, in English, the mental attitude adverbials can take scope over sentence negation, whereas in Mandarin, it is not the case:

(62) a. Mary gladly did not go to school.
    b. *Xiaoming xizizi De mei you/bu qu shangban.
       p.n   glad De no/not go work
       'Xiaoming gladly did not go to work'
    c. Xiaoming mei you/?bu xizizi De qu shangban.
       p.n   no/not glad De go work
       'Xiaoming gladly did not go to work'

That is one of the reasons why such mental attitude adverbials are classified as clausal adverbials in English.

In this section, the characteristics of subject$_1$-oriented [+concomitance] [+participant] [+homogeneity] AAs have been studied, including the typical adjectives occurring as this kind of AAs, the requirements on the aspectual feature match relevant to this kind of AAs, some special features of this kind of AAs, and the difference between this kind of AAs and the English mental attitude adverbs. In the following section, another kind of subject-oriented AAs will be introduced, which differs from subject$_1$-oriented AAs only on the [±homogeneity] feature.

4.3.2 Subject$_2$-oriented AAs

Subject oriented AAs usually express the transitory mental state or attitude, or the transient physical state. The event denoted by the primary predicate usually has no influence on the subject. However, subject$_2$-oriented AAs with [+concomitance] [+participant] [−homogeneity] features require the subject to be affected by the event e. Only a few verbs can have influence on their subjects. As a result, the number of this group of AAs is very small, because the affected thematic role tends to be objects rather than subjects, when the verb is transitive. That relation is called theme-object tendency. This tendency indicates that an adjectival adverbial with the features [+concomitance] [+participant] [−homogeneity] tends to be predicate of objects. But some AAs are exceptions to this rule. There are some transitive verbs with subjects which are affected,[①] such as *chi* 'eat', *he* 'drink', *chuan* 'wear'. When

---

[①] Parsons suggests that a participant can have more than one thematic role. This is illustrated in Chapter 3.

the agent conducts the action denoted by these verbs, the agent him/herself will undergo some changes. If conditions are satisfied, these verbs allow [+concomitance] [+participant] [−homogeneity] subject-oriented AAs.

> (63) a. Xiaoming baobao De chi le yi dun zhaji.
> p.n full De eat Perf one CL fired chicken
> 'Xiaoming got full while eating fried chicken.'
> b. Xiaoli tongkuai De da ku le yi chang.
> p.n comfortable De big cry Perf one CL
> 'Xiaoli got comfortable after crying for a while.'

When stage-level adjectives, such as *baobao de* 'very full', *tongkuai* 'very comfortable' occur as primary predicate, they express transitory state of the referent of the subject. The event e in (63a) and (63b) is telic. At the beginning of the eating event, Xiaoming is hungry or at least not full, and after he ate the fried chicken, he felt full. So the event e' denoted by the adjective is not a static event, but a dynamic process changing from being not full to being full. Similar in (63b), the event e' denoted by *tongkuai* 'comfortable' is the final state of a process of changing from being not so comfortable to being very comfortable. The process of changing is concomitant with the event denoted by the main verb. That is to say, the eventuality of e' has shifted from a static state into a dynamic incremental process with the feature [−homogeneity]. [+participant] means that e and e' in (63) have a shared participant, which is the object of the verb. The [+concomitance] feature indicates that these two events included in the sentences in (63) occur at the same time, which can be expressed as τ(e)=τ(e'), which means the temporal overlap between e and e' is more rigidly stipulated for this group of AAs. The starting and ending points of e totally overlap with those of e'.

It looks like that this kind of AAs also exhibit temporal independence, for (64) is acceptable:

> (64) Xiaoming baobao-De chi le yi dun zha ji, guo -le ban tian, haishi boabaode.
> p.n full De eat Perf one CL fried chicken, pass Perf

half day   still is full
'Xiaoming got full while eating fried chicken, and he was still full several hours later.'

(65) Achievements: λPλe. [(BECOME(P))(e)](baobao de)

(66) States: λPλe.P(e)(baobao de)

However, in (65), the two *baobao-de*, denote two different types of events: the former is a dynamic incremental process represented as (65), while the second denotes a transitory static state represented as (66), which was resulted from the former event. In (64), the event that exists after the culmination of the event denoted by the adjective is a new event, different from e'. So subject-oriented [+concomitance] [+participant] [−homogeneity] AAs don't have temporal independence feature, the event e and e' should culminate simultaneously. The event e that is compatible with this kind of AA should be telic. Otherwise, the sentence will be unacceptable or the AA will be interpreted in another way.

The object of the sentence containing this kind of AA should be indefinite as well as not quantized.

(67) *Zhang San baobao De chi-le na wushi ge jiaozi.
    p.n   full   De eat Perf these 50 CL dumplings.
    'Zhang San got full after eating these 50 dumplings'

In English, it is a very controversial issue whether there are corresponding adverbs expressing similar meaning as the subject$_2$-oriented [+concomitance] [+participant] [−homogeneity] AAs. In German, there is no clear morphological difference between adjectives and adverbs, but the subject-oriented [−homogeneity] adverbials are also restrained, and the reflective is needed to make the sentence acceptable:

(68) a. der Sprinter lauft sich mude
        'the sprinter runs himself tired'
    b. sie schlaft sich schon
        'she sleeps herself beautiful'
            (Richer. M and Roeland van Hout 2010: 2012)

Subject-oriented [+concomitance] [+participant] [−homogeneity] AA is a kind of marked usage of adverbials. In Chinese, only a few verbs are compatible with this kind of AAs. In English, this function is realized by secondary predicates with the assistance of fake reflexives. In German, there is no clear formal difference, but the realization of the corresponding function also depends on reflexives.

4.3.3 Subject$_3$-oriented AAs

In last two sections, two kinds of subject-oriented AAs have been studied, and they are different only on [±homogeneity] feature. As we can see, the difference of [±homogeneity] has great influence on the distribution of subject-oriented AAs. In this section, another kind of subject-oriented AA will be studied.

This kind of subject-oriented AAs belongs to evaluative AAs. Evaluative AAs represent a subjective judgment on person, event, proposition, or fact. Across languages, such evaluations are expressed by different linguistic devices, including bound morphemes (suffixes), free morphemes, or compositional devices. Evaluative adverbials do not affect the truth of the modified target, but rather express the speaker's (positive, negative, or other) evaluation of the state of affairs described in it (Cinque 1999).

Evaluative AAs can be classified into two groups: agent-oriented AAs and evaluative AAs. Agent-oriented AAs indicates that the speaker judges the agent of the event e manifest the property denoted by the adjective with respect to the event denoted by the primary predicate, which is the reason why this kind of AA is called agent-oriented AAs. The notion of agent in this sense is roughly equal to the thematic role Agent. However, the extension is a little bit wider than the agent thematic role. The agent in the agent-oriented sense refers to the individuals that can control the eventuality in question by choosing to take an action, to enter into a state or not.

(69) a. Jim wisely got out of bed.
     b. Jim wisely lay on the bed.

(Ernst 2002: 55)

In (69a), Jim is an agent in the thematic role sense, but in (69b), Jim might have been placed on the bed, and then he just chose to keep on staying there. In this sense, Jim is (69b) is also the agent of the eventuality *staying on the bed*.

According to Chen (1987), he also discusses the control of the agent, and classifies the AAs into controllable and uncontrollable groups, but this control is not related to the eventuality denoted by the main verbs. Control in his sense means the agent can control the state denoted by the adjectival adverbial. However, subjects of states are not agentive, so the classification of AAs based on control over the states denoted by the adjective is misleading.

Now, let's take (70a) as an example to have a look at the agent-oriented AAs:

(70) a. Zhang San mingzhi De zai Beijing maile yitao fangzi.
       p.n   wise   De at Beijing buy one CL apartment
       'Zhang san wisely bought an apartment in Beijing.'

[−concomitance] feature means that e' *mingzhi* 'wise' and e *mai* 'buy" are not happening at the same time. Usually, the occurence of the event e makes the speaker feel that the agent manifests the property denoted by the adjective. Consequently, event e, or at least the initial point of e, is before event e', which is indicated as $\tau(e) > \tau(e')$. [+participant] feature means that the free variable of the event e' is co-indexed with the participant of the event e, and usually its thematic role is the agent of the event e. In this sense, agent–oriented AAs are often categorized as a subset of subject-oriented AAs, but such AAs have some of their own features which differ themselves form other two kinds of subject-oriented AAs. [−homogeneity] feature means that the event e' is not a stative state, but a dynamic eventuality of manifeating the property expressed by the adjective on the agent of e.

4.3.3.1 Typical Adjectives Occur as Subject$_3$-oriented AAs

Usually, the adjectives that describe a person's dispositions can occur as Agent-oriented adjectival adverbials. Scholars have noticed this class of adjectives have different performance when occurring as adverbials (Chen 1987; Zhang 1990; Dong 1991). Zhang (1990) mainly focuses on derived adjective adverbials, and he states that adjectives such as *guaiguaide* 'obedient', *xinxinkuku* 'laborious', *ananfenfen* 'law-abiding' express speaker's evaluation of the subject. However, this kind of adjectival adverbials has not been studied intensively. Representative adjectives that occur as agent-oriented AAs are listed in (71):

(71) Dispositional subject-oriented AAs:
congming 'clever', *yuchun* 'stupidly', *mingzhi* 'wisely', *jizhi* 'tactfully', *shahuhu* 'foolishly', *culu* 'rudely', *kangkai* 'generous', *canren* 'cruel', *manheng* 'violent', *youya* 'elegant', *renrenzhenzhen* 'careful', *keqi* 'polite', *mamahuhu* 'careless', *jinshen*, 'cautious'

These adjectives usually denote a generic, habitual or otherwise permanent property of a person, so they are called dispositional adjectives. These adjectives are often ambiguous between a stage-level reading and an individual-level reading. Stowell (1991: 216) states that in Hebrew, the suffixation -i will indicate the two different interpretations.

When these adjectives occur as primary predicates, they usually express the general and stable personality of the referent of the subject. In this sense, these adjectives belong to the individual-level adjectives in Carlson's (1977) classification of predicates. In Zheng (2000), such adjectives are classified as denoting inherent property of a person.

(72) a. Li Si hen congming.
    p.n very clever
    'Li Si is clever.'
  b. Zhang San shahuhude.
    p.n   foolish
    'Zhang San is foolish.'
(73) a. λx[congming(x)](Li Si)
  b. λx[shahuhu de (x)](Zhang San)

As is indicated in (72), such adjectives are individual-level predicates denoted the permanent property of the subject. The logic form in (73) shows that such adjectives lack the Davidsonian event argument. However, when serving as adjectival adverbials, these individual-level adjectives are coerced to have stage-level interpretation. Agent-oriented AAs don't express the dispositional property that the subjects have, but express the evaluation of the speaker towards the agent because of the occurrence of the event:

> (74) Zhang San yuchun De huida le jizhe de wenti.
> p.n   stupid De answer Perf reporter of question
> 'Zhang San stupidly answered the reporter's question.'
> (agent-oriented reading)

In (74), *Zhang San* was considered to be *yuchun* 'stupid', regardless of how he actually answered the reporter's question. This reading is called agent-oriented reading, for the sentences containing this kind of adjectival adverbials express that the agent of the event e manifests the property denoted by the adjective because of the taking place of the event e. Stowell (1991) notes that such kind of adverbial is in a way temporally bound to the primary predicate. Ernst (2002) names these adverbs derived from dispositional adjectives are as agent-oriented adverbs.

4.3.3.2 Characteristics of Subject$_3$-oriented AAs

The under adjectives of subject$_3$-oriented AAs have some special features, even though these adverbials are included in the category of subject-oriented adverbials. They have a speaker oriented dimension because they reflect the evaluation of the speaker towards the agent.

First, agent-oriented reading demands the agentivity of the subject. The subject should be volitional, and when the subject loses control over the event e, the agent-oriented reading is unacceptable. The other two kinds of subject-oriented AAs are not sensitive to this. Consequently, Bei[①] and some modal expressions are excluded from the scope of the agent-oriented AAs, due to the requirement of controllability over the event e. However, real evaluative AAs are much freer to host modal components in its scope.

---

① It is a passive marker.

(75) a. *Zhang San budebu mingzhi -De tuichule jingxuan.
       p.n   have to wise   De quit Perf election campaign.
       'Zhang San had to wisely quit the election campaign.'
    b. Zhang San budebu shangxin -De tuichu le jingxuan.
       p.n   have to sad   De quit Perf election campaign
       'Zhang San had to sadly quit the election campaign.'
(76) a. Xiaoming keneng hui mingzhi-De fangqi zheci bisai.
       p.n   maybe will wise   De give up this competition.
       'Xiaoming probably will wisely give up this competition.'
    b. *Xiaoming mingzhi De keneng hui fangqi zheci bisai.
       p.n   wise   De maybe give up this competition.
       'Xiaoming will wisely probably give up this competition.'

In (75a), the modality *budebu* 'have to' indicates that the subject lost control over the event *tuichu jingxuan* 'quit the election campaign', so (75a) is not acceptable. However, as is indicated in (75b), mental-attitude AAs are not under this restriction. The minimal pair in (76) indicates that modal expressions inside the scope of agent-oriented AAs will block the agent-oriented interpretation.

Second, subject$_3$-oriented AAs are focus-sensitive and have scope effect. The adjuncts in its scope cannot be dropped.

(77) a. Li Si shahuhu De [zai miaoli]$_{FOCUS}$ mai shuzi[①].
       p.n stupid De at temple   sell comb
       'Li Si stupidly sold combs at a temple.'
    b. Li Si shahuhu De mai shuzi.
       p.n stupid   sell comb
       'Li Si stupidly sold combs.'
    a =//=> b
    c. Li Si shahuhu de.
       p.n stupid

[①] Because people there are usually hairless.

'Li Si is stupid.'

a =//=> c

When the contrast focus [*zai miaoli*] is in the scope of the agent-oriented AA, it can't be dropped. If it is dropped, the two sentences describe different mistakes, and (77a) does not necessarily entail (77b). Furthermore, (77a) does not entail (77c), for in (77c), the predicate is an individual-level predicate, whereas in (77a), the property of being stupid just manifests on *Li Si* temporarily.

What's more, subject$_3$-oriented AAs take scope over negation, while the other two kinds of subject-oriented AAs don't take scope over negation:

(78) a. Li Si hen mingzhi -De meiyou/bu shuochu nage mimi.
   p.n very wise   De no/not   tell   that secret
   'It is wise of Li Si that he did not tell the secret.'
   b. *Li Si gaogaoxingxing De meiyou/bu qu xuexiao.
   p.n happy   De no/not   go school
   'Li Si was happy for he did not go to school'

Third, subject$_3$-oriented AAs are not temporal independent. The event e' denoted by these adjectives cannot have a prolonged existence independent of the relevant event e denoted by the verb:

(79) *Zhang San yuchun -De huida le jizhe de wenti, hui dao jia,
   p.n stupid De answer Perf reporter of question, arrive home, hai shi hen yuchun.
   still is very stupid.
   'Zhang San stupidly answered the reporter's question, and he is still stupid after he went home.'
(80) Individual-level predicate: $\lambda P \lambda x.P(x)$ (yuchun)

The logic form in (80) cannot express the exact meaning the agent-oriented AA *yuchun-De* 'stupid' in (79), for the AA in (79) denotes a dynamic process of presenting the property of being *yuchun*, and the event culminated instantly.

Forth, subject₃-oriented AAs are ambiguous between agent-oriented reading and VP-oriented reading.

(81) a. Zhang San yuchun De huida le jizhe de wenti.
      p.n   stupid De answer Perf reporter of question
      'Zhang San stupidly answered the reporter's question.'
  b. The answer given by Zhang San is very absurd, which manifests stupidity.
                                (VP-oriented reading)
  c. Zhang San was considered stupid to answer the reporter's questions, for he was supposed not to do so, although he might provide decent answers.
                                  (agent-oriented reading)

(82) a. Li Si culu De daduan le yanchu.
      p.n rude De interrupt Perf performance
      'Li Si rudely interrupted the performance.'
  b. Li Si interrupted the performance in a rude manner.
                                  (VP-oriented reading)
  c. Li Si was considered to be rude because he interrupted the performance regardless of how he interrupted it.
                                  (agent-oriented reading)

(81b) is the VP-oriented reading of (81a), in which the agent *Zhang San* is not necessarily to be a stupid person at the moment of performing the answering event. Even if *Zhang San* is always clever, (81a) is acceptable, as long as the event of answering question manifests or shows the typical property of stupidity. Similarly, (82) also has two different interpretations. In (83), the addition of the adverb *guyi* 'intentionally' clearly indicates the VP-oriented reading:

(83) Congming de Zhang San (guyi) yuchun De huidale nage wenti.
     intelligent de p.n (intentionally) stupid de answer that question
     'Intelligent John (intentionally) answered that question

stupidly.'

Negation also can be used to disambiguate the agent-oriented reading and VP-oriented reading:

(84) a. Xiaoming meiyou congming De huida nage wenti.
     p.n   not   clever   De answer that question
    'Xiaoming didn't answer that question cleverly.'
                                (VP-oriented reading)
b. Xiaoming cingming De meiyou huida na ge wenti.
     p.n   clever De not   answer that question
    'Xiaoming cleverly didn't answer that question.'
                                (agent-oriented reading)

In (84a), AA is inside the scope of negation, so it has a VP-oriented reading, while in (84b), negation is inside the scope of AA, which has the agent-oriented reading.

For such ambiguity, some scholars explain it in terms of regular polysemy (Rapport Hovav and Levin 1998). Various approaches have been taken involving lexical (McConnell-Ginet 1982; Geuder 2000; Ernst 2002) or compositional (Thomason and Stalnaker 1973; Rawlins 2008) processes to derive the differences, but the jury is still out. Stowell (1991) has the intuition that when such adjectives appear with an infinitival, the individual-level reading disappears, so he proposes that the event of the SLP reading of such adjectives is contributed by the infinitive. However, Landau (2010) has different opinion that such adjectives are ambiguous in lexicon, which means these adjectives have two lexical entries: one is individual-level, and the other is stage-level. In this work, compositional analysis of the ambiguity of such AAs will be held on, which means that the core semantic of the under adjective is consistent, but they combine with different predicates to get different interpretations.

It has been stated in Chapter 3 that the interpretation of AAs is highly context-sensitive. When the individual-level adjectives are coerced to have stage-level reading in a concrete context, it does not mean the under adjective has been shifted into an SLP, but the introducing of predication operator DO, CAUSE, BECOME, MANIFEST etc., results in the stage-level reading. The reinterpretation process reflects the compositionality principle and the process of coercion is temporary and context-sensitive.

In this work, we will pursue the hypothesis that different interpretations of AAs share the same core meaning, and the variation of interpretation is the result of different way of composition.

4.4 Object-oriented AAs

Object-oriented AAs have long been the focus of the research on adverbials. Object-oriented adjectival adverbials denote perceivable state of the object and only have transparent reading, and they denote the physical state of the referent of the object during the holding or culmination of the event denoted by the main verb. According to the classification system proposed in Section 4.2, two kinds of object-oriented AAs are distinguished. There features are listed in (85):

(85) Two kinds of object-oriented AAs

| d | object$_1$ | +participant | +homogeneity | +concomitance |
| e | object$_2$ | +participant | −homogeneity | +concomitance |

From this form, we can find that these two groups of object-oriented AAs are only different in the feature [±homogeneity]. In the following sections, the features of each kind of object-oriented AAs will be analyzes in details.

4.4.1 Object$_1$-oriented AAs

Object$_1$-oriented [+concomitance] [+participant] [+homogeneity] AAs denote the state of a participant for the duration of the event. This kind of AAs is only compatible with some primary predicates. At the same time, such AAs have some requirements on the objects.

(86) a. Xiaoming rere -De he le yi bei cha.
    p.n   hot De drink one cup tea.

'Xiaoming drank a cup of tea while it was hot.'

Take (86) as an example: the feature [+concomitance] is indicated by $\tau(e) \subseteq \tau(e')$, which means that there is temporal overlap between the drinking event e and the *rere-de* state e'. [+participant] feature means that the free variable x of the event e' should be co-indexed with a participant of the event e, here it is co-indexed with the theme *yibeicha* 'a cup of tea'. [+homogeneity] means that the event e' denoted by *rere-de* is a stative state.

4.4.1.1 Features of Adjectives in Object$_1$-oriented AAs

As we have stated that only the temporal feature of stage-level adjectives are compatible with the temporal feature of event, so they can occur as adverbials. Individual-level predicates expressing long-lasting, immutable characteristics cannot be used as adjectival adverbials regardless of being in reduplicated forms or not. However, most of the object$_1$-oriented AAs are derived from object-related adjectives, and it seems that a lot of individual-level adjectives occur as this kind of AAs. It looks like that the hypothesis that AAs should have with stage-level interpretation.

(87) a. Zhuozishang houhou De fang zhe ji ben shu.
    table   thick De put ASP several CL book.
    'There are several books stacked high on the table.'
 b. * Zhuozishang houhou De fang zhe yi ben shu.
    table   thick De put ASP several CL book.
    'There are several books stacked high on the table.'
(88) a. Xiaoli minghuanghuang De daizhe gen jinxianglian.
    p.n gleaming   De wear ASP gold necklace.
    'Xiaoli wears a gleaming gold necklace.'
 b. *Xiaoli cucu De daizhe gen jinxianglian.
    p.n huge De wear ASP gold necklace.
    'Xiaoli wears a huge gold necklace.'

The default reading of *houhou-de* 'thick' is an individual-level adjective which measures the thickness of an object. However, the interpretation of AAs is highly context-sensitive; as Geuder (2000) states that such elements have 'constructional meanings' and that their interpretation is given by the syntactic structure in which they occur. I assume that his 'constructional meaning' refers to the coercion effect of the context on the interpretation of the adjectival adverbials. In (87a), the AA *houhou-De* refers to the transitory scale of the thickness of a stack of several books. Compared with (87b), the thickness of one book is a permanent property of a book, which is not mutable. In (88a), *minghuanghuang-de* 'gleaming' is a transitory state appearing under specific circumstances, whereas in (88b), the diameter of the gold necklace *cucu-de* 'huge' is a permanent property, which is immutable with the context. That is why (88a) is perfect, and (88b) is unacceptable. These examples support the opinion that the ILP/SLP contrast is not lexicon based, but triggered by the context.

4.4.1.2 Requirement on the Primary Predicate

The eventuality of e modified by this kind of AAs is not restricted to be telic, and some atelic events are also compatible with this kind of AAs, given that they have stage-level predicate interpretation. Verbs that are compatible with object$_1$-oriented AAs are not necessary to have strong transitivity, and the object is not necessarily to be affected by the event. Such event has very weak coercing effect on the event e'. As a result, adjectives occuring as this kind of AAs are usually stage-level adjectives per se.

(89) a. Xiaoming rere De he le yi bei cha.
　　　 p.n　 hot De drink one cup tea.
　　　 'Xiaoming drank a cup of tea while it was hot.'
　 b. zhuozishang houhou De fangzhe jibenshu.
　　　 p.n　 thick　 De wear　 CL sweater.
　　　 'Xiao li wears a thick sweater.'
　 c. *Zhuozishang houhou De you jibenshu.
　　　 p.n　 thick　 De wear　 CL sweater.
　　　 'Xiao li wears a thick sweater.'
　 d.*Xiaoli dada De you yi shuang yanjing.
　　　 p.n　 big De have one pair eyes.

'Xiaoli has big eyes.'

In (89a) the event denoted by the main verb is an accomplishment, and the event denoted by the adjective is a homogeneous state which is concomitant with the drinking event. In (89b), the primary predicate *fangzhe* 'put' refers to the state resulted from the action of putting, which is stative and atelic. However, it is still a stage-level predicate. In (87c), the primary predicate *you* 'have' is an individual-level predicate, which is incompatible with the modification of AA. In (89d), both the verb and the adjective are individual-level predicates, which makes the sentence unacceptable.

4.4.1.3 Requirement on the Object

Different from the other kind of objected-oriented AAs with [−homogeneity] feature, the object-oriented AAs with [+homogeneity] feature put no extra requirements on the quantificational feature of the object.

(90) a. Li Si rere De he cha.
p.n hot De drink tea
'Li Si drinks hot tea.'
b. Li Si rere De he-le yi bei cha.
p.n hot De drink Perf one CL tea
'Li Si drank a cup of tea hot.'
c. Li Si rere De he-le na bei cha.
p.n hot De drink Perf that cup tea
'Li Si drank that cup of tea hot'

In (90a), when the bare noun occurs as the object, the sentence express a long-lasting habit. It is an individual-level predicate, so it is not compatible with AA, which is the reason why (90a) is not well acceptable. The objects that are semantically related to such kind of AAs usually in (number)+CL +n form.

All the requirements on the components of sentences containing [+concomitance] [+participant] [+homogeneity] AAs have been stated, but it doesn't mean that all the components satisfying the requirements can make an acceptable sentence.

> (91) a. Li Si chouhonghong De chi le yi kuai lan rou.
>   p.n smelly   De eat Perf one piece rotten meat.
>   'Li Si ate a piece of rotten meat smelly.'
> b. Li Si bei po chouhonghong De chi le yi kuai lan rou.
>   p.n Bei forced smelly   De eat Perf one piece rotten meat.
>   'Li Si was forced to ete a piece of rotten meat smelly.'

In (91a), both the adjective *chouhonghong-De* 'smelly' and the primary predicate *chi* 'eat' are stage-level predicates, but this sentence is not completely acceptable. The unacceptability of this sentence is the result of many factors. Adjectives with derogatory meanings are restricted to occur as adverbials, for the event is usually under the control of the subject, so the subject will cancel the action if the result is against his/her expectation. The subject has agentivity over the event denoted by the verb, so negative result will be avoided by the subject intentionally, that is the main reason why adjectives with derogatory meaning will decrease the acceptability of the sentence. If the agentivity of the subject is cancelled, the sentence will be much better as indicated in (91b).

4.4.2 Object$_2$-oriented AAs

Most of the researches on adjectival adverbials are centered on the object$_2$-oriented [+concomitance] [+participant] [−homogeneity] AAs. Typical examples are given in (92).

> (92) a. Haizimen gaogao De duile ge xueren.
>   kids   tall De pile CL snowman.
>   'Kids have made a tall snowman.'
> b. Xiaoming cuicui De zha-le yi pan huashengmi.
>   p.n   crispy-DE fry-Perf one plate peanuts
>   'Xiaoming fried a plate of peanuts, and the peanuts were crispy.'

In (92a), the default meaning of the adjective *goagao de* 'tall' is a typical individual-level adjective. However, it was coerced into denoting a dynamic incremental process experienced by its argument for the duration of the event denoted by the verb. The event e is an accomplishment, and the event e' takes place simutaniously and culminates at the same time with the event e. The feature [+concomitance] is expressed as τ(e) =τ(e'), which means that there is complete temporal overlap between e and e'. [+participant] feature means that the free variable x of the event e' should be co-indexed with the theme of the event e. [−homogeneity] means that the event e' denoted by *gaogao De* is a dynamic incremental process of degree increasing to the standard denoted by the reduplicated adjective. This kind of AAs is very demanding for the context. They are only compatible with some primary predicates, at the same time, such AAs have some requirements on the objects. Furthermore, only some adjectives can occur as this kind of adverbials. The requirements on components of the sentence containing such AAs will be analyzed in the following parts.

4.4.2.1 The Components of the Sentence Containing such AAs

Generally speaking, sentences containing object$_2$-oriented AAs require three necessary elements: an affected theme, a property scale, and a bound. Certain property of the affected theme argument changes by degree along a scale due to the event described by the verb, until it reaches a bound (Krifka 1998). The e' denoted by AA is related to certain property of its free variable x, which is co-indexed with the affected theme of the event e. At the same time, the AA also provides a bound. This bound is context-sensitive and subjective. An affected theme requires the verb to have strong transitivity feature, thus verbs denoting stative states and some verbs denoting activities are excluded, for they don't take affected theme.

It has been generally stated that the presence of an argument with some specific features, which is expressed as specified quantity of the argument, is vital for the telic interpretation of the VP (Dowty 1991; Verkuyl 1995; Krifka 1998). The sentences that are compatible with this kind of AAs are required to be telic, so it is generally assumed that the affected themes are often quantitized objects, and the objects are usually in the form 'number + Cl +noun', in which the number is often very small and can be omitted. (Lu, Li 2007). However, according to the observation, we notice that the requirement on the number and definiteness of the affected theme is not so rigid as traditionally assumed:

>(93) a. Xiaoming yanyan De qi le { cha/hu cha/yi hu cha/zhe hu cha/
>p.n strong De cook Perf {one kettle tea/kettle tea/ this kettle tea
>na hu cha}
>that cattle tea}
>'Xiaoming cook {a/ -/this/that} kettle of tea strong.'
>b. Xueshengmen ganganjingjing De dasaole { jiaoshi/ zhejian jiaoshi/
>student   clean   De sweep Perf {classroom/this CL najian jiaoshi/ liangjian jiaoshi}
>/that CL classroom}
>'These students swept a/-/this/that/two classroom clean.'

The aspectual operator $-le$ is often compulsory. Shen (1995) suggests that the aspectual operator $-le$ and the quantification over the theme share the similar function to mark the event as telic. Consequently, the presence of $-le$ relaxes the requirements of quantification over the theme.

The adding of this kind of AAs will not increase extra restrains on the definiteness and quantification of the argument, as long as the VP denotes a telic event, so progressive is incompatible with this kind of AAs.

>(94) a. *Haizimen zhengzai gaogao De dui xueren.
>kids   ASP$_{(progressive)}$ tall   De make snowman
>'The Kids are making a snowman tall.'
>b. *Xueshengmen zhengzai ganganjingjing De dasao jiaoshi.
>students   ASP$_{(progressive)}$ clean   De sweep classroom
>'These students are sweeping the classroom clean.'

Second, the property scale is the property denoted by the adjective. Take the sentences in (92) as examples. In (92a), the property is the height of the snowman, and in (92b), the property is the taste of the peanuts. With the event e going on, the degree will change along the scale of the property. When the degree reaches the bound set by the speaker subjectively, the event e culminates. In this sense, the adjectives in this kind of AAs are related to certain property and at the same time indicate a bound. Simple adjective usually denote extensive scale of certain property, so they are not concrete enough to denote a bound. As a result, under adjectives for this kind of AAs are usually in reduplicated forms, for the reduplication can narrow down the scale denoted by the adjective, and increase the subjectivity.

The entity denoted by the affected theme must change incrementally over the property scale, and the change is directly related to the event denoted by the main verb. Otherwise, the sentence will be unacceptable.

(95) *Li Si hei huhu De chile yizhi kaoji.
    p.n black De ear Perf one CL roask chicken.
    'Li Si ate a roast chicken, which is black.'

In (95), the roast chicken is the affected theme; the color is the property scale, and degree denoted by *heihuhu* 'very black' is the bound. The sentence is not acceptable for that the property scale does not change. Even it changes, the change is not directly related to the event e.

4.5 VP-oriented AAs

In Section 4.3 and Section 4.4, we have analyzed five kinds of AAs with [+participant] feature. Although they are adverbials, they ascribe some property to one of the participants or denote a state of a participant of the event e. In this section, VP-oriented AAs will be analyzed. Modifying VP is the essential function of adverbial, and event adjectives can occur as adverbials with few constraints. This class of adjective adverbials are names as VP-oriented AAs instead of manner AAs, because AAs with manner reading are just a subset of the VP-oriented

AAs (Parsons 1990). Jackendoff (1972) also includes manner adverbs as a subclass of VP adverbs. VP-oriented AAs is the most complex group of AAs among all the AAs, which is exhibited in many ways.

First, the number of syllabal of the under adjectives in VP-oriented AAs is more various than that of other groups. Only a few monosyllabic adjectives can occur as AAs, and almost all of them are VP-oriented. Furthermore, disyllabic adjectives and derived adjectives of various pattern can serve as VP-oriented AAs.

Second, the structural subodinator *-De* is optional for some VP-oriented AAs, while for other groups of AAs, *-De* is compulsary.

Third, if an AA has more than one interpretation, one of which is certianly VP-oriented. Zheng (2000) also suggests that all the AAs are relevant to verbs, so in his classification of AAs, each group of AAs is verb related. However, the verb-relavance in his sense in not the same as the VP-oriented interpretation or manner reading (this term is ambiguous, because some VP interpretataion cannot get a 'in a ADJ manner' paraphrase.). Verb relevance in his sense is the temporal relation between the event denoted by the adjective and the event denoted by the verb.

Some VP-oriented AAs focus on certain property of the verbal process itself or indicate the manner in which an action is performed. In this sense, VP-oriented AAs clearly are more concrete, and less subjective, than the agent-oriented AAs and evaluative AAs. VP-oriented adverbials semantically specify the verb (Jackendoff 1972: 70, Swan 1990: 33-36), and are, therefore, only part of the proposition.

Verb-modification is a dynamic evaluation of an event in the sense of interpreting the event in terms of a scale of the relevant dimension of the event concept, i.e. the specified dimension is evaluated in terms of gradable properties.

(96) a. Shibing men xunsu (De) zhanling le zhe zuo chengshi.
soilders rapid (De) occupy Perf this CL city
'Solders occupied this city rapidly.'
b. Xiaoming xiangxi (De) jieshaole ziji de jihua.
p.n in detail (De) introduce self of plan
'Xiaoming introduced his plan detailedly.'

c. λx∃e[zhanling(e)∧Agt(e)=shibingmen∧Th(e)= chengshi
∧xunsu(De)(e)]

In (96a), the AA *xunsu* 'rapid' is related to the speed of the event *zhanling* 'occupy', and the event e is plotted onto a scale of speed, and the adjective sets a point on the scale. In (96b), the verb *jieshao* 'introduce' denotes an event of bringing out information, and the AA *xiangxi* 'detailed' is related to the quantity of information brought out by the event e, or we can say, the event is mapped on to a scale of quantity of information, and the adjective sets a point on this scale. In this sense, VP-oriented AAs are different form AAs with [+concomitance] [+participant] AAs, for VP-oriented AAs don't express a state. All the VP-oriented AAs have the features [−concomitance] [−participant] and [−homogeneity].

No individual-level primary predicates can be modified by AA. Toril Swan (1997) states that "Manner adverb is to modify a verb, i.e. to specify a type of the action in question. They are dynamic, and do not co-occur with stative verbs for the simple reason that stative events are uniform, temporally stable." He does not define stative verbs in detail.

4.5.1 Classification of VP-oriented AAs

Event, just like object, is a multi-dimensional conceptual structure, and modifiers of event can be easily identified as pertaining to specific sorts of sub-concepts of property values. Ernst (1987) proposes a term Pure Manner Adverb (PMB) to include these adverbials that only allow for VP-oriented reading. He concludes the following common semantic characteristics for PMA:

(97) Pure Manner Adverb
I. PMAs usually involve perceptual qualities.
II. PMAs modify the perceptible dimensions of an event directly, while the manner readings of other adverbs only modify the event indirectly.

(Ernst 1987: 84)

Geuder (2005, 2012) also points out that VP-modification must involve one of the core conceptual dimensions of the event. The core concept of dynamic eventuality usually includes the following dimensions. According to the dimension that adjectives modify, VP-oriented adjectives are divided into seven groups (Chen 1987, Dong 1991; Zhang 2005; Wang 2006):

(98) Classifications of VP-oriented AAs
time: *changjiu*, 'long-lasting', *zao*, 'early', *wan* 'late'
speed; *xunsu* 'rapidly', *manman* 'slow', *kuai* 'fast'
manner: *qiaomiao* 'inginuous', wen 'stable', qing 'gentle'
domain: guangfan, 'extensive', quanmian, 'overall'
frequency: *pinfan* 'frequent', *qin* 'often'
degree: *shidang* 'proper', *yanzhong* 'serious', qingwei 'slight'
result: *yuanman* 'successful', *heli*, 'reasonable'

Most of the adjectives in this list are taken from the event-related adjectives in Zhang (2005). According to Ernst and Geuder, when the adjectives in (98) occur as adverbials, they can be termed as pure VP-oriented AAs. This kind of AAs can only have VP-oriented reading. This classification of event adjectives in (96) reflects the dimensions of the core concept dimensions of event denoted by verb, but it does not mean that every event has these dimensions evenly. For some event, certain dimension is prominent, while certain dimension is missing for some other events, which is closely related to the aspectual features of eventuality.

It has been pointed out in last section that subject$_1$-oriented AAs have manner reading, but such reading is not directly related to certain dimension of the event, they are a kind of evaluation based on certain property of the event.

The number of event-related adjectives is small, but that does not mean the semantic analysis of these AAs is simple. VP-oriented AAs are different from the five kinds of [+participant] AAs we have analyzed in that these five kinds of AAs compulsorily co-occur with *-De*. In Chinese, pure VP-oriented AAs exhibit a special feature that they can modify verbs with -*De* absent.

4.5.2 Restrictive and Descriptive VP-modification

Traditionally, the relation between VP-oriented adverbials and events is analogous to that between attributes and objects (Higginbotham 1985 among others). Bolinger (1967) comments extensively on the fact that the acceptability of an adjectival phrase in the pronominal position is difficult to predict, because it largely depends on pragmatic factors, i.e., on whether the resulting NP is conceived of as a (culturally) relevant characterization. Waltraud Paul (2010) states that in Mandarin, de-less modification usually establishes a new subcategory, which must present a natural, plausible class. Take *tang* 'sugar' as an example, the size, color, taste, etc. are included in the core concept of the denotation of *tang* 'sugar', so *ruantang,* 'soft sweets', *yingtang* 'hard candy'*, fangtang* 'cube sugar'*, shatang* 'granulated sugar'*, baitang* 'white sugar' *hongtang* 'brown sugar', are all plausible subsets of the set denoted by *tang* 'sugar or candy', but whether being dirty or not is not a core dimension of the concept denoted by candy, so 'dirty candy' is not a plausible subset, which is only restrictedly used in certain concrete context.

Analogously, the dimensions of a core concept expressed by an event or object are conventionally decided and only the conventionally accepted core dimension modifiers are employed as criteria for sub-classification. According to the presence and absence of the subordinator "De", Qi Huyang (1997) differentiates combinational AAs (with -*De* present) and bonding AAs (with De absent). Combinational AAs can be separated from verb, while bonding AAs are required to be adjacent to verb. Similarly, Wan (2006) divides VP-oriented AAs into two groups: restrictive VP modifiers and descriptive VP modifiers. Only the adjective that is relevant to the core conceptual dimension of the event can occur as the restrictive VP modifiers. The restrictive VP modifiers modify verb with -*De* absent, and is finally realized as the first order logic predicate of the event variable, and the descriptive VP modifiers with -*De* present describe the event and realized as an independent event denoting the manifesting of the property expressed by the adjective. Compounds composed of monosyllable adjective + monosyllabic verb are not included in this analysis. Pan (2010) also studies the difference resulted from the presence/absence contrast of *-De* between AA and verb. She calls the *-De* -less VP-oriented AAs characteristic-adverb, whose function is to classify the events denoted by the verb. The combinations of characteristic adverbial and adverb are based on semantic compatibility.

As for event, especially for activities and accomplishments, time, speed, and frequency are the core dimension of the concept denoted by the verb, while for some accomplishments, the result is a core dimension, so *shunli wancheng* 'finish successfully', *sunli daoda* 'arrive smoothly', *yuanman jiesu* 'end favorably', are all acceptable subset of events denoted by the verb, while *kuaipao* 'run fast', *zaoqi* 'get up early', *zixiyanjiu* 'study carefully', are plausible subset of the events denoted by corresponding verbs.

The presence/absence of *-De* is not completely decided by the lexical entry of the adjective per se, but decided by both the adjective and the verb. If an adjective modifies certain dimension of the core concept of the verb, *-De* can be absent; otherwise, it must be present. Furthermore, the core dimension of an event is also not completely decided by the verb, for some pragmatic factors and high frequency of usage of the combination of the adjective and the verb will make the *-De* -less combination more acceptable (Lyu 1980). Maybe it is more reasonable to say that all these event-related adjectives are possible to modify VP without *-De*.

> (99) a. Li Si jianjue (De) fandui zhege jihua.
> p.n resolute (De) oppose this plan
> Li Si opposed this plan resolutely.
> b. Xiaoming jianju *(De) yao le yao tou.
> p.n resoluteDe shake PRF shake head.
> Xiaoming shaked his head resolutely.

In (99a), the event denoted by *fandui* 'oppose' is closely related to one's attitude, and the adjective *jianjue* 'resolute' is related to one's attitude. As a result, *jianjue* modifies a dimension of the core concept of the event denoted by *fandui,* so De can be dropped. When an adjective modifies a certain dimension of the core concept of the event denoted by the verb, then the phrase composed of the adjective and the verb denotes a set of events which is the subset of the events denoted by the verb. In (97b), for the action nodding, the adjective *jianjue* doesn't modify a dimension of the core concept, so -*De* is compulsory. The adjective adverbial with -*De* just adds some information about the event.

Restrictive VP-oriented AAs cannot be separated from the verb. The syntactic position of -*De* -less AAs is fixed. They should be immediately adjacent to the verb. It is not the case for descriptive VP-oriented AAs, for some other adjuncts can be inserted between the AAs with -*De* and the verb:

(100) a. Feiji cong kongzhong pingwen (*cong kongzhong) jiangluo.
airplane (stable) from sky   stable land
'The airplane landed from the sky stably'
b. Feiji (pingwen De) cong kongzhong (pingwen De) jiangluo.
airplane (stable De) from sky   stable De land
'The airplane stably landed from the sky.'

As is indicated in (98a), the insertion of the adjunct *cong kongzhong* 'from the sky', will result in the unacceptability of the sentence. In (98b), the descriptive VP-oriented AA *pingwen-De* can be separated from the verb.

In Chinese, most of the event-related adjectives can function as adverbials of some verbs directly, and most of the combinations of monosyllabic event adjectives and monosyllabic verbs have been lexicalized into fix compounds. (Lyu 1980; Wang 2006).

The reason why monosyllabic adjective cannot combine with -*De* to form a depictive phrase is because the monosyllabic adjectives are typical adjectives and denote such a wide scale of value related to certain property of the event, so they can be used as criteria for the classification of the events denoted by verb. They have too weak depictive ability to form a depictive phrase with -*De*. As a result, the monosyllabic adjective should be reduplicated or be substituted by a relevant synonymous disyllabic adjective to form depictive with *-De*. Shen (2011) states that disyllabic adjectives are a kind of quasi-reduplicated forms which denote a relatively narrower scale and have stronger depictive power, so with the help of *-De*, they can form a depictive phrase.

4.5.3 Characteristics of VP modifiers

As a subcategory of adjectival adverbials, VP-oriented AAs have some particular features:

First, VP-oriented AAs, just like other kind of AAs, are veridical. It means that a sentence containing VP-oriented AAs entails the corresponding sentence without the VP-oriented AA. As we have stated in Chapter 3 that the neo-Davidsonian approach is good at presenting such entailment relation.

Second, VP-oriented adverbs are scopeless and not focus-sensitive at all; they do not take scope over an event description in the way agent-oriented AAs do, and they don't take scope over negation.

(101) a. Xiaoming kuaikuai De zai chufang li yong weibolu zuo
p.n quick De at kitchen in with microwave oven make le yidao cai.
cook Perf a dish
'Xiaoming cooked a dish in the kitchen with the microwave oven quickly.'
b. Xiaoming bu/mei renzhen De (*bu /mei) du shu.
p.n not/no careful De (*not/no) read book
'Xiaoming did not read books carefully.'

According to Croft (1984), the relation between VP-oriented AAs and the modified VP is a kind of natural relation. Consequently, the restrictions on the morphological variations and the dependence of *-De* for these event adjectives that occur as adverbials are relatively relaxed. Monosyllabic event adjectives and some disyllabic ones can occur as adverbials directly to classify the events denoted by the verb, or occur as adverbials in derived forms with the aid of *-De* to describe a specific event.

4.6 Clause-oriented AAs

Clause-oriented AAs express a subjective judgment on propositions, or facts. Across languages, such evaluations are expressed by different linguistic devices, including bound morphemes (suffixes), free morphemes, or compositional devices. In Mandarin, evaluative function is realized through some adjectival adverbials or some grammaticalized compositional devices. Such evaluative expressions do not affect the truth of the modified target, but rather express the speaker's (positive, negative, or other) evaluation of the state of affairs described in it (Cinque 1999).

In this section, we will focus on the last kind of AAs with [−concomitance] [−participant] [−homogeneity] features. Typical examples are given in (102):

(102) a. Li Si yihan   De cuoguole mobanche.
　　　　p.n regrettable De miss Perf last bus
　　　　'It is regrettable that Li Si missed the last bus.'
　　b. Wujiaoshou yiwai   De piping-le Xiaoming.
　　　　Wu professor unexpected De critize Perf p.n
　　　　'Unexpectedly, Professor Wu criticized Xiaoming.'

[−concomitance] feature of this kind of AAs can be expressed as $\tau(e){>}\tau(e')$, which means that these two events are not temporally overlapped. The feature [−participant] means that the free variable x of e', that is Arg (e') is not co-indexed with any participant of the event, but co-indexed with the fact involved the verb in. In (102a, b), this fact is roughly expressed as the event combining its participants. The most obvious defect of the logic form is that it does not reflect the [−homogeneity] feature of e'. In (102a, b), the adjectives *yihan* 'regrettable', *yiwai* 'unexpected' do not denote stative state or property, but express a dynamic process of evaluating of the fact.

Toril Swan (1997) states that evaluative adjectives have the entire sentence in their scope, and are subjective, for these adjectives express speaker's comment. Their function is to encode the speaker's evaluation of either the truth of the proposition or the (presupposed) fact expressed by the proposition. The sentences in (102 a, b) can be paraphrased as (103a, b) respectively:

(103) a. (Rang ren)yihan de shi, Li Si cuoguole mobanche.
    make people regret de is, p.n miss last bus
    'It was regrettable that Li Si missed the last bus.'
  b. (Rang ren)yiwai de shi, Wu jiaoshou pipingle Xiaoming.
    make people unexpected de is, Wu professor blame p.n
    'It was unexpected that Professor Wu blamed Xiaoming.'

This kind of AAs is different from the agent-oriented AAs in §4.3.3, for typical agent-oriented AAs cannot be paraphrased in the same pattern:

(104) a. Xiaoli mingzhi De jieshoule jingli de jianyi.
    p.n wise De accept Perf manager of suggestion
    'Xiaoli wisely accepted the manager's suggestion.'
  b. *(Rangren)mingzhi de shi, Xiaoli jieshoule jingli de jianyi.
    make people wise de is, p.n accept manager de suggestion
    'It was wise that Xiaoli accepted the manager's suggestion. '

4.6.1 The relevant Research on Evaluative AAs

The evaluative function of adjectival adverbials has long been noticed (Chen 1987; Zhang 1990; Dong 1991; Zou 2000). Chen (1987), Zhang (1990) discuss the evaluative function of AAs, but the evaluative function of AAs in their works is not distinguished clearly from subject-oriented reading and VP-oriented reading. Chen (1987) lists a few adjectives that occur as evaluative AAs, such as *xingfu* 'happy', *buxing* 'unfortunate', *zhengque* 'correct', *cuowu* 'mistaken'. Dong (1991) states that a subcategory of AAs has evaluative function and semantically orients the whole event instead of just the verb in it, and the speaker instead of the subject of the sentence is the agent of the evaluative action. Example words are given in (105):

> (105) The evaluative adjectival adverbials in Dong (1991)[1]
> *zouyun* 'lucky', *huangdan* 'ridiculous',
> *shenmi* 'mysterious', *daomei* 'unfortunate',
> *yihan* 'regeretable', *qiguai* 'strange'.

In Mandarin, evaluation is not the prominent function of adjectival adverbials. Consequently, research on this kind of AA is much less than that on AAs with [+participant] feature and VP-oriented AAs. In English, the evaluative function is expressed by adverbs, but in Chinese, the corresponding function can be expressed by some adverbs or compositional decoding patterns:

> (106) a. Unbelievably, he's running as fast as the bus.
> b. (Ling ren) nanyi zhixin de shi, ta pao de he gonggong qiche
> make people difficult believe de is, he run DE and bus yiyang kuai.
> same fast
> 'Unbelievably, he's running as fast as the bus.'
> (Kong 2015: 88)
>
> (107) a. Li Si xinghao mei lai.
> p.n fortunate not come.
> 'Fortunately, Li Si did not come.'
> b. Xinghao Li Si meilai.
> fortunate p.n not come
> 'Fortunately, Li Si did not come.'

In (106a), the evaluative function in English is realized by a single adverb, while in (106b), the same function is performed by a clause-

---

[1] Some words are excluded for some these words are judged as dispositional adjectives, such as *zisi* 'selfish', *kaiming* 'liberal'. *hansuan* 'shabby', etc.

like constituent. In (107), the evaluative function is expressed by adverb and different syntactic positions have little effect on the evaluative function. Kong (2015) compares the different decoding pattern of evaluative expressions in Chinese and English, and argues that most evaluative expressions in Chinese are not lexicalized and this function is mainly realized through compositional decoding patterns. Such different decoding patterns reflect the differences between analytic and synthetic languages: inflectional English language exhibits stronger ability in encoding complex event into a single lexical entry than that of isolating Mandarin. Her research does reflect the case in adjectival adverbials in Chinese. However, there are still some adjective adverbials can have the evaluative function.

(108) a. Xiaoli daomei De jiale zheme yi ge huai dan.
   p.n unfortunate De married Perf such a bad man.
   'Unfortunately, Xiaoli married such a bad guy.'
   b. Daomei de shi, Xiaoli jiale zheme yige huaidan.
   unfortunate de is, p.n married Perf such a bad man.
   'Unfortunately, Xiaoli married such a bad guy.'
(109) a. Nage nanhai yiwai De shizong le.
   that CL boy unexpected De got missing
   'Unexpectedly, that boy got missing.'
   b. Yiwai de shi, nage nanhai shizong le.
   unexpected de is, that CL boy missing Perf
   'Unexpectedly, that boy got missing.'

In (108a) and (109a), the adjectival adverbials realize the evaluative function, while in (108b) and (109b), the evaluative function is realized by the clause-like constructions.

From the analysis of the methods of realizing evaluative function, we can find that adjectival adverbials are not the dominant expressions to perform the evaluative function over proposition or facts.

Taking into consideration the difference between English and Chinese, as well as the morphological features of the evaluative expression in Mandarin, Kong (2015: 90) classifies four kinds of evaluation over proposition with typical examples following:

(110) Different kinds of evaluation:
   I Speaker's general impression over the proposition
   nande (de shi)   'uncommon',   *qiguai (de shi)* 'odd',
   xingyun (de shi) 'fortunate'   *kexi (de shi)* 'unlucky',
   yihan (de shi)   'regrettable' *daomei(de shi)* 'hapless'
   II Speaker's emotional changes resulted by the proposition
   lingren jingya de shi   'surprisingly',
   lingren ganga de shi   'embarrassingly'
   III Speaker's cognitive efforts related to the proposition
   nan yi xiangxing de shi 'unbelievably',
   keyi lijie de shi   'understandably'
   IV Speaker's definition over the property of the proposition
   maodun de shi   'paradoxically',
   zhongyao de shi   'importantly'
   Adapted from (Kong 2015: 90)

From this classification, we notice that only the third kind is derived from verbs, whereas all the other three kinds are derived from adjectives. However, only the adjectives from the first kind can occur as adjectival adverbials without the evaluative marker '...*de shi*'. When the adjectives from the second kind occur as AAs, they can only get subject-oriented reading with [+participant] [+homogeneity] [+concomitance] features.

(111) a. Ling ren ganga de shi, Xiaoli da le liang ge baoge.
         embarrassing de is p.n make Perf two CL burp
         'Embarrassingly, Xiaoli burped twice.'
      b. Xiaoli ganga De da le liang ge baoge.
         p.n embarrassing De make Perf two CL burp
         'Xiaoli embarrassingly burped twice.'

In (111a), the fact 'Xiaoli burped twice' makes the speaker feel embarrassed. In (111b), the e' denoted by AA is a homogeneous state which holds over the process of the event e denoted by the verb, and the subject Xiaoli was in that state while event e occurred.

The adjectives from the last kind are individual-level adjectives denote permanent property, so they usually cannot occur as AAs.

(112) a. Zhongyao de shi, zhewei nianqing xuezhe tichule ziji de lilun.
important de is this CL young scholar put forward self de theory
'Importantly, this young scholar put forward his own theory.'
b. *Zhewei niaqing xuezhe zhongyao De tichule ziji de lilun.
this CL young scholar important De put forward self de theory
'This young scholar importantly put forward his own theory.'

From this analysis, we conclude that only the adjectives in the first kind can occur as evaluative AAs. Although adjectives are very restricted in occurring as evaluative AAs, they have some characteristics to make themselves deserved to be analyzed as an independent kind of AAs.

4.6.2 The Features of Clause-oriented AAs

Clause-oriented AAs are a subcategory of evaluative AAs. According the target of evaluation, evaluation can be divided into evaluation over object and evaluation over speech. The agent-oriented AAs we talk about in Section 4.3.3 are evaluation over object, and the clause-oriented we are dealing with here are evaluation over speech. This kind of AAs have some features which make them different from other kinds of AAs.

First, evaluative AAs are factive, presupposing the truth of the rest of the sentence. On the clausal reading of the evaluative adverbials, the AA takes the whole clause in its scope, so clause-oriented AAs have scope effect and are focus-sensitive. The adjuncts which are scoped over cannot be dropped.

(113) a. Li Si yiwai De [zai jaioshi li] tuodiaole chenyi.
p.n unexpected De at classroom in take off shirt
'Unexpectedly, Li Si took off his shirt in the classroom.'
b. Li Si yiwai De tuodiaole chenyi.
p.n unexpected De take off shirt
'Unexpectedly, Li Si took off his shirt.'

a =//=> b

(114) a. Xiaozhang hennande De zai da hui shang biaoyangle Zhang San.
headmaster uncommon De at dig meeting praise Perf p.n.
'Uncommonly, the headmaster praised Zhang San at the general membership meeting.'
b. Xiaozhang hennande De biaoyang le Zhang San.
headmaster uncommon De praise Perf p.n.
'Uncommonly, the headmaster praised Zhang San.'

a =//=> b

In (113a), the PP *zai jiaoshi li*, is the focus, which means that because the event taking off his shirt happened in classroom made the speaker feel unexpected. (113a) does not entail (113b), even though without the AA '*yiwai De*', the entailment relation can be maintained. Similarly, (114a) does not entail (114b). In addition, negation and modal expressions are also in the scope of this kind of AAs:

(115) a. Laoban henyiwai De keneng hui gei dajia fa jiangji.
boss unexpected De possible will give everyone deliver bonus
'Unexpectedly, the boss probably will give premium to everyone.'
b. Zheci, Xiaoming nande De meiyou shuo fenglianghua.
this time p.n uncommon De not say wind cool word
'Uncommonly, Xiaoming did not say any sarcastic words.'

Second, this kind of AAs is not temporal independent, for such AAs not denote a state of any participant. They just denote an achievement which manifests of the property denoted by the adjective.

Third, some clause-oriented AAs are ambiguous between clause-oriented reading and VP-oriented reading:

(116) a. Li Si xingyun De huodele jinpai.
   p.n lucky De get Perf gold medal
   'Li Si luckily got the gold medal.'
b. Xingyun de shi, Li Si huode le jinpai.
   lucky de is p.n got Perf gold medal
   'Luckily, Li Si got the gold medal.'
c. Li Si yi yizhong xingyun de fangshi huode le jinpai.
   Li Si in a kind lucky de manner got Perf gold medal
   'Li Si got the gold medal in a lucky manner.'

Forth, the default reading of the adjectives that occur as clause-oriented AAs are individual-level adjectives. When occurring as clause-oriented AAs, they don't denote a property any longer, but denote a dynamic eventuality of manifesting the property.

4.6.3 Agent-oriented Reading and Evaluative Reading

Both agent-oriented AAs and clause-oriented AAs express speaker's evaluation. Judging from the classification criteria we set in Section 4.2, these two kinds of AAs are only different in the [±participant] feature. However, they have obvious differences in the demanding of the context. Clause-oriented AAs are not very selective as to the content of their complement, as well as their subject, while agent-oriented AAs strictly require the subject of the sentence to have agentivity:

(117) a. Na ge huaping yiwai De shuai sui le.
   that CL vase unexpected De fall break Perf
   'Unexpectedly, that vase broke into pieces.'
b. *Najian huaping mingzhi De shuang suile.

that CL vase wise De fall break Perf
'That vase wisely broke into pieces.'

Expressing evaluation is not the main function of AAs and only a few adjectives can occur as clause-oriented AAs. However, clause-oriented AAs exhibit some features which make them deserve to be analyzed as an independent kind of AAs. The under adjectives of this kind of AAs denote property of objects or facts, and the ILP/SLP contrast is not clearly reflected in this group of adjectives. When they occur as clause-oriented AAs, they uniformly denote a dynamic eventuality of manifesting the property denoted by the adjective.

4.7 Summary

AAs are identified as a kind of downgraded predicates, and all kinds of AAs have Davidsonian argument for they are interpreted as stage-level predicates. Based on the three features [±concomitance]. [±homogeneity] [±participant], and the value of the free variable of event e' denoted by the AA, AAs are classified into seven kinds. Through the classification of AAs in this chapter, the features of each kind are stated clearly. All these features of each kind of AAs are summarized in the following chart:

(118) Features of seven kinds of AAs

	subject$_1$	object$_1$	subject$_2$	object$_2$	VP	subject$_3$	Clause
[±concomitance]	+	+	+	+	−	−	−
[±participant]	+	+	+	+	−	+	−
[±T independence]	+	+	−	−	−	−	−
[±homogeneity]	+	+	−	−	−	−	−
[±Transparency]	+	+	−	−	−	−	−
[±Ambiguity]	−	−	−	−	±	+	+
[±scope effect]	−	−	−	−	−	+	+
[±Evaluative]	−	−	−	−	±	+	+

Notes on the chart: [±T independence] means whether this kind of

AAs is temporal independent. [±Ambiguity] means whether this kind of AAs is regularly ambiguous between VP-oriented reading and the specific reading belong to this kind.

We can notice from this chart that each kind of AAs has different requirements on the morphological forms and the aspectual features of the under adjectives. The degree of the dependency on the structural subordinator –*De* is also different. At the same time, AAs exhibit different performances concerning the following features: including whether have scope effect; whether have evaluative function; whether have transparent reading; whether have temporal independence; whether present regular ambiguity between VP-oriented reading and other FEO-oriented reading.

From Section 4.2 to Section 4.6, all the seven kinds of AAs in Mandarin have been analyzed. From the analyses of these seven kinds of AAs, we can see that the semantic of AAs are compositional, and the acceptability of the sentence containing AA is not decided by the AA alone, the verb, and the argument of the verb and the aspectual of the eventuality of the event denoted by the VP all have their contributions. The hypothesis that only stage-level primary predicates can be modified by AAs and all AAs must get stage-level interpretation has been verified in the process of analyzing these seven kinds of AAs.

The classification of AAs is also useful for the research on the relative order of different kind of AAs. The relative order of adverbial has been widely studied both in English and in Chinese (Cinque; Ernst, Zhang; Pan 2010). Based on the classification and the analysis for each kind of AA, the rules that decide the relative order of these seven kinds of AAs can be roughly listed as:

1. The AAs with scope effect goes before those AAs with no scope effect.
2. AAs with [+concomitance][+homogeneity]features go before AAs with [+concomitance][−homogeneity]features.
3. Subject-oriented AAs go before object-oriented AAs and VP-oriented AAs.
4. Pure VP-oriented AAs (without -De) should be adjacent to the verb.

This classification of AAs is also helpful in explaining the AAs with more than one interpretation. In the traditional researches on AAs, scholars generally support the fixed type hypothesis. Adjective adverbials are divided into different classes in terms of the target they modify and they implicitly assume that these types are fixed: that is, once an adjective adverbial is ascribed to certain type, it cannot be changed.

Actually, it is not the case in language facts, for some AAs potentially have multi-interpretations on condition of semantic compatibility. As we have stated that the interpretation of AAs is highly context-sensitive, and many adjectives are ambiguous between object-oriented reading and event-oriented reading. For example, agent-oriented AAs reflect regular ambiguity between agent-oriented reading and VP-oriented reading, while clause-oriented AAs are often ambiguous between clause-oriented reading and VP-oriented reading. However, the VP-oriented reading of these kinds is different from the AAs with pure manner reading. Some AAs are ambiguous between subject-oriented reading and object-oriented reading in a proper context. Different interpretations of AAs are the consequence of the different compositional pattern and the apparent difference of semantic orientation of AAs is the result of combination of various different features.

Chapter Five

Semantic Analysis of AAs

This chapter mainly focuses on the event semantic analyses of the seven kinds of AAs. The organization of this chapter is as follows. In Section 5.1, features of each kind of AAs are summarized and the questions that we will work on are put forth. In Section 5.2, the status of the event denoted by the AA is treated as an embedded event and its aspectual features are represented. The function of the structural subordinator -*De* is the focus of Section 5.3. -*De* is analyzed as a functional head, and the under adjective combines with different kind of -*De* to form different kinds of AAs. In Section 5.4, based on the initially proposed semantic analyses and the function head -*De*, the semantic derivation process of each kind of AA is presented. In the derivation process, the compositionality and context-sensitivity of AAs is reflected clearly. In Section 5.5, AAs with more than one interpretation is analyzed as the result of the under adjective combines with different functional head -*De*. Some compounds and idioms that cannot be analyzed compositionally are discussed in Section 5.6. The summary of the chapter is given in section 5.7.

5.1 Features of Each Kind of AAs

The tenet of the "neo-Davidsonian" framework of semantics is that verbs and adjectives denote sets of events---in the same way as countable nouns denote sets of concrete individuals, and thematic roles introduce functions from events to participants. It is believed that one of the greatest benefits of introducing an event argument into the logic form is that adverbial modifiers can be analyzed as simple first-order predicates of the underlying event variable to add information to this event variable on the conjunction-based semantics. Such an account of adverbial modifier will represent straightforward the entailment between the sentences with adverbial modifiers and the corresponding ones with the adverbial modifiers being dropped. This is also one of the motivations that AAs in Mandarin will be analyzed from the perspective of event semantics.

It has been indicated that not all AAs in Mandarin are semantically related to the primary predicates, so it is not appropriate to analyze all the AAs as the predicates of the underlying event argument introduced by the main verb, for besides the VP-oriented AAs, the other kinds of AAs are not semantically related to the event argument of the main verb. Based on the semantic natures of AAs, some kinds of AAs will be analyzed as downgraded predicates. These AAs, instead of being analyzed as the predicates of the underlying event argument of the main verb, have their own Davidsonian event argument. As for what kind of predicates can introduce an underlying event argument, we hold that only stage-level predicate is capable of introducing a Davidsonian event argument.

In previous chapters, the contrast between individual-level predicates and stage-level predicates has been verified to be very important for the interpretation of AAs in Mandarin. All the AAs must receive stage-level interpretation, and all the primary predicates that are compatible with AAs should also have stage-level interpretation. Based on these theoretical backgrounds and the analyses in chapter 4, the features of each kind of AAs will be concluded in (1—7). For the convenience to compare, All these typical examples of each kind of AA and their features will be repeated here for further improvement:

(1) Subject$_1$-oriented [+participant] [+homogeneity] [+concomitance] AA
   a. Xiaoming shengqi De rengdiao le shouji.
      p.n   angry De throw Perf cellphone
   'Xiaoming angrily threw his cell phone away.'

b. τ(e)⊆τ(e')
c. e' has the [+homogeneity] feature.
d. The shared element of e and e' is the subject of the sentence.

(2) Subject₂-oriented [+concomitance] [+participant] [−homogeneity] AA
   a. Xiaoming baobao De chi le yi dun zhaji.
      p.n   full   De eat Perf one CL fried chicken
      'Xiaoming got full while eating fried chicken.'
   b. τ(e)=τ(e')
   c. e' has the [−homogeneity] feature.
   d. The shared element of e and e' is the subject of the sentence.

(3) Subject₃-oriented [−concomitance] [+participant] [−homogeneity] AA
   a. Zhang San mingzhi De maile   yi tao fangzi.
      p.n   wise   De buy Perf one CL apartment
      'Zhang san wisely bought an apartment in Beijing.'
   b. τ(e) >τ(e')
   c. e' has the [−homogeneity] feature.
   d. The shared element of e and e' is the subject of the sentence.

(4) Object₁-oriented [+concomitance] [+participant] [+homogeneity] AA
   a. Xiaoming rere De he le yi bei cha.
      p.n   hot De drink Perf one cup tea.
      'Xiaoming drank a cup of tea while it was hot.'
   b. τ(e)⊆τ(e')
   c. e' has the [+homogeneity] feature.
   d. The shared element of e and e' is the object of the sentence.

(5) Object₂-oriented [+concomitance] [+participant] [−homogeneity] AA
   a. Haizimen gaogao De duile ge xueren.
      kids   tall   De pile CL snowman.
      'Kids have made a tall snowman.'

b. τ(e) =τ(e')
c. e' has the [−homogeneity] feature.
d. The shared element of e and e' is the object of the sentence.

(6) VP-oriented [−concomitance] [−participant] [−homogeneity] AA
  a. Shibing men xunsu (De) zhanling le zhe zuo chengshi.
     soilders   rapid (De) occupy Perf this CL city
     'Solders occupied this city rapidly.'
  b. τ(e) >τ(e')
  c. e' has the [−homogeneity] feature.
  d. The shared element of e and e' event argument of the verb.

(7) Clause-oriented [−concomitance] [−participant] [−homogeneity] AA
  a. Li Si yihan De cuoguole mobanche.
     p.n regrettable De miss last bus
     'It is regrettable that Li Si missed the last bus.'
  b. τ(e) >τ(e')
  c. e' has the [−homogeneity] feature.
  d. The shared element of e and e' is the fact involved the verb in.

From (1) to (7), feature (b) indicates the temporal relation between the run time of e and that of e'; feature (c) indicate the aspectual feature of e'; feature (d) expresses the shared element between e and e'. In this section, we are expected to answer the following questions:

First, a sentence containing AA is a simple sentence, which usually includes a sigle event. However, both these two predicates in these sentence are stage-level predicates which introduce Davidsonian event argument. What is the realationship between these two events and how to represent it?

Second, we suppose that all the adjective adverbials should have stage-level interpretation, but the default reading of adjectives in (3),(5), and (7) are not typical stage-level predicates. Why they can occur as adverbials? Furthermore, e' in (2), (3), (4), (5) and (7) has [−homogeneity] feature. How to represent the [−homogeneity] feature? Where does the marked [−homogeneity] feature come from? Is it included in the lexical entry of the adjective, or is it the result of compositionality?

Third, as far as the AA in (6) is concerned, whether it is appropriate to analyze the VP-oriented AAs uniformly as the predicate of the event arguemnt introduced by the main verb, considering obvious difference resulted from the presence/absence contrast of *-De*?

Forth, *-de* is often a necessary part of the under complex adjectives, such as in (2),(4),(5), what happened to *-de*? Furthermore,what is the exact function of *-De* in the interpretation of AAs?

In the following sections, appropriate logic forms will be constructed for each kind of AAs to answer these questions we are confronted with in this section.

5.2 Formalizing the Features of AAs

Appropriate logic forms will be constructed to reflect more accurately the semantic and syntactic features of AAs, mainly concerning the relationship between these two events denoted by the two predicational constituents, and the aspectual feature of the event denoted by the AA in order to reflect the compositionality and the context-sensitivity of AAs.

5.2.1 Embedding or Summing?

As far as the two events in a simple sentence with an AA are concerned, there are two possible patterns to represent the relation between them: one is to embed one event into the other; the other one is to form a new event by a summing operation. In Rothstein (2004), summing operation is defined as an operation from E x E to E, which sums two atomic events e_1 and e_2 and then a new singular event $^S(e_1 \cup e_2)$ is derived. Such a summing operation means that the event e_2 denoted by the adjective is parallel to the event e_1 denoted by the main event and is an indispensible part of the derived new singular event.

Parsons holds that atomic formulas which are made of subatomic structures are combined to produce a non-atomic formula mainly by the operation of embedding. Most of the relevant researches on the relation between two events are conducted around the secondary predicates. AAs in Mandarin are different from secondary predicates. However, valuable references can be got from the analyses of secondary predicates. In this section, these two different pattens of arranging events will be compared and evaluated to get a pattern which is more suitable for the analyses of AAs in Mandarin.

5.2.1.1 Embedding

Parsons provides a very detailed analysis for the resultative secondary predicate following the lexical decomposition theory in Dowty (1979). David Dowty provides an analysis of causative and inchoative structure within the symbolism of Montague Grammar. His logic form of (8a) is (8b):

(8) a. Mary closes the door.
b. $(\exists P)[(P(Mary))CAUSE(BECOME(The\ door\ is\ closed))]$

In (8b), 'CAUSE' connects two propositions: $(\exists P)[(P(Mary))$ and (BECOME (The door is closed)), and indicates the causal relation between these two propositions. 'BECOME' maps the proposition (the door is closed) onto the proposition (the door became closed). Parsons took over the idea behind this proposed analysis, and incorporated this idea into a framework with underlying events.

(9) a. Mary hammered the metal flat.
b. $(\exists e)[Cul(e) \wedge Agent(e,\ Mary) \wedge Hammering(e)$
$\wedge Theme(e,\ metal)$
$\wedge (\exists e')\ [Cul(e') \wedge Theme(e',\ metal) \wedge CAUSE(e,\ e') \wedge \exists s[Being\text{-}flat(s) \wedge Theme(s,\ metal) \wedge Hold(s)$
$\wedge BECOME(e',\ s)]]]$

Parsons(1990; 122)

The surface forms of (8a) and (9a) are similar; however, 'close' and 'hammer' differ in that 'close' indicates a causative-inchoative reading while 'hammer' just indicates an activity. The meaning of causative-inchoative in (9a) is compositional which comes from the adding of the adjective struck on the end of the activity. The adjective stuck on the end of the sentence in (9a) is entitled as "resultative tag" by Parsons and such modifiers pick out kinds of states instead of being predicated of events. A resultative, holding for the whole time that the culmination of the matrix event is going on, denotes an event which is the result or consequence of the event denoted by the primary predicate.

It is indicated in (9b), that the event is composed of three components: an event e denoted by verb hammering, and a caused event e' and a resultant state being-flat. All these three components are called atomic events which are embedded in the event e.

This pattern is also applied to the analysis of predicational adverbs in English by Geuder (2000: 29-30). He presents a detailed analysis of the emotional adverbs. He labels adverbials including *angrily, sadly* as transparent adverbs and introduces a new ontology f and semantic links such as CAUSE and MOTIVE to illustrate the semantic relation between the transparent adjective and the verb.

(10) a. X leave sadly
b. $\exists e(leave(e)(x) \& \exists s[sad(s)(x) \& f \psi$ CAUSE s & f≈ leave(e)(x)])
ψ- CAUSE(s,e) →e $_o$ s
(11) a. He angrily wrote a letter.
b. $\exists e \exists y letter(y) \& [write(e)(x,y) \& \exists s[angry(s)(x) \&$ $R_{motive}(s, e))]$

Geuder (2000: 198-200)

For the transparent reading of such emotion adverbs, no matter it is related to the event denoted by the main verb by CAUSE, or R_{motive}, it is required that the psychological state holds when the event occurs, which is represented as e $_o$ s, in which o means overlap.

From the logic forms given by Parson or Geuder, the adjectives when occurring as resultative tags or as the roots of the predicational adverbs, are analyzed as independent predicate introducing its own Davidsonian event argument, and this event is embedded in the event denoted by the primary predicate.

The advantage of this pattern is that the entailment relation is maintained, and it also reflects that the adjunct is droppable.

5.2.1.2 Summing Operation

Rothstein treats a sentence which includes more than one predicate as a singular event. The events denoted by these predicates compose a singular event by a summing operation. Summing in Rothstein sense is defined as an operation sums two atomic events e_1 and e_2 to form a new singular event $^s(e_1 \cup e_2)$, in which the superscript s means S-cumulativity. Susan Rothstein (2001, 2004) argues that secondary predicates are aspectual modifiers in the sense that they introduce a new event and define a relation between it and the event introduced by the main predicate. Secondary predication must involve a summing operation of the two events introduced by the secondary predicate and the matrix verb respectively. There are two constraints on the relation between the summed events in secondary predication. The first is a constraint about temporal dependency, and the second is about the shared participants. When an AP occurs as a depictive secondary predicate, the state it expresses must hold of the denotation of its subject for the whole time that the matrix event is going on. Besides the constraint of temporal dependency, another constraint which must be adhered to is that the secondary predicate and the matrix verb must share a thematic argument (Williams 1980, Rothstein 1983). These two constraints together form the content of a relation which Rothstein named "Time-Participant Connected" (TPCONNECT for short). The TPCONNECT of a depictive is TPCONNECT (e_1,e_2,y), which means that:

>(12) Two events are TPCONNECT iff:
> a. $\tau(e_1)= \tau(e_2)$ (the run time of e_1 is the same as the run time of e_2)
> b. e_1 and e_2 share a participant y.
>
>   (Rothstein 2004: 71)

This TPCONNECT relation is reflective and symmetrical, but not transitive. If e_1 and e_2 have the same run time and share a same participant x, and e_2 and e_3 have the same run time and share a same participant y, then e_1 and e_3 will have a same run time but not necessarily a same participant. The form of subject-oriented depictive is given in (13) and the sentence in (14a) serves as an example of subject-oriented depictive with its logic form represented as (14b):

(13) a. SSUM $[\alpha_{<e,t>}, \beta_{<d,<e,t>>}(x)] = \lambda e. \exists e_1 \exists e_2 [e =^s (e_1 \cup e_2) \wedge \alpha(e_1)$
$\wedge (\beta(x))(e_2) \wedge \text{TPCONNECT}(e_1, e_2, x)]$

(14) a. John drove the car drunk.
b. $\exists e \exists e_1 \exists e_2 [e =^s (e_1 \cup e_2) \wedge \text{Drive}(e_1) \wedge \text{Ag}(e_1) = \text{John} \wedge \text{Th}(e_1) = \text{The car}$
$\wedge \text{Drunk}(e_2) \wedge \text{Arg}(e_2) = \text{John TPCONNECT}(e_1, e_2, \text{John})$
$\wedge \text{Past}(e)]$

"There was a singular event which was the sum of an event of John driving the car and John being drunk where the driving event was time-participant connected to the drunk event"

Different form the TPCONNECT relation of depictives, the TPCONNECT relation of resultative is expressed as TPCONNECT $(\text{cul}(e_1), e_2, y)$. '$\text{Cul}(e_1)$' refers to the culmination of the matrix predicate.

(15) RSUM $[\alpha, \beta] = \lambda y \lambda e. \exists e_1 \exists e_2 [e =^s (e_1 \cup e_2) \wedge \alpha(e_1, y) \wedge \beta(e_2, y)$
$\wedge \text{TPCONNECT}(\text{Cul}(e_1), e_2, y)]$

Rothstein(2004: 76)

TPCONNECT $(\text{Cul}(e_1), e_2, y)$ indicates that the TPCONNECT relation holds between the culmination of the event denoted by the verb and event introduced by the adjectival predicate. The detailed logic form of (16a) is (16b):

(16) a. Mary painted the house red.
b. $\exists e \exists e_1 \exists e_2 [e =^s (e_1 \cup e_2) \wedge \text{paint}(e_1) \wedge \text{Ag}(e_1) = \text{Mary} \wedge \text{Th}(e_1) = \text{The house} \wedge \text{red}(e_2) \wedge \text{Arg}(e_2) = \text{The}$

house∧ TPCONNECT(Cul(e₁), e₂, The house)]]

"There was a singular event which was the sum of an event of Mary painting the house and an event of the house being red, and the culmination of the painting event was time-participant connected to the event of the house being red."

Rothstein(2004: 80)

In Rothstein's interpretation of resultative, the causal relation between these two events is not represented, as she indicates that the causal relation is entailed in the temporal relation between these two events. Such a model of analysis is very suitable for the semantic and syntactic feature of secondary predicates:

First, the temporal relation between these two events e_1, e_2 is clearly represented by the TPCONNECT relation: TPCONNECT(e_1, e_2) indicate the concomitant relation and TPCONNECT(Cul(e_1), e_2) indicates the temporal precedence relation.

Second, the semantic orientations of these secondary predicates have been obviously represented as the shared argument of the two events.

Third, the summing operation indicates that the secondary predicate, which is different from predicational adverb, is an indispensible part of the predicate,

Wu (2009) analyzes some constructions in Mandarin Chinese in the framework of underlying events, such as Shi-Construction in (17a), V-DE construction in (17b), Ba-Construction in (17c), verb-copying construction in (17d),

(17) a. Zhejianshi shi Liuqiang hen bu man.
    this matter make p.n very not satisfied
    'This matter made Liuqiang unsatisfied.'
  b. Liuqiang zou DE lei le.
    p.n walk DE tired Perf
    'Liuqiang got tired from walking.'
  c. Yi ping jiu ba Liuqiang guan zui le.
    one bottle alcohol Ba p.n pour drunk Perf
    'Liuqiang got drunk after drinking a bottle of

alcohol.'
d. Liuqiang ca chuanghu ca lei le.
   p.n wipe window wipe tired Perf.
   'Liuqiang got tired after wiping the window.'

There are two predicates in every sentence in (17), and each one contributes an event to the logic forms in (18):

(18) a. $\exists e[\exists e_1[\exists e_2[e=^S(e_1 \cup e_2) \wedge shi(e_1) \wedge Causer(e_1)=$ zhejianshi
$\wedge Th(e_1)=$Liuqiang very buman$(e_2) \wedge Arg(e_2)=$Liuqiang
$\wedge$ TPCONNECT(Cul(e_1), e_2, Liuqiang)]]]
b. $\exists e[\exists e_1[\exists e_2[e=^S(e_1 \cup e_2) \wedge zou(e_1) \wedge Ag(e_1)=$ Liuqiang $\wedge lei(e_2)$
$\wedge Arg(e_2)=$Liuqiang$\wedge$ TPCONNECT(Cul(e_1), e_2, Liuqiang)]]]
c. $\exists e[\exists e_1[\exists e_2[e=^S(e_1 \cup e_2) \wedge Cause(e_1)=$guan
$\wedge Causer(e_1)=$yi ping jiu$\wedge Th(e_1)= \wedge$Become-zui(e_2)
$\wedge Th(e_2)=$Liuqiang$\wedge$ INCR$(e_1, e_2, C(e_2))$]]]
d. $\exists e[\exists e_1[\exists e_2[e=^S(e_1 \cup e_2) \wedge wipe(e_1) \wedge Ag(e_1)=$ Liuqiang
$\wedge Th(e_1)=$chuanghu$\wedge lei(e_2) \wedge Arg(e_2)=$Liuqiang
$\wedge$ TPCONNECT(Cul(e_1), e_2, Liuqiang)]]]

Wu (2009)

In Chinese traditional grammar, the adjectival predicates after verbs are termed as *buyu* 'complement'. According to the criteria set by Jin (2009) to identify secondary predicates in Chinese, all the adjectives in (17) conform to these criteria. In the last chapter, it has been made clear that AAs are different from the *buyu*[1] after the verb.

First, adjectival adverbials are adjuncts, which is droppable, while buyu is a part of the matrix predicate. AA is not the focus of a sentence,

---

[1] *Buyu* is usually translated into complement, but it is different from the complement in Generative Grammar. Jing (2009) suggests a dichotomy of *buyu*: secondary predicates and post-positing adverbials.

but sometimes can be made as the contrast focus. *buyu* is the natural focus of a sentence, sometimes, even the main verb can be omitted. Consequently, the *buyu* will be more prominent and become the main predicate (Liu and Xu 1998, Xian2007, Pan 2012).

Second, adjective adverbials mainly focus on concomitant temporal relationship with the matrix predicate, while the resultant relationship is often what the *buyu* emphasizes. All the sentences in (17) include the inchoative relation between two events.

Wu (2009) analyzes *buyu* as a coordinate event, which accurately reflects the semantic and syntactic features of *buyu*. If AAs are analyzed in the same pattern, the subordinate semantic feature and the adjunct syntactic status of AAs will be blurred. Taking the semantic and syntactic features of adjective adverbials in Mandarin Chinese into consideration, we will take in nutrients from both Parsons and Rothstein to provide an analysis in the framework of underlying event.

5.2.1.3 A Comparison Between These Two Patterns

Both Parsons (1990) and Rothstein (2001, 2004) analyze secondary predicates in the "neo-Davidsonian" framework, but they take different strategies to arrange the relation between the two events included in a clause. Take the sentence "Mary hammered the metal flat." as an example, and the (19a) is the form in Parsons' style, while Rothstein represents it as (19b).

(19) A comparison between embedding and summing:
  a. $(\exists e)[Cul(e) \wedge Agent(e, Mary) Hammering(e) \wedge Theme(e, metal)$
  $(\exists e')[Cul(e') \wedge Theme(e', metal) \wedge CAUSE(e, e') \wedge$
  $\exists s[Being\text{-}flat(s) \wedge Theme(s, metal) \wedge Hold(s)$
  $\wedge BECOME(e', s)]]]$

  Parsons(1990; 122)

  b. $\exists \ e \exists e_1 \exists e_2 [e =^S (e_1 \cup e_2) \wedge hammer(e_1) \wedge Ag(e_1) =$ Mary
  $\wedge Th(e_1) =$ The metal flat$(e_2) \wedge Arg(e_2) =$ The metal
  $\wedge \ TPCONNECT(Cul(e_1), e_2, \text{The metal})]]$

  Adapted from Rothstein(2004: 80)

The most striking difference between these two logic forms is the difference between the embedding and summing operation. Besides that, in Parsons' form, adjective denotes a state, while an adjective denotes an event in Rothstein's logic form. In the following analyses, we will ignore this difference and treat all the eventuality denoted by adjective and verb equally as an event. Parsons' form shows the temporal feature of the matrix event and that of the embedded event respectively, while Rothstein explicitly exhibits the temporal relation between the two sub-events. Moreover, the shared argument is also clearly indicated.

Firstly, the state denoted by the adjective is embedded in the matrix event in Parsons' proposal while the event introduced by the adjective is connected to the verb event by summing operation in Rothstein's interpretation.

Secondly, Parsons takes over Dowty's idea and introduces DO, CAUSE, BECOME to present the dynamic process of the whole event while Rothstein provides the term TPCONNECT to exhibit the exact temporal dependency and argument sharing relationship between these two events.

Thirdly, Rothstein presents the derivation of the logic form which embodies compositionality principle and the isomorphism between syntactic structure and semantic structure while Parsons focuses more on the entailment between the sentences with and without the adjective modifier.

Although secondary predicates are quite different from the adjective adverbials in syntactic and semantic status, Parsons and Rothstein provide us with great inspirations for exploring the essential characteristics of adjective adverbial in Mandarin Chinese. Should we take over Parsons' stand or accept Rothstein's proposal? This is a question.

5.2.1.4 AAs denote embedded event

In Chapter 4, comparisons between AAs and the secondary predicates as well as predicational adverbs in English have been conducted, and we concluded that AAs share more features in common with corresponding predicational adverbs, for AAs are not indispensible parts of the primary predicates. Following this line of reasoning, Parsons' style is inclined to be followed to analyze AAs. Take the AAs with [+participant]

[+concomitance] features in (1), (2), (4) and (5) as examples, their corresponding representations are listed in (20):

(20) a. (∃e)[rengdiao(e)∧Ag(e)= Xiaoming∧Th(e)=shouji
∧(∃e')[shengqi-De(s) ∧Th(s)=Xiaoming ∧Hold(e')]]
b. (∃e)[chi(e)∧Ag(e)=Xiaoming∧Th(e)=zhaji
∧(∃e')[baobao-De(e') ∧Arg(e')=xiaoming∧
Hold(e')]]
c. (∃e) [he(e)∧Ag(e)=Xiaomin∧Th(e)=yibeicha
∧(∃e')[rere-De(e') ∧Arg(e')=yibeicha] ∧Hold(e')]]
d. (∃e)[dui(e)∧Ag(e)=haizimen∧Th(e)=xueren
∧(∃e') [Cul(e')∧ Th(e')=xueren∧CAUSE(e, e')
∧(∃e'')[Being-gaogao-De(e'') ∧Th(e'')=xueren
∧Hold(e'')
∧BECOME(e', e'')]]]

It is indicated in the logic forms in (20) that the event denoted by the adjectival adverbial is treated as an embedded event. Such an analysis reflects the theoretical advantage that the neo-Davidsonian approach has in representing the entailment and the feature of being droppable of the AAs. Rothstein's term "Time-Participant Connected" (TPCONNECT for short) is considered to be very effective in representing the temporal relationship and the co-argument of the two events. Consequently, TPCONNECT will be introduced to indicate the temporal dependency and the shared thematic argument between these two events. The representations in (20) will be amended as (21):

(21) a. ∃e[rengdiao(e)∧Ag(e)= Xiaoming∧Th(e)=shouji
∧(∃e')[shengqi-De(e')∧Th(e')=Xiaoming]
∧TPCONNECT(e, e', Xiaoming)] ∧Past(e)]
b. ∃e[chi(e)∧Agt(e)=Xiaoming∧Th(e)=zhaji
∧(∃e')[baobao-De(e')∧Arg(e')=xiaoming
∧ TPCONNECT(Cul(e), e', xiaoming)] ∧Past(e)]
c. ∃e[he(e)∧Ag(e)=Xiaomin∧Th(e)=yibeicha ∧(∃e')
[rere-De(e')
∧Arg(e')=yibeicha] ∧ TPCONNECT(e, e', yibeicha)

$\wedge$Past(e)]

d. ∃e[dui(e)$\wedge$Agt(e)=haizimen$\wedge$Th(e)=xueren
$\wedge$ (∃e') [gaogao-De(e') $\wedge$Th(e')=xueren $\wedge$Hold(e')
$\wedge$TPCONNECT(Cul(e), e', xueren)] $\wedge$Past(e)]

The logic forms in (21) indicate that the event e' is embedded in the atomic event e. In this way, the entailment relation between sentence with AA and corresponding sentence with AA dropped is represented. Furthermore, the temporal dependence between e and e' and the semantic orientation of AA are clearly indicated through the TPCONNECT relation between e and e'. The features of these AAs concluded in chapter 4 has been almost represented by combining Parsons' pattern of arranging the relation between e and e', and Rothstein's TPCONNECT to represent the temporal relation and the shared argument between e and e'. However, Such analyses are still not the desired ones, for the logic forms (21b) and (21d) fail to reflect the [+concomitant] [−homogeneity]features of these kinds of AAs.

5.2.2 Represent the [±homogeneity] Feature of e'

It has been noticed that in Mandarin, the semantic of some adjectives will alter when they appear as adverbials (Zhu 1956; Lyu 1966; Hu 1991; Han 2001). Zhu (1956) states that when modifying verbs, the meaning of the property adjectives will change to some degree. These adjectives don't express the property, but describe manner or state of actions. That is to say, they change from property adjectives to state adjectives. Although in his classification of adjectives, property adjectives are not equal to ILPs and state adjectives are not equal to SLPs, his observation indeed reflects the requirement of changing the temporal features of adjectives.

Lyu (1966) also states that when some adjectives modify verbs, the meaning of these adjectives usually shifts, and sometimes, the alternation of meaning is very dramatic. Hu (1991) concludes that generally speaking, property adjectives, because of their semantic property, are not suitable for adverbials. Once they occur as adverbials, the meaning of these adjectives will change, which is the consequence of the contrast between the semantic property and the syntactic position.

However, not all simple adjectives will undergo such semantic alternation when acting as adverbial modifiers, such as *zao* 'early', *wan* 'late', *yuan* 'far', *jin* 'near', *duo* 'much', *shao* 'little', *jiandan* 'simple', *xiangxi* 'detailed'. Han (2001: 49) states that some property adjectives can act as attributes, primary predicate, and adverbial modifiers, But these adjectives don't express properties, they are closely related to verbs, mainly express the meaning of number, time, location, frequency, domain, manner, and state, such as, *anquan* 'safe', *anxin* 'reassuring', *bubian* 'inconvenient', *canku* 'cruel', *chengzhuo* 'imperturbable'. Han names such adjectives as *qingzhuang xingrongci* 'situation adjectives'. These adjectives roughly correspond to the event-related adjectives in Zhang (2005).

The phenomenon of the meaning shift of adjective when occurring as adverbials has been described in length, but a satisfying explanation has not been provided for the motivation of such alternation. According to the definition of property adjective and state adjective given by Zhu Dexi, the alternation between property adjective and state adjective is equal to the alternation between ILPs and SLPs. From the examples provided by Hu (1991), adjectives that occur as adverbial modifiers without semantic alternation are mainly adjectives that describe transitory states, so it can be initially proposed that adjectives which express transitory states can occur as adverbial modifiers naturally, while those denote permanent properties can act as adverbial modifiers only after they undergo semantic alternation.

Dowty (1979) extends the application of Vendler's four-way classification of verbal predicates into adjectival predicates.

(22) Classification of adjectival predicates
State: be tall, be big, be Chinese, be green, be true,
Activity: be grave, be greedy, be rude/polite/ obnoxious to NP
Achievement: become adj/adj-er
Accomplishment: hammer NP flat, wipe NP clean, wiggle NP loose.
                                    (Dowty 1979: 66-70)

The stative reading with [+homogeneity] feature is the unmarked or default reading of an adjective. However, as it has been pointed out in previous chapters that adjective is underspecified and its interpretation is highly context-sensitive. The contextual pressure can coerce adjective out of a particular aspectual class and into any other aspectual classes easily. From the examples listed in each aspectual class of adjectival predicates in (22), we can see that the first class is roughly equal to the typical individual-level predicates, and all the other three classes are stage-level predicates. The classification of adjectival predicates is context-sensitive, for some markers, such as copula or some verbal predicates have effect on the aspectual features of the adjectival predicates.

Rothstein (2001) develops Dowty's idea of adjectival predicates classification. She suggests that both verbs and adjectives denote eventualities. The difference is that the underlying event argument of verb ranges over atomic, count-like eventualities, and the verb denotes the properties of these eventualities. Rothstein names the denotation of verbs as 'c-eventualities' (for count-eventualities). Adjectives denote sets of non-atomic, non-countable, state-like eventualities, which is named as 'm-eventualities' (for mass eventualities). Adjectives are predicated of such M-states. The differences between the 'c-eventualities' and 'm-eventualities' are analogous to these between count and mass entities in the nominal domain.

In Chinese, simple adjectives are supposed to denoted permanent properties which are unbounded, similar to the M-eventualities in Rothstein's sense. Let's take *keqi* 'polite' and *gao* 'tall' as examples to illustrate the alternation of the aspectual class of adjectival predicates in the neo-Davidsonian approach:

(23) The aspectual class of *keqi* 'polite' and gao 'tall'
    a. Property: $\lambda P \lambda x.P(x)$
       gaolou 'tall buliding'
       $\lambda x.lou(x) \wedge gao(x)$
    b. States: $\lambda P \lambda s.P(s)$
       Zhang San hen keqi.
       'Zhang San is polite.'
       $P\lambda s[P(s) \wedge Arg(s)=Zhang\ San](keqi)$

c. Activities: λPλe. (DO(P))(e)
Keqi dian!
polite a little
'be polite, Please!'
Pλe. [(DO(P))(e) ∧Arg(e)=x](keqi)
d. Achievements: λPλe. (BECOME(P))(e)
Haizimen zhang gao le.
kids   grow tall Perf
'Kids are becoming taller'
λPλe. [(BECOME(P))(e) ∧ Arg(e)=haizimen](gao)
e. Accomplishments: λPλQ λe. [(Q)(e_1)
∧(BECOME(P))(e_2)
∧Cul(e)=e_2]
Haizimen gaogao De duile ge xueren.
kids   tall   De pile CL snowman.
'Kids have made a tall snowman.'
λP ∃e[dui(e)∧Ag(e)=haizimen∧Th(e)=xueren
∧ (∃e') [(BECOME(P))(e') ∧Th(e')=xueren
∧ Cul(e)=e']](gaogao-De)

From above analyses of the aspectual features of adjectival predicates, we get a very rough impression that the aspectual feature of verbal predicate is more inherent, than that of the adjectival predicates. Although the contextual pressure can also shift the aspectual class of verbal predicates, the aspectual class of adjectival predicates exhibits more flexibility and stronger context-sensitivity. It has been emphasized that the ILP/SLP distinction is very important for the acceptability of the AAs. However, from the semantic derivation of the sentences containing, we can find that as Gallego and Uriagereka (2011) suggest the ILP/SLP is not lexical (contra Kratzer 1995), but rather lexico-syntactic. Any adjectives, ILP or SLP, can combine with the structural subodinator -*De*, and produce a SLP event.

In the following sections, the focus is to find out the way to present the aspectual feature of e' for each kind of AAs.

5.2.2.1 [+homogeneity] feature of subject1-oriented AAs

The AA in (1a) derived from psychological adjectives has the features of [+concomitance] [+homogeneity] (Repeated here as (24) for convenience).

(24) Xiaoming shengqi -De rengdiao le shouji.
  p.n   angry De throw Perf cellphone
  'Xiaoming angrily threw his cell phone away.'

The adverbial modifier *shengqi-De* 'angry' in (24) expresses a homogeneous emotional state of the animate subject and the state holds concomitantly with the event denoted by the verb. Such AAs are temporal independent, which means that after the culmination of the event denoted by the verb, the emotional state can last for a prolonged period independent of the event denoted by the verb. Furthermore, the adjective adverbial has transparent reading, which means that the subject is actually in the mental state expressed by the adjective in question.

The default reading of *shengqi* 'angry' is a state, which is unbounded, can exist anywhere for a period of any length of time. However, once it occurs as adjectival adverbial, it denotes a transitory state of the subject while the event e takes place, no matter what aspectual class the verbal predicate belongs to, as long as it has stage-level interpretation.

(25) $\exists e[rengdiao(e) \wedge Ag(e) = Xiaoming \wedge Th(e) = shouji$
  $\wedge (\exists e')[shengqi(e') \wedge Th(e') = Xiaoming]$
  $\wedge TPCONNECT(e, e', Xiaoming) \wedge Past(e)]$

"There was a singular event *Xiaoming throwing away his cell phone* in which another event *Xiaoming being angry* is embedded, where the event *throwing his cell phone away* was time-participant connected to the *being angry* event".

In this analysis, the features [+concomitance] [+homogeneity] of the AAs are represented, and the causal relation between these two events is derived from pragmatic reasoning, which is not included in the logic form. Such a logic form clearly indicates the temporal relation between events and the semantic orientation of the AA is indicated by the shared argument.

5.2.2.2 [−homogeneity] Feature of Subject₂-oriented AAs

The default reading of *baobao-de* 'full' in (26) is an unbounded state with [+homogeneity] feature. However, once it occurs as adverbial to modify certain verbs, it is coerced out of the aspectual class of state. In (26), the adjectival adverbial *baobao-De* doesn't denote a homogeneous state, but a dynamic process of changing from ¬P→P. We represent this event as ∃e(BECOME (*baobao-de*))(e), and the run time of event denoted by the main verb and the run time of this (BECOME (*baobao-de*))(e) event overlap.

(26) Xiaoming baobao De chi le yi dun zhaji.
    p.n   full   De eat Perf one CL fried chicken
    'Xiaoming got full while eating fried chicken.'

The event of Xiaoming eating fried chicken is accompanied by the event Xiaoming BECOME full, which indicates that the AA has the feature of [+concomitance]. What's more, the event denoted by the adjectival adverbial has the feature [−homogeneity], which means that at the initial instant of the eating event, Xiaoming was not full, but at the end of the eating event, Xiaoming was full, so the event of being full is a dynamic and incremental process of (¬P→P) or a BECOME P event. Rothstein (2004) states that such BECOME P process is composed of ordered incremental chains, and she defines incremental chain as:

(27) Incremental chain:
    Let e be a BECOME event. An incremental chain C(e)
    is a set of parts of e such that:
    1. the smallest event in C(e) is the initial bound of e
    2. For every e_1, e_2 in C(e) $e_1 \subseteq e_2$ or $e_2 \subseteq e_1$
    3. e∈C(e)

                                                   Rothstein (2004: 107)

In (26), the [+concomitance] feature is strictly defined: the initial bound of the incremental process e' temporally overlaps with the beginning of the event e, and both e and e' culminate at the same time. The culmination of an incremental process is defined as:

(28) Let C(e) be an incremental chain in e.
ub(C(e))={ub(e'): e'∈C(e)}(the set of upper bounds)
The culmination of e is defined as: Cul(e)$_{def}$=ub(e)

The two events e and e' in (26) are connected together via an incremental relation, which is marked as INCR(e, e',C(e')). The logic form of (26) is represented as (29):

(29) ∃e [chi(e)∧Agt(e)=Xiaoming∧Th(e)=zhaji
∧(∃e')[(BECOME(baobao-de))(e')∧Arg(e')= xiaoming]
∧INCR(e, e', C(e'), Xiaoming)] ∧Past(e)]

"There was an event *Xiaoming chi zhaji* in which an incremental process BECOME(baobao-de) is embedded, and the culmination of the eating event and the event BECOME (baobao-de) temporally overlap. These two events have Xiaoming as co-argument".

In this logic form, the INCR(e, e', C(e')) clearly indicate that the two events take place simultaneously, and the predicate BECOME reflects the [−homogeneity] feature of the event e'.

5.2.2.3 [−homogeneity] of subject3-oriented AAs

Adjectives occur as this kind of AAs usually denote dispositions of the subject, so they are typical individual-level predicates. However, contextual pressure easily coerces such predicates into having [−homogeneity] feature, for the interpretation of AAs is highly context-sensitive.

(30) Zhang San mingzhi De zai Beijing maile yitao fangzi.
p.n   wise De at Beijing buy one CL apartment
'Zhang san wisely bought an apartment in Beijing.'

This kind of AAs expresses speaker's subjective judgment over the subject based on the occurrence of the event e. Although this kind of AAs expresses the evaluation of the speaker over the agent, the evaluation is on behalf of the agent, not based on the speaker's value or preference. For example, in (30), the fact "Zhang San bought an apartment in Beijing" has brought out benefits for Zhang San, so Zhansan is evaluated as *mingzhi* 'wise'.

Subject$_3$-oriented AAs are usually ambiguous between agent-oriented reading and VP-oriented reading. Many scholars provide different explanations for such ambiguity.

McConnell-Ginet (1982) states that this ambiguity is resulted from different syntactic positions of the adverb. She supposes there is an abstract light verb ACT present at a higher position in the structure of the clause and the agent-oriented adverb is the predicate of this abstract light verb ACT. The corresponding VP-oriented adverb is the predicate of the main verb. Such a proposal tactfully takes the scope effect of agent-oriented adverbial into consideration and at the same time maintains the uniform analyses of predicational adverbs. Cristophor Piñón (2010) further develops this idea and he uses the relation "decide to do A" to substitute the higher abstract verb ACT. As Piñón states that his innovation maintains the uniform status of the manner adverbs and avoids the flaw of Ginet's proposal in paraphrasing some verbs.

More scholars try to explain this ambiguity from semantic perspective (Moore 1995; Geuder 2000; Ernst 2002; Wyner 2008). Both Moore and Wyner introduce new ontology to describe the meaning of agent-oriented adverbs. Moore suggests that VP-oriented adverb is the predicate of event while agent-oriented adverb is the predicate of situation. Similarly, Wyner proposes that manner adverb is the predicate of event, and agent-oriented adverb is the predicate of fact. Take *stupidly* as an example, Wyner's analysis of agent-oriented adverb is represented as (31):

(31) $\lambda P \, \exists f \, (\text{Fact}(P) = f \wedge \text{stupid}(f))$
Where P is a literal and f is an individual fact

Such an analysis can reflect the difference between VP-oriented adverb and agent-oriented adverb and scope effect of agent-oriented adverb. However, as a dispositional adjective, stupid is more naturally related to an individual instead of a fact.

Ernst (2002) suggests that Agent-oriented adverbs are two-place ADJ predicate: one argument is an event and the other is the agent. The semantic representation of agent-oriented adverb *rudely* is in (32a) and the corresponding VP-oriented reading is represented as (32b):

(32) a. rudely(e)=e[$_{REL}$ warrants positing] rudeness in Agent.
b. rudely(e)=e[$_{REL}$ manifest] rudeness in Agent
Ernst (2002: 57)

According to the FEO Calculus proposed by Ernst, in (32a) e refers to something like Wyner's fact or Moore' situation, and the e in (32b) is the event denoted by the verb, or we can understand it as the event argument. However, what is the difference between [$_{REL}$ warrants positing] and [$_{REL}$ manifest]? Why not use the [$_{REL}$ manifest] term as a more general one to unify these two representations? Cristophor Piñón (2010) also questions the value to keep these two different terms.

For the analysis of agent-oriented AAs in Mandarin, the predicate [$_{REL}$ manifest] is more appropriate. Agent-oriented AA denotes a transitory manifesting of the property denoted by the adjective on the agent who is intentionally involved in the event denoted by the main verb. The target of the modification is the agent of the event not the fact or situation which involved in the event denoted by the main verb. So subject$_3$-oriented AA in (30) is analyzed as following:

(33) $\exists$e[mai(e)$\land$Ag(e)=Zhang San$\land$Th(e)= fangzi$\land$Loc(e)= Beijing
$\exists$e' [(MANIFEST(mingzhi))(e') $\land$Arg(e')=Zhang San]
$\land\tau$(e) >τ(e')$\land$Past(e)]

"There was an event e *Zhang San zai Beijing maile tao fangzi* in which an event e' MANIFEST(mingzhi) is embedded, and the culmination of the event e is usually prior to the culmination of e'. These two events have *Zhang San* as co-argument".

In this from, MANIFEST(mingzhi) reflects the [−homogeneity] feature of the event e', and τ(e) >τ(e') indicates that the [−concomitance] temporal relation between these two events.

5.2.2.4 [+homogeneity] feature of object1-oriented AAs

Adjectives occurring as this kind of AAs usually denote transitory homogeneous state, and this state holds concomitantly with the event denoted by the verb. Such AAs are temporal independent, which means that the run time of the event e is a part of the holding period of the event e'. Typical AA of this kind in (34a) is represented as (34b):

(34) a. Xiaoming rere De he le yi bei cha.
        p.n   hot De drink one cup tea.
        'Xiaoming drank a cup of tea while it was hot.'
    b. ∃e [he(e)∧Ag(e)=Xiaomin∧Th(e)=yibeicha ∧(∃e')
       [rere-De(e')
       Arg(e')=yibeicha] ∧ TPCONNECT(e, e', yibeicha)
       ∧Past(e)]

"There was a singular event *Xiaoming he le yibeicha*, in which another event e' *Cha rere de* is embedded. The *he* 'drinking' event was time-participant connected to the *rere-de* 'being hot' event".

5.2.2.5 [−homogeneity] Feature of Object₂-oriented AAs

In Mandarin Chinese, it is very common for adjectival adverbials to be predicate of the object, while in English, the resultant state of the object is usually expressed by the resultative secondary predicates. When analyzing resultative secondary predicate in English, the CAUSE relation between these two events are usually highlighted (Parsons 1990; Stechow 1993; Kratzer 2004). However, Rothstein takes a different stand. She does not emphasize the causal relation between these two events.

Different from the resultative secondary predicate, this kind of AAs highlights the temporal concomitant relation between e and e'.

(35) Haizimen gaogao De duile ge xueren.
    kids   tall   De pile CL snowman.
    'Kids have made a tall snowman.'

The default reading of *gaogao-de* 'be tall' in (35) is an individual-level predicate denoting an unbound state with [+homogeneity] feature. However, once it occurs as adverbial, it is coerced out of the aspectual class of state. In (35), the adjectival adverbial *gaogao-de* doesn't denote a homogeneous state, but a dynamic process of changing from ¬P→P. In this process, the degree of *gao* 'tall' is always increasing until it reaches the upper bound which is denoted by the reduplicated form of the adjective. This event is represented as (BECOME (*gaogao-de*))(e), and the run time of the event denoted by the main verb and the run time of this (BECOME (*gaogao-de*)(e)) event overlap. In Section 5.2.2.2, I introduce the concept of incremental process, and the event e' (BECOME(*gaogaode*))(e') is an incremental process. According to Krifka (1998), such incremental processes require three necessary elements: an affected theme, a property scale, and a bound. The property related to the adjective of the affected theme argument changes along a scale due to the event described by the verb, until it reaches a bound. Based on such analysis, (35) is represented as (36):

(36) ∃e [dui(e)∧Ag(e)=haizimen∧Th(e)=xueren
    ∧(∃e') [(BECOME(gaogao-de))(e') ∧Th(e')=xueren]
    ∧INCR(e, e', C(e'), xueren)] ∧Past(e)]

"There was an event *Haizimen duile ge xueren* in which an incremental process BECOME(gaogao-de) is embedded, and the culmination of the event e and the event BECOME (gaogao-de) temporally overlap. These two events are connected by the incremental chain C(e'), and have *xueren* 'snowman' as co-argument".

Such a representation in (36) clearly reflects the [+concomitance] [−homogeneity] features of this kind of AAs.

5.2.2.6 VP-oriented AAs

Five kinds of AAs with [+participant] feature have been analyzed. These AAs have [+participant], which means that although they are adverbials, they are semantically related to certain participant of the event. All these five kinds of AAs are analyzed as embedded events which are temporally related to the event denoted by the primary predicate, and they share a participant with the event denoted by the verb.

VP-oriented AAs[①] are different from the above-mentioned five kinds of AAs in that VP-oriented AAs are typical adverbials, which are not only temporally but also semantically related to VP. What's more, for above-mentioned five kinds of AAs, -De is compulsory, but for some VP-oriented AAs, -De is optional. Consequently, the present/absent contrast of -De, the number of syllables of the adjective and the contrast between event–related and object-related adjectives make the VP-oriented AAs much more complex. In this section, the focus is how to represent the difference formally.

Jackendoff (1972) proposes the projection rule of P_{manner} for the VP adverb:

(37) If Adv/pp is dominated by VP, attach its semantic markers to the reading of the verb without changing its functional structure.

This rule for manner reading of adverbs indicates that manner adverbs function as predicates of predicates, and add information or modify the meaning of the verb. The manner adverbs, not like the subject or object-oriented adverbs, are part of the proposition expressed by the sentence, which means that the sentences containing manner adverbs just express a singular proposition.

Jackendoff's idea of the manner adverbs is reflected in Parsons (1990) analyses of VP modifiers as the predicate of the underlying event variable of the verb. Cristophor Piňón (2007) argues that neo-

---

[①] We use the VP-oriented interpretation instead of the manner reading, because manner-reading is only a small part of the VP-oriented reading.

Davidsonian approach treats both manner adverb and verb as predicates of events. Therefore, the semantic difference between adverb and verb is overlooked. He suggests that, in order to distinguish adverb from verb, manner should be introduced as a concrete particular and adverb is the predicate of this newly-introduced ontology. Manners are concrete particulars ontologically dependent on an event, and event as well as a function determines what the manner is. He represents (38a) as (38b):

(38) a. John spoke clearly.
   b. $\exists e \exists m(speak(e) \wedge agent(e)=John \wedge articulation(e)= mclear(m))$

The introduction of manner as a new ontology has been controversial. Both object and event denote concepts with a number of properties. When adnominal modifiers modify NP, it is not necessary to express what dimension an adjective is related to. It seems that there is an automatic process of matching the adjective with certain property of the object that is modified. For example, when we say "red flower", it is not necessary to express that red modifies the color of the flower, for adjective "red" is automatically matched with the color property. Analogously, in (38a), when the adverb *clearly* modifies the verb *speak*, the default reading of the adverb is related to the manner of articulation. If not, different languages will employ various methods to mark this mismatch. In English, the syntactic position of the adverb will indicate the non-default reading of the adverb. In Chinese, some lexical methods will be used to indicate the unnatural reading of the adverbials. Therefore, it is not necessary to introduce extra ontology to mark the difference between adverb and verb, for the difference is inherently lexical. Generally speaking, analyzing VP modifiers as predicates of underlying event argument is nowadays very much the standard view. Before we can find a better pattern to represent the manner modification, neo-Davidsonian approach is still an efficient and accurate one to indicate the modification relationship. However, in Mandarin, the VP-oriented AAs are not so easy to be dealt with in an uniform pattern.

Based on the analyses in Chapter 4, we assume that the *De*-less VP-oriented AAs, except for some lexicalized compounds①, are pure manner adverbials in Ernsts' sense, so they can be uniformly treated as the predicates of the underlying event argument of the verb.

(39) a. Xiaoming naixin dengdai xinde zhiling.
P.n   patient wait new instruction
'Xiaoming waited for new instruction patiently.'
b. Xiaoming naixin De dengdai xinde zhiling.
xiaoming patient De wait new instruction
'Xiaoming patiently waited for new instruction.'
(subject-oriented reading)
'Xiaoming waited for new instruction patiently.'
(VP-oriented reading)

(39a) only has manner reading corresponding to the English translation, and (39b) is ambiguous between a subject-oriented transparent interpretation and VP-oriented interpretation. What is the difference between the pure manner adverbial in (39a) and the manner reading of the AA in (39b)? Should we analyze both of these two VP oriented readings in the neo-Davidsonian approach?

(40) a. $\exists e[dengdai(e) \wedge Ag(e)=Xiaoming \wedge Th(e)=xin\ zhiling \wedge naixin(e)]$
b. $\exists e[dengdai(e) \wedge Ag(e)=Xiaoming \wedge Th(e)=xin\ zhiling \wedge naixin\text{-}De(e)]$

(40a) is the representation of pure manner adverbial reading of (39a), and (40b) is the representation of the manner interpretation of (39b). The difference between them is centered on the absent/present contrast of -De in the downgraded predicate of the the underlying event variable. However, the representations in (40) haven't accuately reflected the semantic difference between (39a) and the manner reading of (39b). Now, we will try to apply the proposal in dealing with AAs having [+participant]

---

① Here, some highly lexicalized monosyllabic adjective + monosyllabic verb compounds are excluded.

feature. The two interpretations of (39b) will be represented in (41):

(41) a. ∃e [dengdai(e)∧Ag(e)=Xiaoming∧Th(e)=xin zhiling
∧∃e'[naixin-de(e')∧Arg(e')=Xiaoming]
∧TPCONNECT(e, e', Xiaoming)∧PAST(e)]
b. ∃e [dengdai(e)∧Ag(e)=Xiaoming∧Th(e)=xin zhiling
∧∃e'[naixin-de(e')∧Arg(e')=e]∧PAST(e)]

(41a) is the subject-oriented transparent reading of (39b), which is in agreement with the proposed analysis for the Subject$_1$-oriented [+homogeneity] [+concomitance] AAs. (41b) is the VP-oriented interpretation of (39b). However, such a representation does not completely reflect the [−concomitance] [−participant] [−homogeneity] features of VP-oriented AAs. The default reading of *naixin* is a homogeneous state. However, it is weird to say an event is in a certain state or an event is *naixin* 'patient'. The VP-oriented reading expressed in (41b) is actually the speaker's evaluation over the event. Compared with other events denoted by the same verb, the speaker assumes that the specific event in (41b) manifests the property of *naixin* 'patience'. So the event denoted by this kind of VP-oriented AAs is a dynamic eventuality of manifestation of the property expressed by the adjective. Similarly, the predicate MANIFEST will be introduced. (41b) can be innovated as following:

(42) ∃e [dengdai(e)∧Ag(e)=Xiaoming∧Th(e)=xin zhiling
∧(∃e')[(MANIFEST(naixin))(e')∧Arg(e')=e] ∧τ(e) > τ(e')∧PAST(e)]

"There was an event e *Xiaoming dengdai xinde zhiling*, in which an event e' MANIFEST(naixin) is embedded, and the culmination of the event e is usually prior to the culmination of e'. These two events have the event argument of the verb as co-argument".

The representation in (42) completely reflects the [−concomitance] [−participant] [−homogeneity] features of VP-oriented AAs, and the underlying event argument is fully used in this analysis. Up to now, we get two different representations for the VP-oriented AAs which can reflect the difference resulted from the presence/absence contrast of -*De*.

5.2.2.7 Clause-oriented AAs

In Mandarin, the evaluation over facts is usually realized through some compositional devices, with some pragmatic markers. Just a few adjectives can occur as evaluative adjectival adverbials. Adjectives occur as evaluative AAs usually denote properties, so they are typical individual-level predicates. However, when these adjectives occur as evaluative adjectival adverbials, they are easily coerced into having [−homogeneity] feature, for the interpretation of AAs are highly context-sensitive. Sentences containing this kind of AAs usually can be paraphrased as (43a) or (43b):

(43) a. Speaker evaluates the fact F as ADJ.
b. It is ADJ that F.

(43a) indicates that interpretation of evaluative AAs is subjective, which is based on the speakers subjective judgment. Papafrago (2006) defines subjectivity in terms of a set that is composed of the speaker's believes. Ernst (2009) formulates the definition of subjectivity in (44):

(44) Subjectivity (for evaluative AAs)
Where a speaker asserts Q=ADJ(p)(thus Q is in $M_B(s)$)[①], ADJ is subjective iff all worlds by which Q is evaluated are consistent with respect to $M_B(s)$ at the time of utterance; otherwise, this ADJ is objective.

It has been stated in Section 5.2.2.3 and Section 5.2.2.6, that agent-oriented AAs and some VP-oriented AAs express speaker' subjective evaluation over agent and event, and a predicate MANIFEST is introduced to represent that the subjective evaluation is a dynamic eventuality of manifestation of the property denoted by the adjective over the target modified by the AAs. Following this line of reasoning, the [−homogeneity]

[①] $M_B(s)$ refers to the speaker's belief set.

feature of clause-oriented AAs will be represented in the similar pattern.

(45) a. Li Si yihan De cuoguole mobanche.
p.n regrettable De miss last bus
'It is regrettable that Li Si missed the last bus.'
b. ∃e [∃f [∃e (cuoguo(e)∧Agt(e)=Li Si∧Th(e)=mobanche ∧Past(e))] ∧
∃e'[(MANIFEST(yihan))(e')∧Arg(e')=f]]∧τ(e) >τ(e')]
c. ∃e [cuoguo(e)∧Agt(e)=Li Si∧Th(e)=mobanche∧Past (e)∧
(∃e') [(MANIFEST(yihan))(e')∧Arg(e')=(cuoguo(e) ∧Agt(e)=Li Si
∧Th(e)=mobanche∧Past(e))]∧τ(e) >τ(e')]

"There was an event e *Li Si cuoguole mobanche,* in which an event e' MANIFEST(yihan) is embedded, and the culmination of the event e is usually prior to the culmination of e'. These two events have the whole event as co-argument".

For the representations of (45a), two alternations are provided here: in (45b), a new ontology "fact" is introduced to express the target of the modification of evaluative AAs; in (45c), there is no newly-introduced ontology. Compare these two alternations, the latter one is preferred. Although it seems that (45b) is much simpler, the newly introduced ontology will greatly decrease the economy of this proposal.

This section is centered on representing the [±homogeneity] feature of event e'. For all these seven kinds of AAs, only two kinds have [+homogeneity] feature, and they express that certain participant of the event e is/was in the state denoted by the adjective. All the other five kinds of AAs have [−homogeneity] feature. Among them, two kinds are represented as incremental processes which express that certain participant of the event e undergoes a change along the degrees scaled relevant to the property denoted by the adjective and the event culminates when the degree lives up to the scale denoted by the AA. At the same time, the event denoted by the verb also culminates. The other three kinds of AAs with [−homogeneity] feature are uniformly treated as an instant accomplishment of manifesting the property expressed by the adjective, for these three kinds of AAs express the subjective evaluation over different targets based on the speaker's belief set. That they are subjective means that in the speaker's belief set, the evaluated target manifests more or stronger property than the average corresponding target.

It has been verified from the analyses in this section that the interpretation of adjectival adverbials in Mandarin is highly sensitive to the context. Context-sensitive is exhibited in two aspects: all these seven kinds of AAs have shifted away from their default reading, even these two kinds with [+homogeneity] feature; and the semantic orientation of these AAs are decided in the context instead of being decided before hand.

In the re-analyses of these seven kinds of AAs, the TPCONNECT relation proposed by Rothstein is only applied to the four kinds of AAs with [+concomitance] features, and for the other three kinds of AAs with [−concomitance] feature, the temporal relation between these two events is still marked as $\tau(e) > \tau(e')$. Furthermore, for VP-oriented AAs and clause-oriented AAs, there is no shared participant between these two events, so the remaining problem is whether it is necessary to keep the TPCONNECT in the logic forms? In the following section, we will focus on exploring the function of the structural subordinator -*De*, and maybe this marker will provide a better solution than the TPCONNECT relation in analyzing AAs.

5.3 -*De*

In last section, all the seven kinds of AAs have been analyzed in details. For all these seven kinds of AAs in Mandarin, except for some pure manner AAs, -*De* is compulsory. In Chapter 2, and Chapter 4, the significance of -*De* has been introduced. In this section, the main task is to discover the function of -*De* for the adjectival adverbials. What is the reason that when adjectives occur as primary predicates, they denote homogeneous state, but when they occur as adverbials with -*De*, they can only denote transitory and dynamic eventuality? Another puzzle is that in previous analyses, -*De* is marked as a part of the predicate of the underlying event e'. However, when adjectives occur as predicates, only some derived adjectives are in need of the clitic of –*de*. After finding out the function of -*De*, we can decide whether it is necessary to include -*De* as a part of the predicate of the underlying event argument of e' in the logic form.

Zhu (1982: 142) states that de is divided into de$_1$, de$_2$ and de$_3$ in grammatical analysis, but in written system they correspond to – *de*(的) and -*De*(地)①. -*De* usually appears after adverbs, and adjectival adverbials. It has long been controversial whether it is necessary to differentiate '-*de*' from '-*De*'. Lyu (1962) suggests that the different written forms of -de " 的 "and -De" 地 "should be unified as -de" 的 ", because "-*de*" and "-*De*" are just variations of one word with no difference in pronunciation and meaning. Gan (1984), Sun(1995)oppose to such a proposal and argue that the unification of "de" and "-*De*" will lead to ambiguity in some constructions. In this work, we maintain the distinction between -*de* and -*De*.

5.3.1 Similarities Between -*De* and -*de*

Although it is a common practice in Mandarin written system to distinguish -*de* from-*De*, the significant similarity in semantic and syntactic and even in pragmatic between these two morphemes cannot be neglected. -*de* usually appears in front of NP, while -*De* appears in front of VP. Both *de* and -*De* represent the modification relation between modifier and the head, and the difference between them is resulted from the difference of the head. It is very interesting to notice that in natural language, modifiers appear in an exactly parallel fashion. Actually, there are a lot of similarities between adjective attributive modification and adjective adverbial modification:

The Davidsonian analysis introduces an underlying event argument into the logical form of the verb, which is a particular ontology of semantic objects. Events are treated as objects that can be described by

---

① For the convenience, 的 is represented as de, and 地 is represented as De.

event predicates and referred to by deictic expression. The introduction of the event argument makes it possible that events can be treated on a par with concrete individuals, and in turn *-de* and *-De* are analyzed in a parallel pattern. *-de* modifies the sets of individuals denoted by the noun instead of the word per se, and *-De* modifies the sets of events denoted by the verb instead of the verb per se.

Although objects are ontologically different from events, the difference exists only in their relation to time. Objects usually exist permanently, while events are temporally delimited. Both event concept and object concept are multi-dimensional, which means that they are composed of a number of properties, and adjectives, occurring as attributives or adverbials, are related to one dimensional property. Modification, in Gärdenfors' (2000) sense, is an operation that restricts the allowed range of property values of a concept in one dimension. Both object[1] and event are complex concepts, which are composed of a number of properties. Some of these properties are core properties, while some are peripheral. If the dimension being modified is one of the properties of the core concept, the modification marker is not compulsory; otherwise, the marker is needed. Whether a property is core or peripheral is decided conventionally. When monosyllabic adjectives match with certain properties and set the value on the scale of that dimension sands for, the modifier and the head can form a relatively stable combination without the modification marker *-de* or *-De*.

If a monosyllabic adjective does not relate to certain core property of the concept denoted by the head, the combination is less acceptable, such as *zangtang* 'dirty candy', *lianglian* 'cold face' (Zhu 1956, 1982, 1993), but some are recoverable by the context[2]. Furthermore, when adjective matches with certain dimension of the core concept of the noun denotes, 'de' is not needed, and the combination of the adjective and the noun denote a plausible subset of the denotation of the noun. If 'de' is inserted between the adjective and the noun, the derived complex phrase usually

---

[1] Here, object is not a grammar concept, and it is roughly equal to the denotation of noun.

[2] Chao (1968) suggests that this kind of restriction is not a rigid grammatical one, so the context will improve the degree of acceptability of such combination. Because the dimensions the core concept denoted by the noun is not fixed, but a conventionally.

has some pragmatic effects. The denotation of the adjective becomes prominent and the function of the adjective is not for sub-classification, but for description. When adjective does not modify certain core property of the concept, de is compulsory.

In the adverbial modification relation, the principle is similar. The event denoted by verb is also a multi-dimensional core concept. If an adjective indicate the value of scale of certain dimension of the core concept, the adjective can modify the verb without -*De*, and the combination denotes the subset of events denoted by the verb. If -*De* is inserted between the combinations, the function of the adjective will change from classifying to description. Similarly, when an adjective doesn't modify a certain dimension of the core concept of the event denoted by the verb, -*De* is necessary. The insertion of -*De* in front of the verb will significantly enlarge the number of adjectives that can modify the verb, because the modification of the verb with -*De* is not limited to the evaluation of the dimension of the core concept.

The number of monosyllabic adjectives that are capable of modifying nouns and verbs are limited, and a lot of monosyllabic adjective + monosyllabic noun are compounds, and -*de* is not necessary, while a lot of monosyllabic adjective + monosyllabic verb are also compounds, -*De* is repelled. Derived adjectives are supposed to occur as primary predicates freely. However, according to Sui (2014), when reduplicated adjectives occur as predicates, -*de* is compulsory.

The modification is a process in which the one-dimensional adjective matches itself with the corresponding specific dimension of the object or event concept and set a relatively fixed scale on this dimension. Both individual and events are ontologies. The verb's underlying argument is a suitable target for adverbial modifiers. As Davidson states that this allows adverbial modifiers to be treated analogously to adnominal modifiers, because both the adnominal modifier and adverbial modifiers target the referential argument of their verbal or nominal host. In this way, we can get more inspirations from the attributive modification, and test it in the adjective adverbial modification.

5.3.2 The Function of -*De*

Some researchers try to explain the mismatches represented by AAs with the particle -*De* as a breakthrough. Many scholars have realized the importance of -*De* (Liu 1983; Zhang 2005; He 2006; Pan 2013). Zhang (1991) even argues that it is -*De* that results in the syntactic/semantic mismatch. But the exact function is not clearly stated. In this work, the potential function of -*De* in the analyses of AAs will be revealed with the adnominal modification maker -*de* as reference.

Pan (2013) states that, similar to –*de*, -*De* is also an overt marker of modification relation. However, he does not give more explanation for the function of this overt marker. The presence of -*De* does change the perspective of a sentence; specifically, a dynamic aspect may be introduced, and the verbal activity is therefore often focused on to some extent, even if the subject is the primary scope, and in spite of the stativeness of the under adjective. The existing researches on -*De* mainly describe the distribution of -*De* and give a very subtle description of the function of -*De*. Based on the analysis of the AAs, we can conclude the functions of -*De* as following:

5.3.2.1 Indicate the Pattern of Composition

According to the compositionality principle: the meaning of an expression is derived from the meaning of its parts and the syntactic rule by which these parts are combined, -*De* is the overt marker indicating the operation by which two predicates are included in one clause. In Chapter 2, the syntactic function of -*De* has been stated. According to the analyses of the seven kinds of AAs in this chapter, the syntactic function of -*De* can be concluded as: -*De* marks the adjective in front of the verb as a downgraded predicate and embeds the event e' denoted by this downgraded predicate into the event e denoted by the primary predicate. When -*De* is absent from the position between the adjective and verb, the structure of the sentence is changed. We can either get a pure manner adverbial which classify the events denoted by the verb, or we can get two parallel predicates, and therefore two clauses.

5.3.2.2 Anchor the Event e' Around e Temporally

One of the functions of -*De* is to provide a time anchor for the event e' denoted by the AA. When adjectives like these in (48) occur as adverbials and are related to the verb by -*De*, the run time of the state denoted by the stage-level predicates are anchored around the run time of the event e denoted by the verb. Being anchored around the event e indicates various temporal relations, and two kinds of situations are roughly distinguished based on the feature [±concomitance].

(46) a. Xiaoming hen shengqi.
 b. Zhang san gaogaoxingxing de.

The transitory states denoted by the adjectives in (46) are not bounded, which means that they are not overtly temporally anchored. Without the context, it is difficult to get to know when the subject is in the state denoted by the adjective and how long the states last. In Chapter 4, AAs are categorized as a kind of downgraded predicates, which differ from primary predicates in that they do not need independent time anchor. They can be temporally anchored indirectly by the event argument of the primary predicate.

5.3.2.3 Diversify the Aspectual Feature of e'

Adjectives denote a permanent properties or states with [+homogeneity] feature. However, among the seven kinds of AAs we have analyzed, only two kinds of AAs keep the default [+homogeneity] feature, whereas the other five kinds are coerced out of the default feature and into [−homogeneity] aspectual feature. An adjective denotes a permanent property or an unbounded state. Unboundedness in this sense is different from Shen (1995). Shen states that simple adjectives denote very extensive ranges of scale related to certain property, while derived adjectives denote relatively narrower range or even a fixed point along the scale of certain property. Boundedness/unboundedness contrast in his sense is closely related to the range of scale that an adjective can denote.

Before the adjective can modify the atomic and count-like eventuality denoted by verb, the M-state denoted by the adjective should also be divided. This dividing function is performed by -*De*, which packages① a set of atomic eventualities from the M-state denoted by the adjectives. '-De' cuts a slice from the M-state denoted by the adjective and packs it into a C-eventuality. That means -De denotes a function from the domain of M-states to the domain of C-eventuality. This function is called instantiation relation, which maps from the domain of M-states to the domain of located countable eventualities.

(47) INST=λSλe. ∃s∈S: e=I(s)

(Rothstein 1999: 372)

The domain of I is the set of M-states and its range is the set of events. Adjectives denote M-states and -De locates eventuality from the M-states to match with the event denoted by the main verb. Take *xizizi* 'happy' as an example to illustrate the process form M-state to C-eventuality:

(48) xizizi: λs. xizizi(s) ∧Arg(s)=x
     xizizi -De;   λe ∃s[xizizi(s) ∧Arg(s)=x∧e=I(s)]

For some other adjectives, -De pass the contextual pressure onto the adjective and coerce the event denoted by the adjective present various aspectual features. Agent-oriented AAs, some VP-oriented AAs and clause-oriented AAs denote MANIFEST(adj) events, and subject$_2$-oriented AAs and object$_2$-oriented AAs denote incremental process of BECOME(adj) events.

5.3.2.4 Limit the Potential Orientations of the Adjective

When an adjective occurs as primary predicate, the subject of it can be anything. However, when it occurs as adverbial, the only argument of the event e' denoted by the adjective is restricted. The potential value of free variable x of the event e' is the subject of the verb, the object of the verb, the underlying event argument of the verb, or the fact involved the verb in.

---

① The term 'Package' was originated from Pelletier (1979). This packaging function allows a uncountable mass noun to be used as a count term.

-*De* has all these above-mentioned functions, and all the information related to these functions is included in this structural subordinator. In the following section, -*De* will be analyzed as the functional head of -*De* Phrase, and the feasibility of such a proposal will be evaluated.

5.3.3 -*De* as the Functional Head of DeP

In last section, the functions of -*De*, as an overt modification marker, have been clearly stated. It is well-motivated to establish a DeP. The adjectival adverbial with -*De* projects a -*De* Phrase, and -*De* is the functional head of the -*De* Phrase, which takes in the adjective and forms a *De* Phrase. The difference between these seven kinds of AAs is brought out by the semantic specification of this functional head. All the information, such as: the temporal relation between e and e', the aspectual feature of e', as well as the semantic orientation of the adjectival adverbial, is included in the semantics of the functional head.

The idea of assuming that the adjectival adverbial is introduced by a functional head -*De* is supported empirically. In spite of the similarity between -*de* and -*De*, -*De* still has some specific features, for example, -*de* is only a necessary part for some complex adjectives, but for AAs, -*De* is compulsory except for pure VP-oriented AAs. In this sense, -*De* is not a part of the adjective. The presence of -*De* is not the requirement of the semantic of the adjective, but to realize the adverbial modification function, so it is reasonable to treat it as a functional head, which is similar to the depictive head in Pylkkänen (2002, 2008). She states that:

> *The presence of a separate depictive head is empirically plausible since in many languages depictives are morphologically distinct from their underlying adjectives. For examples, in Finnish, depictive secondary predicates carry essive case.*
>
> Pylkkänen (2002: 28)

Pylkkänen (2002, 2008) decomposes a depictive secondary predicate phrase (DepP) into an adjective and a depictive head (Dep). This depictive head relates the event denoted by the adjective and the event denoted by the matrix predicate. (51a) is the logic form of a depictive, and (51b) illustrates the formation of a depictive phrase:

(49) a. Dep: $\lambda f_{<e,<s,t>>}.\lambda x. \lambda e. (\exists s)f(s,x)\& e_o s$

b.   DepP $\lambda x. \lambda e. (\exists s)$tired (s) & in (x, s) & $e_o s$

tired   Dep
$\lambda x. \lambda e. (\exists s)$tired $(s,)$ & in (x,s) $\lambda f_{<e,<s,t>>}.\lambda x. \lambda e. (\exists s)f(s, x)\&$
                                                $e_o s$

Pylkkänen (2008: 23)

The representation '$e_o s$' indicates temporal relation between these two events. Pylkkänen's theory is very inspiring for the research on AAs in Mandarin.

Pan Haihua (2013) suggests that both -*De* and -*de* are overt markers of modification relation in Chinese and he analyzes –*de* as the head of deP. If -*de* can be analyzed as a functional head, we have stronger motivation to analyze -*De* as a functional head of a -*De* Phrase (short for DeP). Based on the analysis above, we propose that -*De* in front of the verbal predicate is the marker of adverbial modification, which relates the AAs to the main verb, and its main function is to add information to the event denoted by the main verb.

Projecting -*De* as a separate adverbial functional head is empirically plausible since in Mandarin Chinese, the adjectival adverbial modification is morphologically distincted from the under adjective in that '-*De*' is compulsory marker of adjectival adverbial modification.

The semantic type of the functional head -*De* is $<<e, t>,<<e, t>,<e, t>>>$. The complement of the head is an adjective, whose semantic type is $<e, t>$. After functional application, we get the adjectival adverbial with-*De*, whose semantic type is $<<e, t>,<e, t>>$.

The adjectival adverbials are downgraded predicates, and they are semantically unsaturated, and the semantic type of it is $<d, t>$. The primary predicate is also semantically unsatarated, the semantic type of it is also $<d, t>$, which will be saturated by its subject. The logic forms and the type of the adjectives in (1-7) are expressed in (50):

(50) a. *shengqi*:   x, λs [*shengqi* (s) ∧Arg(s)=x]   <d, t>
    b. *baobao-de*: λx, λs [*baobao-de* (s) ∧Arg(s)=x] <d, t>
    c. *mingzhi*:   λx. mingzhi (x)   <d, t>
    d. *rere-de*:   λx, λs [*rere-de* (s) ∧Arg(s)=x]   <d, t>
    e. *gaogao-de*: λx. gaogao-de (x)   <d, t>
    f. *xunsu*:   λx. xunsu (x)   <d, t>
    g. *yihan*:   λx. yihan (x)   <d, t>

From (50), we notice that the underlying adjectives of these seven kinds of AAs are all of type <d, t>, and there is a free variable x to be saturated. According the theory of predicate in Rothstein (2001), there is a distinguished free variable x of type d, which has the external thematic role. As is indicated in (50), all these adjectives are one-place predicates, and the thematic role of the only one argument of the predicate is not decided yet. Before the predicate formation operation, the only argument in the logic form is a free variable, so the semantic type of the adjective is <d, t>, and here d refers to an individual argument.

What's more, we can notice that these adjectives are not uniform in morphological forms. (50b, d. e) are reduplicated adjectives, and *-de* is compulsory for these three adjectives. Sui Na (2014) suggests that the process of reduplication of adjectives is conducted in lexical syntax and the reduplicated adjectives are semi products which cannot undergo syntactic operation without the clitic of *-de*. Take (50b) as an example, when this under adjective combines with the functional head *-De*, the resulted form will be (51):

(51) *baobao-de -De*

The two *-de* and *-De* have same pronunciation, and languages usually avoid two adjacent constituents with same pronunciation. Consequently, these two elements are either separated by another element or haplology will take place to cancel one of these elements with identical pronunciation (Ke 2006; Si 2005; Sui 2014). Usually, the *–de* will be cancelled, and those adjectives without the clitic of *–de*, will incorporate with *-De* directly. As a result, all the AAs are uniformly marked with *-De*

Furthermore, form the logic forms of these adjectives, we can see that (50a, b, d) are stage-level predicates denoting transitory M-states and the free variable x is uniformly marked as Arg(e)=x,[①] whereas (52c. e.f.g) are individual-level predicates which denote permanent properties. Then, these adjective will enter the DeP, with *-De* as the functional head, and these adjectives as the complements. After the under adjectives enter the DeP, the functional head *-De* will exert its effect on the adjective. Consequently, all these adjectives are coerced to denote temporally delimited states or dynamic eventuality with a Davidsonian event argument. From the analyses of the seven kinds of AAs, we find that all these adjectives in (50) are coerced to be stage-level predicates denoting events with different aspectual features as indicated in (52):

(52) a. $(\exists e')$ [shengqi(e')$\wedge$Arg(e')=x]
b. $(\exists e')$ [(BECOME(baobao-de))(e')$\wedge$ Arg(e')=x]
c. $(\exists e')$ [(MANIFEST(mingzhi))(e') $\wedge$ Arg(e')=x]
d. $(\exists e')$ [rere-de(e') $\wedge$ Arg(e')=x]
e. $(\exists e')$ [(BECOME(gaogao-de))(e') $\wedge$ Arg(e')=x]
f. $(\exists e')$ [(MANIFEST(xunsu))(e')$\wedge$ Arg(e')=x]
g. $(\exists e')$[(MANIFEST(yihan))(e')$\wedge$ Arg(e')=x)

All these under adjectives now are coerced to denote different events and the process of coercion is compositional, which means that the semantic nature of the under adjective does not change, but combine with different predicate to denote different events.

As has been suggested, one of the functions of *-De* is to anchor the run time of e' around the run time of the event denoted by the verb. However, this information is not reflected until now. As we have analyzed, the temporal relation between e and e' are reflected by the feature [±concomitance], and [+concomitance] feature can be represented as $\tau(e) \subseteq \tau(e')$ or $\tau(e)=\tau(e')$, while [−concomitance] can be represented as $\tau(e) > \tau(e')$. Until now, all the information included in the function head *-De* has been represented. In the following section, the compositional

---

[①] Arg is the short for argument. Before the application of the predication formation rule, the thematic of this argument is not decided, so it is just marked as an argument.

process of the formation of DeP will be illustrated.

5.3.4 Compositional Analysis of Seven Kinds of DeP

In this section, the process how adjectives combine with different functional head *-De* to form different kinds of AAs will be illustrated, and the information in different functional head *-De* will be stated.

5.3.4.1 Subject$_1$-oriented DeP

The DeP *shengqi-De* 'angry' in (1) will be taken as an example to illustrate the information included in the functional head of subject$_1$-oriented [+homogeneity] [+concomitance] AAs and the derivation process:

(53) a. De$_1$: $\lambda Q[\lambda P[\lambda e[P(e) \wedge Ag(e)=x \wedge \exists e'[Q(e') \wedge Arg(e')=Ag(e) \wedge \tau(e) \subseteq \tau(e')]]]]$

b. DeP. *shengqi-De*   <<e,t>,<e,t>>
    $\lambda P[\lambda e[P(e) \wedge Ag(e)=x \wedge \exists e'[shengqi (e') \wedge Arg(e')= Ag(e) \wedge \tau(e) \subseteq \tau(e')]]]]$

    De'

    AP. *shengqi* <e,t>   De. <<e,t>,<<e,t>,<e,t>>>
    $\lambda s[shengqi (s) \wedge Arg(s)=x]$ $\lambda Q[\lambda P[\lambda e[P(e) \wedge Ag(e)=x \wedge \exists e'[Q(e') \wedge Arg(e')=Ag(e) \wedge \tau(e) \subseteq \tau(e')]]]]$

From the derivation process, we can see that the under adjective denotes Mass state and when it combines with the functional head, the packing function of *-De* packs a slice of the Mass state and temporally anchors it around the event denoted by the verb. The event e' is embedded in the event e. At the same time the only argument of the packed event is decided to be co-indexed with the agent of the event e. The clitic *–de* is not necessary for the under adjective *shengqi*, so it incorporates directly with the functional head *-De* to form DeP. However, in the logic form, *-De* is not a part of the predicate of the underlying event e'.

5.3.4.2 Subject$_2$-oriented DeP

The DeP *baobao-De* 'full' in (2) is taken as an example to illustrate the information included in the functional head of subject$_2$-oriented [−homogeneity] [+concomitance] AAs and the derivation process:

(54) a. De$_2$: $\lambda Q[\lambda P[\lambda e[P(e) \wedge Ag(e)=x \wedge \exists e'$ [(BECOME(Q))(e') $\wedge Arg(e')=Ag(e) \wedge \tau(e)=\tau(e')]]]]$

b. *D*e*P*. *baobao-De* <<e,t>,<e,t>>
$[\lambda P[\lambda e[P(e) \wedge Ag(e)=x \wedge \exists e'$ [(BECOME(*baobao-de*))(e') $\wedge Arg(e')=Ag(e) \wedge \tau(e)=\tau(e')]]]]$

De'

AP. *baobao-de* <e,t>
$\lambda s[baobao-de(s) \wedge Arg(s)=x]$

De. <<e,t>,<<e,t>,<e,t>>>
$\lambda Q[\lambda P[\lambda e[P(e) \wedge Ag(e)=x \wedge \exists e'$ [(BECOME(Q))(e') $\wedge Arg(e')=Ag(e) \wedge \tau(e)=\tau(e')]]]]$

It is indicated that before the under adjective *baobao-de* combines with the functional head *-De*, it denotes a Mass state and then the information included in functional head *-De* coerses the Mass state into an incremental process e', which is temporally anchored rigidly concomitant with the event denoted by the verb. The clitic *–de* of the under adjective is cancelled out of haplology. The event e' is embedded in the event e and the only argument of the coersed event e' is decided to be co-indexed with the agent of the event e.

5.3.4.3 Subject$_3$-oriented DeP

The DeP *mingzhi-De* 'wise' in (3) is a typical agent-oriented AA and let's take it as an example to illustrate the information included in the functional head of subject$_3$-oriented[−concomitance] [−homogeneity] AAs and the derivation process:

(55) a. De$_3$: $\lambda Q[\lambda P[\lambda e[P(e) \wedge Ag(e)=x \wedge \exists e'$ [(MANIFEST(Q))(e')

                    ∧Arg(e')=Ag(e) ∧τ(e)>τ(e')]]]]
b. *DeP.*   *mingzhi-De* <<e,t>,<e,t>>
  | λP[λe[P(e) ∧Ag(e)=x∧∃e'[(MANIFEST
  | (*mingzhi*))(e')
  | ∧Arg(e')= Ag(e) ∧τ(e) >τ(e')]]]]
  De'
  ╱╲
 ╱ ╲
AP. *mingzhi* <e,t>   *De.* <<e,t>,<<e,t>,<e,t>>>
                       λQ[λP[λe[P(e)∧Ag(e)=x∧∃e'
λx. mingzhi (x)   [(MANIFEST(Q))(e')
                       ∧Arg(e')=Ag(e) ∧τ(e) >τ(e')]]]]

The adjective *mingzhi* is a typical individual-level predicate denoting a person's disposition. When it combines with the functional head -*De*, the information included in this functional head coerces it into denoting a dynamic event e' of manifesting the property denoted by the adjective. This event e' is embedded in the event e and temporally anchored around the event e. The only argument of the coersed event e' is decided to be co-indexed with the agent of the event e.

5.3.4.4 Object₁-oriented DeP

DeP *rere-De* 'hot' in (4) is to be taken as an example to state the information included in the functional head of object₁-oriented [+homogeneity] [+concomitance] AAs and the derivation process of this kind of DeP:

(56) a. De₄: λQ[λP[λe[P(e)∧Th(e)=y∧∃e'[Q(e')
               ∧Arg(e')=Th(e)]∧τ(e)⊆τ(e')]]]
     b. *DeP.* *rere-De* <<e,t>,<e,t>>
       | λP[λe[P(e) ∧Ag(e)=x∧∃e'[*rere-de*(e')
       | ∧Arg(e')= Th(e) ∧ τ(e) ⊆τ(e')]]]]
       De'
       ╱╲
      ╱ ╲
AP. *rere-de* <e,t>   *De.* <<e,t>,<<e,t>,<e,t>>>
λs[*rere-de* (e)∧Arg(s)=x]   λQ[λP[λe[P(e)∧Ag(e)=x∧∃e'[Q(e')
                       ∧Arg(e')=Th(e) ∧ τ(e) ⊆τ(e')]]]]

It is indicated in the derivation process that the under adjective denotes Mass state and when it combines with the functional head, the packing function of *-De* packs a slice of the Mass state and anchors it around the event denoted by the verb and the temporal information is expressed as $\tau(e) \subseteq \tau(e')$. The event e' is embedded in the event e and the only argument of the packed event is decided to be co-indexed with the theme of the event e.

5.3.4.5 Object₂-oriented DeP

The DeP *gaogao-De* 'tall' in (5) is taken as an example to illustrate the derivation process and the information included in the functional head of Object₂-oriented [+concomitance] [−homogeneity]AAs:

(57) a. De₅: $\lambda Q[\lambda P[\lambda e[P(e) \wedge Th(e)=x \wedge \exists e'\ [(BECOME(Q))(e')$
$\wedge Arg(e')=Th(e) \wedge \tau(e) \subseteq \tau(e')]]]]$

b. *DeP.*   *gaogao-De* <<e,t>,<e,t>>
$[\lambda P[\lambda e[P(e) \wedge Ag(e)=x \wedge \exists e'\ [(BECOME(baobao-de))(e')$
$\wedge Arg(e')= Th(e) \wedge \tau(e) =\tau(e')]]]]$

De'

AP. *gaogao-de* <e,t>   *De.* <<e,t>,<<e,t>,<e,t>>>
$\lambda x.\ gaogao\text{-}de\ (x)$ $\lambda Q[\lambda P[\lambda e[P(e)\ Ag(e)=x$
$\wedge \exists e'\ [(BECOME(Q))(e')$
$\wedge Arg(e')=Th(e) \wedge \tau(e) =\tau(e')]]]]$

It is indicated that before the under adjective *gaogao-de* combines with the functional head *-De*, it denotes a property expresed by the reduplicated adjective and clitic *–de* is necessary for such reduplicated adjective. When the adjective incorporates with the functional head, there are two particles with identical pronouncation. Consequently, *–de* is cancelled as the result of haplology. The information included in functional head *-De* coerses the under adjective into expressing an incremental process e', which is temporally anchored rigidly concomitant with the event denoted by the verb. The event e' is embedded in the event e and the only argument of the coerced event e' is to be co-indexed with the theme of the event e.

5.3.4.6 VP-oriented DeP

For pure manner AAs, *-De* is optional. However, the presence/absence contrast of *-De* will result in semantic variations. In this section, we mainly focus on the VP-oriented AA with *-De*. The DeP *xunsu-De* 'rapid' in (6) is taken as an example to illustrate the information included in the functional head and the derivation process of VP-oriented [−concomitance] [−participant] [−homogeneity]AAs:

(58) a. De_6: $\lambda Q[\lambda P[\lambda e[P(e) \wedge Ag(e)=x \wedge \exists e'[(MANIFEST(Q))(e') \wedge Arg(e')=e \wedge \tau(e) > \tau(e')]]]]$

b. *DeP.* *xunsu-De* $<<e,t>,<e,t>>$
$\lambda P[\lambda e[P(e) \wedge Ag(e)=x \wedge \exists e'[(MANIFEST(xunsu))(e') \wedge Arg(e')=e \wedge \tau(e) > \tau(e')]]]$

De'

AP. *xunsu* $<e,t>$ *De.* $<<e,t>,<<e,t>,<e,t>>>$
$\lambda Q[\lambda P[\lambda e[P(e) \wedge Ag(e)=x \wedge \exists e'[(MANIFEST(Q))(e') \wedge Arg(e')=e \wedge \tau(e) > \tau(e')]]]]$

x. *xunsu* (x)

The adjective *xunsu* is a typical individual-level predicate denoting the speed of an event. When it combines with the functional head *-De*, the information included in this functional head coerces it into denoting a dynamic event e' of manifesting the property denoted by the adjective. This event e' is embedded in the event e and temporally anchored around the event e. The only argument of the coersed event e' is decided to be the underling event argument of the verb.

5.3.4.7 Clause-oriented DeP

The DeP *yihan-De* 'regrettable' in (7) is a typical clause-oriented AA and it will be taken as an example to illustrate the information included in the functional head of Clause-oriented [−concomitance] [−participant] [−homogeneity] AAs and the derivation process:

(59) a. De_7 : $\lambda Q[\lambda P[\lambda e[P(e) \wedge \exists e'[(MANIFEST(Q))(e')$
$\wedge Arg(e')=P \wedge \tau(e) > \tau(e')]]]]$

b. $DeP.\ <<e,t>,<e,t>>$
$\lambda P[\lambda e[P(e) \wedge Ag(e)=x \wedge \exists\ e'\ [(MANIFEST$
$(yihan))(e')$
$\wedge Arg(e')= P \wedge \tau(e) > \tau(e')]]]]$

De'

AP. *yihan* $<e,t>$ $De.\ <<e,t>,<<e,t>,<e,t>>>$
$\lambda Q[\lambda P[\lambda e[P(e) \wedge Ag(e)=x \wedge \exists e'$
$[(MANIFEST(Q))(e')$
$\lambda x.\ yihan\ (x)$ $\wedge Arg(e')=P \wedge \tau(e)>\tau(e')]]]]$

The adjective *yihan* is a typical individual-level predicate denoting a relative permanent property of an event based on evaluation made by the speaker. When it combines with the functional head -*De*, the information included in this functional head coerces the adjective into denoting a dynamic event e' of manifesting the property denoted by the adjective. This event e' is embedded in the event e and temporally anchored around the event e. The fact involved in the main verb is the only argument of the coersed event e'.

5.3.5 Advantages of Introducing the Functional head -*De*

By decomposing the adjectival adverbial into an adjective and a -*De* functional head, it is possible to provide a fully compositional analysis for the AAs in Mandarin. The functional head -*De* takes an adjective as its complement to form an adverbial -*De* Phrase and then the head -*De* relates the event e' denoted by the adjective to the event denoted by the primary predicate. There are seven kinds of AAs in Mandarin, which means that there are seven different functional *Des*. From the derivation of these seven kinds of *DeP*, we find that although the type of the functional head *-De* is always <<e, t>,<<e, t>,<e, t>>> , but the information in it is different and *-De* has many functions.

From the information containing in the functional head *-De*, we can conclude constrains for an adjective to form an acceptable AA.

The first constraint is the meaning compatibility. Up to now, we can see that the coercion of the adjectives is a semantic operation derived from compositionality. The coercion is very powerful mechanism, but it does not mean all adjectives can be coerced to occur as AAs to match with the primary predicate. Adjectives that denote inherent and permanent properties cannot be coerced to express transitory state, thus can't occur as adverbials. Coercion is allowed only if certain structural requirements are met.

The second constraint is about the temporal dependency. For all the AAs with [+concomitance] feature, *-De* Phrase introduce a temporal overlap relation, whereas for all the AAs with [−concomitance] feature, *-De* Phrase introduce a tempral linear order relation, but the two event should be temporally related.

The third constraint is the embedding status of the e'. *-De* decides the compositional pattern between these two events.

The forth constraint is the shared constituent of e and e'. *-De* limits the potential possibilities of the semantic orientation of the AAs.

In this way, the function of *-De* is similar to the "Time-Participant Connected Relation" (TPCONNECT for short) in Rothstein's theory. However, the functions of *-De* is more various and stronger than that of the TPCONNECT.

Firstly, the shared element between e and e' for AAs is not restricted in participants, even the underlying event argument of the verb, and the fact involved the verb in can be the shared element of the two events.

Secondly, the coercing effect of the functional head is stronger. In English, only stage-level adjective can occur as depictive secondary predicates (Rappaport 1991), and the function of the depictive head (Dep) in Pylkkänen (2008) or the TPCONNECT relation in Rothstein(2004) is just to relate the two events. However, certain kinds of functional head

-De in Mandarin can coerce some individual-level adjectives to occur as AAs.

For all the seven kinds of AAs, all the information between these two events is included in the functional head *-De*, so TPCONNECT relation is redundant in the logic form. Consequently, the TPCONNECT relation will not be presented in the logic form. The logic forms of (1-7) will be represented as:

(60) Subject$_1$-oriented [+participant] [+homogeneity] [+concomitance] AA
    a. Xiaoming shengqi De rengdiao le shouji.
        p.n   angry De throw Perf cellphone
        'Xiaoming angrily threw his cell phone away.'
    b. $\exists e[rengdiao(e) \wedge Ag(e)=Xiaoming \wedge Th(e)=shouji$
        $\wedge (\exists e')[shengqi(e') \wedge Arg(e')=Ag(e)] \wedge \tau(e)$
        $\subseteq \tau(e') \wedge Past(e)]$

(61) Subject$_2$-oriented [+concomitance] [+participant] [−homogeneity] AA
    a. Xiaoming baobao De chi le yi dun zhaji.
        p.n   full   De eat Perf one CL fried chicken
        'Xiaoming got full while eating fried chicken.'
    b. $\exists e\ [chi(e) \wedge Ag(e)=Xiaoming \wedge Th(e)=zhaji$
        $\wedge (\exists e')[(BECOME(baobao\text{-}de))(e') \wedge Arg(e')=$
        $Ag(e) \wedge \tau(e)=\tau(e')]$
        $\wedge Past(e)]$

(62) Subject$_3$-oriented [−concomitance] [+participant] [−homogeneity] AA
    a. Zhang San mingzhi De zai Beijing maile yitao fangzi.
        p.n   wise De at Beijing buy one CL apartment
        'Zhang san wisely bought an apartment in Beijing.'
    b. $\exists e\ [mai(e) \wedge Ag(e)=Zhang\ San \wedge Th(e)=$
    fangzi$\wedge Loc(e)=Beijing$
    $\wedge \exists e'[(MANIFEST(mingzhi))(e') \wedge Arg(e')=$
    $Ag(e) \wedge \tau(e) > \tau(e')]$
    $\wedge Past(e)]$

(63) Object₁-oriented [+concomitance] [+participant] [+homogeneity] AA
   a. Xiaoming rere De he le yi bei cha.
      p.n   hot De drink one cup tea.
      'Xiaoming drank a cup of tea while it was hot.'
   b. ∃e [he(e)∧Ag(e)=Xiaomin∧Th(e)=yibeicha ∧(∃e') [rere-de(e')
      ∧Arg(e')=Th(e)]∧τ(e)⊆τ(e')]∧Past(e)]
(64) Object₂-oriented [+concomitance] [+participant] [−homogeneity] AA
   a. Haizimen gaogao De duile ge xueren.
      kids   tall   De pile CL snowman.
      'Kids have made a tall snowman.'
   b. ∃e [dui(e)∧Ag(e)=haizimen∧Th(e)=xueren ∧ (∃e') [gaogao-de(e')
      ∧Arg(e')=Th(e)]∧τ(e) =τ(e')]∧Past(e)]
(65) VP-oriented [−concomitance] [−participant] [−homogeneity] AAs
   a. Shibing men xunsu De zhanling le zhe zuo chengshi.
      soilders   rapid De occupy Perf this CL city
      'Solders occupied this city rapidly.'
   b. ∃e [zhanling(e)∧Ag(e)=shibingmen∧Th(e)=zhezuo chengshi
      ∧∃e'[(MANIFEST(xunsu))(e')∧Arg(e')=e] ∧τ(e)
      >τ(e')∧PAST(e)]
(66) Clause-oriented [−concomitance] [−participant] [−homogeneity] AA
   a. Li Si yihan De cuoguole mobanche.
      p.n regrettable De miss last bus
      'It is regrettable that Li Si missed the last bus.'
   b. ∃e [cuoguo(e)∧Ag(e)=Li Si∧Th(e)=mobanche∧Past (e)∧
      ∧e'[(MANIFEST(yihan))(e')∧Arg(e')=(cuoguo(e)∧ Ag(e)=Li Si
      ∧Th(e)=mobanche)]∧τ(e) >τ(e') ∧Past(e)]

In Section 5.1, questions need answing are listed, including the relation between e and e'; whether -*De* should be presented in the logic form; how to represent different kind of VP-oriented AAs, as well as how to express the [±homogeneity] feature of e'. In the logic formulas in (60-66), all these questions have been answered and the compositionality principle and the context-sensitivity of AAs are reflected. The interpretation of AAs is not only dependent on the meaning of the adjective per se. It is the result of different compositional pattern, and the semantic features of the adjective, the type of the event denoted by the main verb and the information in the functional head of DeP that contribute to the interpretation of the AAs.

Up to now, we have got the logic forms of sentences containing these seven kinds of AAs. However, these logic forms are static and they are the final products. In the following parts, the dynamic and incremental semantic derivation process of the sentences containing these seven kinds of AAs will be presented to illustrate how different under adjectives get adjectival adverbial interpretation.

5.4 Semantic derivation process of sentences containing AAs

In Chapter 3, the predicate theory proposed by Rothstein (2001, 2004) has been briefly introduced. Rothstein doesn't presuppose a variable x in predicate, no matter whether there is one or not, the λ-abstraction operation can be conducted by the so-called predication formation operation. The syntactic predicates and semantic predicates are connected through the operation of predication formation.

(67) Predicate Formation:
If α is the translation of a syntactic predicate then
$\alpha \rightarrow \lambda x.\alpha$

(Rothstein 2001: 138)

Functional application involving internal argument is lexically triggered, but the functional application of the external argument is not. Take the transitive verb *zha* 'fry' as an example:

(68) $zha_V: <\theta_{Ag}, \theta_{Th}> \to \lambda y \lambda e.zha(e) \wedge Ag(e)=x \wedge Th(e)=y$

The internal argument and the external argument show up in the logical form in different ways: the internal argument introduces a conjunct and the value of the function is a variable bounded by a lambda operator, but the value of the function of the conjunct introduced by the external argument is a free variable. A verbal or adjectival predicate which has assigned all its internal arguments, denotes a set of events and the type is <e, t>. Such a syntactic predication must be saturated syntactically at the maximal projection level, so there is a predicate formation operation in which a semantic expression is prefixed by λx, which will shift a verbal/adjectival expression of type <e, t> into <d,<e, t>>. The benefit of her predicate theory is that in the semantic derivation, frequent type alternation can be avoided, so the types of adverbials will be much simpler to work with.

Different from the expressions in type theory, in the event semantic analysis, the type of individual is d, e is for the type of event, and t is truth value. Based on the predicate theory of Rothstein, (69) will be taken as a sample to illustrate the event semantic derivation process:

(69) a. Xiaoming zha le yi pan huashengmi.
       p.n   fry Perf one plate peanuts
      'Xiaoming fried a plate of peanuts.'

    b. $[zha]_V \to \lambda y \lambda e.zha(e) \wedge Ag(e)=x \wedge Th(e)=y$
    c. $[zha\ yi\ pan\ huashengmi]_{V'} \to [\lambda y \lambda e.zha(e) \wedge Ag(e)= x \wedge Th(e)=y]$
      (yi pan huashengmi)
      $=\lambda e.zha(e) \wedge Ag(e)=x \wedge Th(e)=$ yi pan huashengmi
    d. $\wedge[zha\ le\ yi\ pan\ huashengmi]_{VP} \to \lambda x[\lambda e.[zha(e) \wedge Ag(e)=x$
      $\wedge Th(e)=$ yi pan huashengmi $\wedge PAST(e)]$ (by predicate formation)
    e. $[zha\ le\ yi\ pan\ huashengmi]_{I'} \to \lambda x[\lambda e.[zha(e) \wedge Ag(e)=x$
      $\wedge Th(e)=$ yi pan huashengmi $\wedge PAST(e)]$

f. [Xiaoming zha le yi pan huashengmi]IP→ λx[λe.
[zha(e)
∧Ag (e)=x ∧Th(e)= yi pan huashengmi∧PAST(e)]
(Xiaoming)
=λe[zha(e)∧Ag (e)=Xiaoming∧Th(e)= yi pan huashengmi
∧PAST(e)]
g. Existential quantification leads to: ∃e [zha(e)
∧Ag(e)=Xiaoming
∧Th(e)= yi pan huashengmi∧PAST(e)]

(70) The derivation tree:

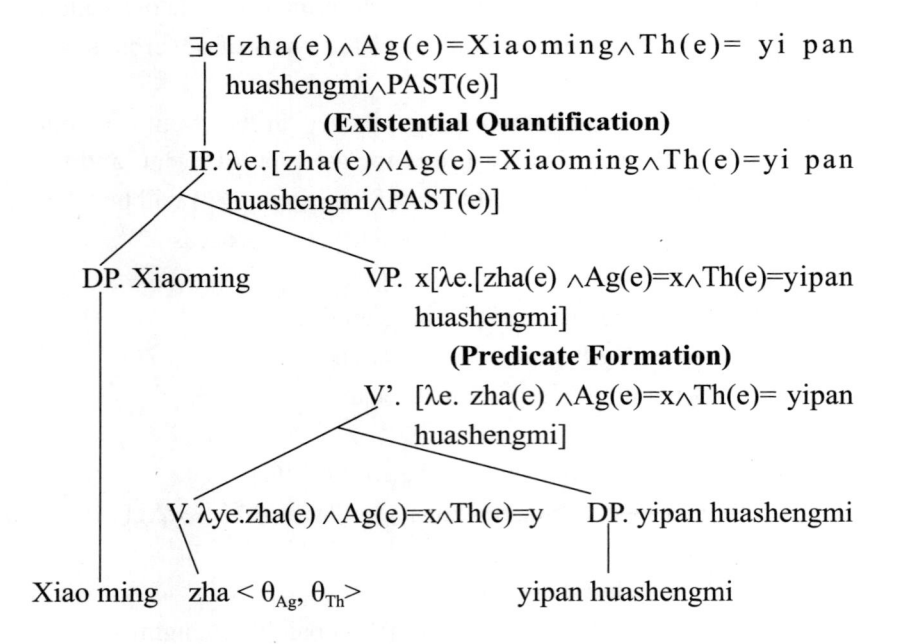

∃e [zha(e)∧Ag(e)=Xiaoming∧Th(e)= yi pan huashengmi∧PAST(e)]
(Existential Quantification)
IP. λe.[zha(e)∧Ag(e)=Xiaoming∧Th(e)=yi pan huashengmi∧PAST(e)]

DP. Xiaoming   VP. x[λe.[zha(e) ∧Ag(e)=x∧Th(e)=yipan huashengmi]
(Predicate Formation)
V'. [λe. zha(e) ∧Ag(e)=x∧Th(e)= yipan huashengmi]

V. λye.zha(e) ∧Ag(e)=x∧Th(e)=y   DP. yipan huashengmi

Xiao ming   zha < θ$_{Ag}$, θ$_{Th}$>   yipan huashengmi

"There was a singular event *Xiaoming zha le yi pan huashengmi*, in which *Xiaoming* is the agent, *yipan huashengmi* is the theme". In the derivation process, the agent is always a free variable x, and it is unbounded until the operation of predicate formation. The underlying event argument is always bounded by the lambda operator, until the last existential quantification operation. At the IP level, the event existential closure over the event argument takes place, and type *t* is finally brought

Chapter Five Semantic Analysis of AAs 249

out. The "existential closure" is a type-shifting operator applied in order to produce a sentence of type t (Landman 2000). Sentences come to describe eventualities via an operation over an unsaturated event variable.

In this section, the derivation process of a sentence without AA has been stated. In the following sections, the derivation process of the sentences with seven kinds of AAs will be provided.

5.4.1 Subject$_1$-oriented AAs

Compositionality principle states that the components of the sentence and the pattern in which these components are put together form the semantic of the sentence. The components of (71a) have been analyzed respectively: (71b) is the logic form of the whole sentence. (71c) is the logic form of the functional head of De. (71d) is the logic form of the main verb. (71e) is the logic form of the adjective:

(71) a. Xiaoming shengqi De rengdiao le shouji.
      p.n   angry De throw Perf cellphone
     'Xiaoming angrily threw his cell phone away.'
  b. $\exists e[rengdiao(e) \wedge Ag(e)=Xiaoming \wedge Th(e)=shouji$
     $\wedge (\exists e')[shengqi(e') \wedge Arg(e')=Ag(e)] \wedge \tau(e) \subseteq \tau(e') \wedge$
     $Past(e)]$
  c. De$_1$: $\lambda Q[\lambda P[\lambda e[P(e) \wedge Ag(e)=x \wedge \exists e'[Q(e')$
                 $\wedge Arg(e')=Ag(e) \wedge \tau(e) \subseteq \tau(e')]]]]$
  d. rengdiao: $\lambda y \lambda e\ [rengdiao(e) \wedge Ag(e)=x \wedge Th(e)=y]$
  e. shengqi: $\lambda s\ [shengqi\ (s) \wedge Arg(s)=x]$

These components in (71c, d, e) will be combined together in a compositional pattern to form the logic expression of (71a), and the derivation process is exhibited in (72) and the derivation tree is in figure (73):

(72) a. [rengdiao]$_V \rightarrow \lambda y \lambda e.rengdiao(e) \wedge Ag(e)=x \wedge Th(e)=y$
    b. [rengdiao shouji]$_{V'} \rightarrow \lambda y \lambda e.rengdiao(e) \wedge Ag(e)=x \wedge Th(e)=$
       y(shouji)

$=\lambda e.\ rengdiao(e) \wedge Ag(e)=x \wedge Th(e)=shouji$

c. $[shengqi]_A \rightarrow \lambda s.shengqi(s) \wedge Arg(s)=x$

d. $[shengqi]_{AP} \rightarrow \lambda x\ \lambda s.shengqi(s) \wedge Arg(s)=x$ (by predication formation)

e. $[shengqi\text{-}De]_{DeP} \rightarrow \lambda Q[\lambda P[\lambda e[P(e) \wedge Ag(e)=x \wedge \exists e'[Q(e') \wedge Arg(e')=Ag(e) \wedge \tau(e) \subseteq \tau(e')]]]](shengqi)$
$= \lambda P[\lambda e[P(e) \wedge Ag(e)=x \wedge \exists e'[shengqi(e') \wedge Arg(e')=Ag(e) \wedge \tau(e) \subseteq \tau(e')]]]$

f. $[shengqi\text{-}De\ rendiao\ shouji]_{V'} \rightarrow \lambda P[\lambda e[P(e) \wedge Ag(e)=x \wedge \exists e'[shengqi(e') \wedge Arg(e')=Ag(e) \wedge \tau(e) \subseteq \tau(e')]]]$ (rengdiao shouji)
$= \lambda e\ [rengdiao(e) \wedge Ag(e)=x \wedge Th(e)= shouji \wedge \exists e'\ [shengqi(e') \wedge Arg(e')=Ag(e)] \wedge \tau(e) \subseteq \tau(e')]$

g. $[shengqi\text{-}De\ rengdiao\ shouji]_{VP} \rightarrow \lambda x[\lambda e\ [rengdiao(e) \wedge Ag(e)=x \wedge Th(e)= shouji \wedge \exists e'[shengqi(e') \wedge Arg(e')=Ag(e)]]$ (by predication formation)

h. $[shengqi\text{-}De\ rengdiao\text{-}le\ shouji]I' \rightarrow \lambda x \lambda e.[rengdiao(e) \wedge Ag(e)=x \wedge Th(e)= shouji \wedge \exists e'\ [sehngqi(e') \wedge Arg(e')= Ag(e) \wedge \tau(e) \subseteq \tau(e')] \wedge PAST(e)]$

i. $[Xiaoming\ shengqi\text{-}De\ rengdiao\text{-}le\ shouji]IP \rightarrow \lambda x \lambda e.\ [rengdiao(e) \wedge Ag(e)=x \wedge Th(e)=shouji \wedge (\exists e')[shengqi(e') \wedge Arg(e')=Ag(e) \wedge \tau(e) \subseteq \tau(e')] \wedge Past(e)]](Xiaoming)$
$= \lambda e[rengdiao(e) \wedge Ag(e)=Xiaoming \wedge Th(e)=shouji \wedge (\exists e')[shengqi(e') \wedge Arg(e')=xiaoming \wedge \tau(e) \subseteq \tau(e')] \wedge Past(e)]$

j. Existential quantification leads to:
$\exists e\ [rengdiao(e) \wedge Ag(e)=Xiaoming \wedge Th(e)=shouji \wedge (\exists e')[shengqi(e') \wedge Arg(e')=Xiaoming \wedge \tau(e) \subseteq \tau(e')] \wedge Past(e)]$

In (72e), when the under adjective incorporates with the functional head, the Mass state denoted by the adjective *shengqi* is packed into an event with bounded run time which includes the run time of the

Chapter Five Semantic Analysis of AAs   251

event denoted by the verb. The value of free variable x of e' is decided, therefore, the event e' is existential closed.

(73) ∃e [rengdiao(e)∧Ag(e)=Xiaoming∧Th(e)=shouji
   ∧(∃e')[shengqi(e')∧ Arg(e')=Xiaoming ∧τ(e)
   ⊆τ(e')]∧Past(e)]
   (Existential Quantification)

IP, λe[rengdiao(e)∧Ag(e)=Xiaoming∧Th(e)=shouji
   ∧(∃e')[shengqi(e')∧Arg(e')=xiaoming∧τ(e)⊆τ(e')]
   ∧Past(e)]

DP, Xiaoming   VP, λx[λe [rengdiao(e)∧Ag (e)=x∧Th(e)= shouji
   ∧∃e'[shengqi(e') ∧Arg(e')=Ag(e)
   ∧τ(e) ⊆τ(e')]]]
   (Predicate Formation)

V', λe [rengdiao(e)∧Ag (e)=x∧Th(e)= shouji
   ∧∃e' [shengqi(e')∧Arg(e')=Ag(e)
   ∧τ(e)⊆τ(e')]]

DeP, λP[λe[P(e)∧Ag(e)=   V', e.rengdiao(e) ∧Ag(e)=x
x∧∃e'[shengqi(e')∧Arg(e')=   ∧Th(e)=shouji
Ag(e) ∧τ(e) ⊆τ(e')]]]

De'   V. λyλe.rengdiao(e)   DP.shouji
   ∧Ag(e)=x∧Th(e)=y

AP, λx λs.[shengqi(s)∧Arg(s)=x]   De₁, λQ[λP[λe[P(e) ∧Ag(e)=x
   ∧∃e'[Q(e')
   (predicate formation)   ∧Arg(e')=Ag(e) ∧τ(e) ⊆τ(e')]]]]
A, λs.shengqi(s)∧Arg(s)=x

The derivation process and the tree exhibits clearly how the information included in the functional head -De decides the relation between the event denoted by the adjective and the event denoted by the main verb. It is indicated that before the AP incorporates with the functional head -De, the event argument of the AP is bounded by a lambda operator. After the functional application, the event argument is existentially closed and the free variable of the event e' gets its value from the context provided by the verb. For the event denoted by the AA, the functional head has dual functions: introducing existential quantification over the event argument and deciding the value of the free variable of the event. All the event denoted by the predicates must be bounded, but in different ways. The event denoted by the primary predicate is brought under existential quantification by the temporal information in the INFL, whereas the event introduced by the adjectival adverbial is brought under existential quantification indirectly through the functional head *De*.

Functional application is the basic mechanism for the combination of expressions in the derivation process. The derivation tree can be simplified as (74), and all the process of semantic derivation is driven by functional application:

(74) The simpified semantic structure of the derivation tree:

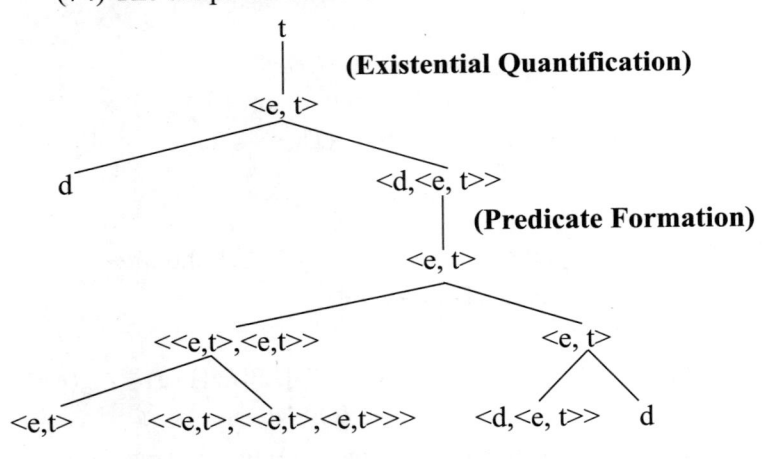

```
                        t
                        |           (Existential Quantification)
                      <e, t>
           ┌────────────┴────────────┐
           d                      <d,<e, t>>
                                     |      (Predicate Formation)
                                   <e, t>
                          ┌──────────┴──────────┐
                    <<e,t>,<e,t>>             <e, t>
                    ┌─────┴─────┐          ┌────┴────┐
                  <e,t>   <<e,t>,<<e,t>,<e,t>>>   <d,<e, t>>   d
```

5.4.2 Subject₂-oriented AAs

(75) is composed of the event denoted by the main verb, the functional head *-De*, and the event denoted by the adjectival. The logic form of each component is given in (77a,b,c):

(75) Xiaoming baobao De chi le yi dun zhaji.
       p.n   full   De eat Perf one CL fired chicken
       'Xiaoming got full while eating fried chicken.'

(76)   ∃e [chi(e)∧Ag(e)=Xiaoming∧Th(e)=zhaji
       ∧(∃e')[(BECOME(baobao-de))(e')∧ Arg(e')= Xiaoming
       ∧τ(e)⊆τ(e')] ∧Past(e)]

(77) a. De_2: λQ[λP[λe[P(e)∧Ag(e)=x∧∃e' [(BECOME(Q))(e')
       ∧Arg(e')=Ag(e)∧τ(e) ⊆τ(e')]]]]
   b. chi: λyλe [chi(e) ∧Ag(e)=x∧Th(e)= y]
   c. baobao-de: λs [*baobao-de* (s) ∧Arg(e)=x]

The following derivation process in (78) exhibits how these components are combined to form (76):

(78) a. $[chi]_V$ → λyλe.chi(e) ∧Ag(e)=x∧Th(e)=y
   b. $[chi\ yidun\ zhaiji]_{V'}$ →λyλe.chi(e) ∧Ag(e)=x∧Th(e)= y(yidun zhaji)
      =λe. chi(e) ∧Ag(e)=x∧Th(e)=yidun zhaiji
   c. $[baobao-de]_A$ →λs.baobao-de(s)∧Arg(s)=x
   d. $[baobao-de]_{AP}$ →λx λs.baobao-de(s)∧Arg(s)=x
      (by predication formation)
   e. $[baobao-de-De]_{DeP}$→λQ[λP[λe[P(e)∧Ag(e)=x
      ∧∃e'[(BECOME(Q))(e') ∧Arg(e')=Ag(e)
      ∧τ(e) =τ(e')]]]] (baobao-de)
      =λP[λe[P(e)∧Ag(e)=x∧∃e'[(BECOME(baobao-de))(e')
      ∧Arg(e')= Ag(e)∧τ(e)=τ(e')]]]
   f. $[baobao-De\ chi\ yi\ dun\ zhaji]_{V'}$ →λP[λe[P(e)∧Ag(e)=x
      ∧∃e'[(BECOME(baobao-de))(e')
      ∧Arg(e')= Ag(e)∧τ(e)=τ(e')]]](chi yi dun zhaji)
      =λe [chi(e)∧Ag(e)=x∧Th(e)=yi dun zhaji
      ∧(∃e')[(BECOME(baobao-de))(e')∧ Arg(e')= Ag(e)∧τ(e)=τ(e')]]

g. [baobao-De chi yi dun zhaji]$_{VP}$ →λx[λe[chi(e)∧
Ag(e)=x
∧Th(e)=yi dun zhaji∧(∃e')[(BECOME(baobao-de))(e')
∧ Arg(e')= Ag(e)τ(e)=τ(e')]](by predication formation)

h. [baobao De chi le yi dun zhaji]I' → λxλe.[chi(e)∧
Ag(e)=x
∧Th(e)=yi dun zhaji∧(∃e')[(BECOME(baobao-de))(e')
∧ Arg(e')= Ag(e)∧τ(e)=τ(e')]∧ PAST(e)]

i. [Xiaoming baobao De chi le yi dun zhaji]IP→xλe.
[chi(e)∧Ag(e)=x
∧Th(e)=yi dun zhaji∧(∃e')[(BECOME(baobao-de))(e')
∧ Arg(e')= Ag(e)∧τ(e)=τ(e')]]∧ PAST(e)]](Xiaoming)
=λe[chi(e)∧Ag(e)=x∧Th(e)=yi dun zhaji
∧(∃e')[(BECOME(baobao-de))(e')
∧ Arg(e')=Xiaoming∧τ(e)=τ(e')]]∧ PAST(e)]

j. Existential quantification leads to:
∃e [chi(e)∧Ag (e)=Xiaoming∧Th(e)=yi dun zhaji
∧(∃e')[(BECOME(baobao-de))(e')∧ Arg(e')= Xiaoming
∧τ(e)=τ(e')] ∧Past(e)]

(78e) represents how the clitic –*de* is cancelled out of hapology when it is parallel with the functional head –*De*. The derivation tree of the processin in (78) is in figure (79):

(79) ∃e [chi(e)∧Ag (e)=Xiaoming∧Th(e)=yi dun zhaji
∧(∃e')[(BECOME(baobao-de))(e')∧ Arg(e')=
Xiaoming
∧τ(e)=τ(e')]∧Past(e)]
(Existential Quantification)

IP, λe[chi(e)∧Ag(e)=x∧Th(e)=yi dun zhaji
∧(∃e')[(BECOME(baobao-de))(e')
∧ Arg(e')= Xiaoming∧τ(e)=τ(e')]]∧ PAST(e)]

DP, Xiaoming   VP, λx[λe[chi(e)∧Ag(e)=x∧Th(e)=yi dun zhaji
∧(∃e')[(BECOME(baobao-de))(e')
∧ Arg(e')= Ag(e)τ(e)=τ(e')]]
(Predicate Formation)

V', λe [chi(e)Ag(e)=x∧Th(e)=yi dun zhaji
∧(∃e')[(BECOME(baobao-de))(e')
∧ Arg(e')= Ag(e)∧τ(e)=τ(e')]]

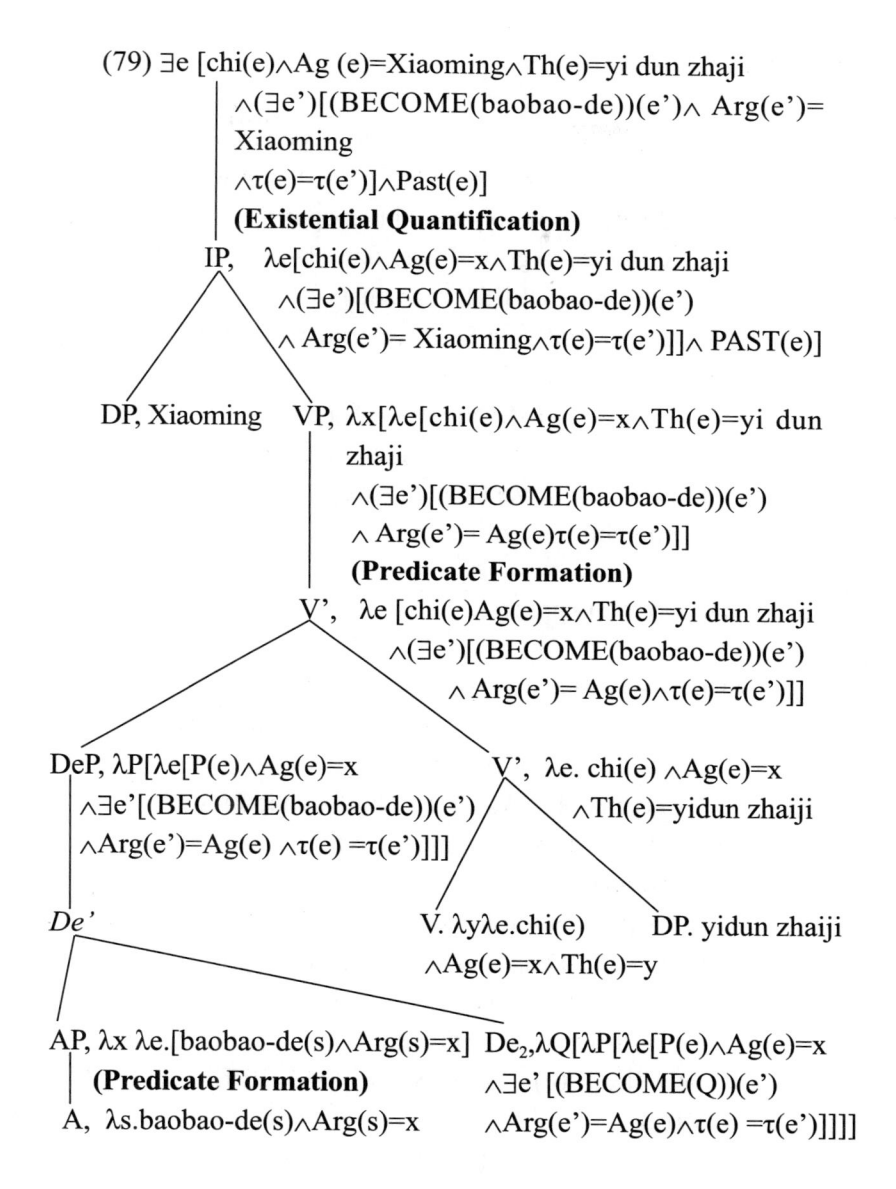

DeP, λP[λe[P(e)∧Ag(e)=x   V', λe. chi(e) ∧Ag(e)=x
∧∃e'[(BECOME(baobao-de))(e')   ∧Th(e)=yidun zhaiji
∧Arg(e')=Ag(e) ∧τ(e) =τ(e')]]]

De'   V. λyλe.chi(e)   DP. yidun zhaiji
                       ∧Ag(e)=x∧Th(e)=y

AP, λx λe.[baobao-de(s)∧Arg(s)=x]   De₂,λQ[λP[λe[P(e)∧Ag(e)=x
(Predicate Formation)   ∧∃e' [(BECOME(Q))(e')
A, λs.baobao-de(s)∧Arg(s)=x   ∧Arg(e')=Ag(e)∧τ(e) =τ(e')]]]]

5.4.3 Subject₃-oriented AAs

This kind of AA is also known as agent-oriented AA. We will take (80a) as an example to illustrate the compositional process of this kind of AAs. (80b) is the logic form of (80a). (80c) is the logic form of the functional head of this kind of AA. (80d) is the logic of the verb and (80e) is the form of the adjective.

(80) a. Zhang San mingzhi De maile yi tao fangzi.
   p.n   wise De buy Perf one CL apartment
   'Zhang san wisely bought an apartment in Beijing.'
b. $\exists e[mai(e) \wedge Ag(e)=Zhang\ San \wedge Th(e)=yi\ tao\ fangzi$
   $\wedge \exists e'[(MANIFEST(mingzhi))(e')$
   $\wedge Arg(e')=Zhang\ San \wedge \tau(e) > \tau(e')] \wedge Past(e)]$
c. De_3: $\lambda Q[\lambda P[\lambda e[P(e) \wedge Ag(e)=x \wedge \exists\ e'$
   $[(MANIFEST(Q))(e')$
   $\wedge Arg(e')=Ag(e) \wedge \tau(e) > \tau(e')]]]]$
d. mai: $\lambda y \lambda e\ [mai(e) \wedge Ag(e)=x \wedge Th(e)= y]$
e. mingzhi: $\lambda x.\ mingzhi\ (x)$

(81) is the derivation process:

(81) a. $[mai]_V \rightarrow \lambda y \lambda e.mai(e) \wedge Ag(e)=x \wedge Th(e)=y$
b. $[mai\ yitao\ fangzi]_{V'} \rightarrow \lambda y \lambda e.mai(e) \wedge Ag(e)=x$
   $\wedge Th(e)=y(yitao\ fangzi)$
   $= \lambda e.\ mai(e) \wedge Ag(e)=x \wedge Th(e)=\ yitao\ fangzi$
c. $[mingzhi]_A \rightarrow \lambda x.\ mingzhi\ (x)$
d. $[mingzhi]_{AP} \rightarrow \lambda x\ s.[mingzhi(s) \wedge Arg(s)=x]$
   (by predication formation)
e. $[mingzhi\text{-}De]_{DeP} \rightarrow \lambda Q[\lambda P[\lambda e[P(e) \wedge Ag(e)=x$
   $\wedge \exists e'[(MANIFEST(Q))(e') \wedge Arg(e')=Ag(e)$
   $\wedge \tau(e) > \tau(e')]]]]$ (mingzhi)
   $= \lambda P[\lambda e[P(e) \wedge Ag(e)=x \wedge \exists e'[(MANIFEST(mingzhi))$
   (e')
   $\wedge Arg(e')= Ag(e) \wedge \tau(e) > \tau(e')]]]$
f. $[mingzhi\ De\ mai\ yitao\ fangzi]_{V'} \rightarrow \lambda P[\lambda e[P(e)$
   $\wedge Ag(e)=x$
   $\wedge \exists e'[(MANIFEST(Q))(e')$
   $\wedge Arg(e')=Ag(e) \wedge \tau(e) > \tau(e')]]]($ mai yitao fangzi$)$
   $= \lambda e\ [mai(e) \wedge Ag(e)=x \wedge Th(e)=yitao\ fangzi$
   $\wedge\ \exists e'[(MANIFEST(mingzhi))(e')$
   $\wedge Arg(e')=Ag(e) \wedge \tau(e) > \tau(e')]]$

g. [mingzhi De mai yitao fangzi]$_{VP}$ →λx[λe[mai(e)∧
Ag(e)=x
∧Th(e)=yitao fangzi∧ ∃e'[(MANIFEST(mingzhi))
(e')
∧Arg(e')=Ag(e)∧τ(e)>τ(e')]](by predication formation)
h. [mingzhi De maile yitao fangzi]$_{I'}$ →
  λxλe.[mai(e) Ag(e)=x∧Th(e)=yitao fangzi
  ∧∃e'[(MANIFEST(mingzhi))(e')
  ∧Arg(e')=Ag(e)∧τ(e)>τ(e')]∧Past(e)]
i. [Zhang San mingzhi De maile yitao fangzi]$_{IP}$→
  λxλe.[mai(e) ∧Agt(e)=x ∧Th(e)=yitao fangzi
  ∧∃e'[(MANIFEST(mingzhi))(e')
  ∧Arg(e')=Ag(e)∧τ(e)>τ(e')]∧Past(e)]](Zhang San)
  =λe[mai(e) ∧Agt(e)=Zhang San ∧Th(e)=yitao fangzi
  ∧∃e'[(MANIFEST(mingzhi))(e')
  ∧Arg(e')=Zhang San∧τ(e)>τ(e')]∧Past(e)]
j. Existential quantification leads to:
  ∃e [mai(e) ∧Agt(e)=Zhang San ∧Th(e)=yitao fangzi
  ∧∃e'[(MANIFEST(mingzhi))(e')
  ∧Arg(e')=Zhang San∧τ(e)>τ(e')]∧Past(e)]

(81c,d) indicates that the adjective *mingzhi* denotes relatively permanent property, when it incorporats with the functional head De, it is coerced to denote a pounctual eventuality of manifesting the property denoted by the adjective. The derivation tree is in figure (82):

(82) ∃e [mai(e) ∧Agt(e)=Zhang San ∧Th(e)=yitao fangzi
       ∧∃e'[(MANIFEST(mingzhi))(e')
       ∧Arg(e')=Zhang San∧τ(e)>τ(e')]∧Past(e)]
     (Existential Quantification)
     IP, λe[mai(e) ∧Agt(e)=Zhang San ∧Th(e)=yitao fangzi
           ∧∃e'[(MANIFEST(mingzhi))(e')
           ∧Arg(e')=Zhang San∧τ(e)>τ(e')]∧Past(e)]

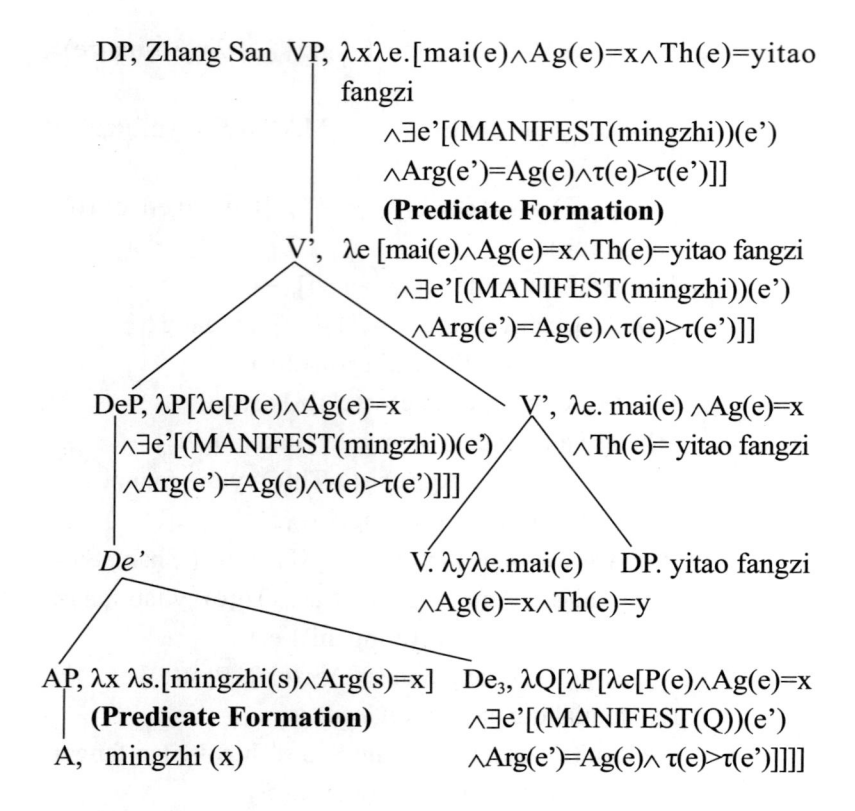

258 A Study Of Adjectival Adverbials In Mandarin Chinese: An Event Semantics Perspective

```
DP, Zhang San   VP, λxλe.[mai(e)∧Ag(e)=x∧Th(e)=yitao
                    fangzi
                        ∧∃e'[(MANIFEST(mingzhi))(e')
                        ∧Arg(e')=Ag(e)∧τ(e)>τ(e')]]
                    (Predicate Formation)
                V', λe [mai(e)∧Ag(e)=x∧Th(e)=yitao fangzi
                     ∧∃e'[(MANIFEST(mingzhi))(e')
                     ∧Arg(e')=Ag(e)∧τ(e)>τ(e')]]

   DeP, λP[λe[P(e)∧Ag(e)=x          V', λe. mai(e) ∧Ag(e)=x
   ∧∃e'[(MANIFEST(mingzhi))(e')        ∧Th(e)= yitao fangzi
   ∧Arg(e')=Ag(e)∧τ(e)>τ(e')]]]

       De'                    V. λyλe.mai(e)    DP. yitao fangzi
                              ∧Ag(e)=x∧Th(e)=y

   AP, λx λs.[mingzhi(s)∧Arg(s)=x]   De₃, λQ[λP[λe[P(e)∧Ag(e)=x
       (Predicate Formation)              ∧∃e'[(MANIFEST(Q))(e')
   A,  mingzhi (x)                        ∧Arg(e')=Ag(e)∧ τ(e)>τ(e')]]]]
```

From the derivation of these three kinds of subject-oriented AAs, we can see that the value of the free variable x of e' is initially decided when the adjective incorporates with the functional head, but only after the operation of predicate formation on the primary predicate is conducted, the free variable x of e' is finally decided.

5.4.4 Object₁-oriented AAs

The representations of the components (83a) have been given: (83b) is the representation of the whole sentece, (83c) is the representation of the functional head of object-oriented [+concomitance] [+homogeneity] DeP, (83d) is the logic form of the main verb, and (83e) is the form of the adjective:

(83) a. Xiaoming rere De he le yi bei cha.
         p.n   hot De drink one cup tea.

'Xiaoming drank a cup of tea while it was hot.'
b. ∃e [he(e)∧Ag(e)=Xiaomin∧Th(e)=yibeicha∧(∃e')
[rere-de(e')
∧ Arg(e')=yibeicha]∧τ(e)⊆τ(e')]∧Past(e)]
c. De₄: λQ[λP[λe[P(e)∧Th(e)=y∧∃e'[Q(e')
∧Arg(e')=Th(e)]∧τ(e)⊆τ(e')]]]
d. he: λe [he(e) ∧Ag(e)=x∧Th(e)= y]
e. rere-de: λs[*rere-de*(s) ∧Agt(s)= x]

These components will be combined in the derivation process in (84) and the derivation tree is as (85):

(84) a. [he]ᵥ → λyλe.he(e)∧Ag(e)=x∧Th(e)=y
b. [he yibeicha]ᵥ' →λyλe.he(e) ∧Ag(e)=x
∧Th(e)=y(yibeicha)
=λe. he(e) ∧Ag(e)=x∧Th(e)=yibeicha
c. [rere-de]_A →λs.rere-de(s)∧Arg(s)=x
d. [rere-de]_AP →λx λs.rere-de(s)∧Arg(s)=x
(by predication formation)
e. [rere-de-De]_DeP→λQ[λP[λe[P(e)∧Th(e)=y∧∃e'[Q(e')
∧Arg(e')=Th(e)∧τ(e) ⊆τ(e')]]]](rere-de)
=λP[λe[P(e)∧Ag(e)=x∧∃e'[rere-de(e')∧Arg
(e')=Th(e)
∧τ(e) ⊆τ(e')]]]
f. [rere De he yi bei cha]ᵥ' →λP[λe[P(e)∧Ag(e)=x
∧∃e'[rere-de(e')∧Arg(e')=Ag(e)∧τ(e) ⊆τ(e')]]]
(he yibeicha)
=λe [he(e)∧Ag(e)=x∧Th(e)=yi bei cha
∧∃e' [rere-de(e')∧Arg(e')=yi bei cha]∧τ(e) ⊆τ(e')]
g. [rere De he yi bei cha]_VP → λx[λe [he(e)
∧Ag(e)=x∧Th(e)= yi bei cha ∧∃e' [rere-de(e')
∧Arg(e')=yi bei cha]∧τ(e) ⊆τ(e')]] (by predication formation)
h. [rere De he le yi bei cha]I' →x[λe [he(e)
∧Ag(e)=x∧Th(e)= yi bei cha ∧∃e' [rere-de(e')
∧Arg(e')=yi bei cha]∧τ(e) ⊆τ(e')] ∧ PAST(e)]

i. [Xiaoming rere De he le yi bei cha]IP→λxλe. [he(e)
∧Ag(e)=x∧Th(e)= yi bei cha ∧∃e' [rere-de(e')
∧Arg(e')=yi bei cha∧τ(e) ⊆τ(e')] ∧ PAST(e)]
(Xiaoming)
=λe [he(e)∧Ag(e)=x∧Th(e)= yi bei cha ∧∃e' [rere-de(e')
∧Arg(e')=yi bei cha∧τ(e) ⊆τ(e')] ∧ PAST(e)]

j. Existential quantification leads to:
∃e [he(e)∧Ag(e)=Xiaomin∧Th(e)=yibeicha∧(∃e')
[rere-de(e')
∧ Arg(e')=yi bei cha∧τ(e)⊆τ(e')]∧Past(e)]

It is indicated in (84e), when the under adjective incorporates with the functional head, the clitic –de is cancelled because of hapology. The figure in (85) exhibits the derivation tree:

(85) ∃e[he(e) ∧Ag(e)= Xiaoming∧Th(e)=yi bei cha
∧(∃e')[rere-de(e')∧ Arg(e')=yi bei cha∧τ(e)
⊆τ(e')]∧Past(e)]
     (Existential Quantification)
 IP, λe[he(e) ∧Ag(e)= Xiaoming∧Th(e)=yi bei cha
  ∧(∃e')[rere-de(e')∧Arg(e')=yi bei cha∧τ(e)⊆
  τ(e')]∧Past(e)]

DP,Xiaoming VP, λx[λe [he(e)∧Ag(e)=x∧Th(e)= yi bei cha
     ∧(∃e')[rere-de(e')∧ Arg(e')=yi bei cha
     ∧τ(e) ⊆τ(e')]]](Xiaoming)
     (Predicate Formation)
   V', λe [λe [he(e)∧Ag (e)=x∧Th(e)= yi bei cha
      ∧∃e'[rere-de(e')∧Arg(e')=
      yibeicha∧τ(e)⊆τ(e')]]]

DeP, λP[λe[P(e)∧Th(e)=y∧∃e'[rere-de(e') V', λe.he(e) ∧Ag(e)=x
∧Arg(e')=Th(e)∧τ(e) ⊆τ(e')]]]   ∧Th(e)=yi bei cha

De'   V. λyλe.he(e) DP.yi bei cha
    ∧Ag(e)=x∧Th(e)=y

AP, λx λe.[rere-de(s)∧Arg(s)=x]   De₄, λQ[λP[λe[P(e) ∧Ag(e)=x ∧∃ e' [Q(e')
  (Predicate Formation)   ∧Arg(e')=Th(e) ∧τ(e) ⊆τ(e')]]]]
A, λs [*rere-de*(s)∧Arg(e)=x]

Different from subject-oriented AAs, the value of the free variable x of e' is finally decided as soon as the V' incorporates with the DeP.

5.4.5 Object₂-oriented AAs

The components of (86a) have been analyzed respectively: (86b) is the logic form of the whole sentence. (86c) is the logic form of the functional head of DeP. (86d) is the logic form of the main verb. (86e) is the logic form of the adjective:

(86) a. Haizimen gaogao De duile ge xueren.
     kids   tall De pile CL snowman.
     'Kids have made a tall snowman.'
  b. ∃e [dui(e)∧Ag(e)=haizimen∧Th(e)=yi ge xueren
     ∧ (∃e')[(BECOME(gaogao-de))(e')∧Arg(e')=yige xueren)]
     ∧τ(e) =τ(e')]∧Past(e)]
  c. De₅: λQ[λP[λe[P(e)∧Th(e)=x∧∃e'[(BECOME(Q))(e')
                ∧Arg(e')=Th(e)∧τ(e) =τ(e')]]]]
  d. dui: λyλe [dui(e) ∧Ag(e)=x∧Th(e)= y]
  e. gaogao-de: λs[*gaogao-de*(s)∧Agt(s)= x]

(87) Darivation process of (86a):
  a. [dui]ᵥ → λyλe.dui(e) ∧Ag(e)=x∧Th(e)=y
  b. [dui yige xueren] ᵥ· →λyλe.dui(e) ∧Ag(e)=x
     ∧Th(e)=y(yi ge xueren)
     =λe. dui(e) ∧Ag(e)=x∧Th(e)=yi ge xueren
  c. [gaogao-de]ₐ →λs.gaogao-de(s)∧Arg(s)=x
  d. [gaogao-de]ₐₚ →λx λs.gaogao-de(s)∧Arg(s)=x

(by predication formation)

e. [gaogao-de-De]$_{DeP}$→λQ[λP[λe[P(e)∧Ag(e)=x
∧∃e'[(BECOME(Q))(e') ∧Arg(e')=Ag(e)
∧τ(e) =τ(e')]]]](gaogao-de)
=λP[λe[P(e)∧Ag(e)=x∧∃e'[(BECOME(gaogao-de))
(e')
∧Arg(e')=Ag(e)∧τ(e) =τ(e')]]]

f. [gaogao De dui yi ge xueren]$_{V'}$ →λP[λe[P(e)∧Ag(e)=x
∧∃e'[(BECOME(gaogao-de))(e')
∧Arg(e')= Th(e)τ(e)=τ(e')]]](dui yi ge xueren)
=λe [dui(e)∧Ag(e)=x∧Th(e)=yi ge xueren
∧(∃e')[(BECOME(gaogao-de))(e')∧ Arg(e')= yige xueren
∧τ(e)=τ(e')]]

g. [gaogao De dui yi ge xueren]$_{VP}$ →λx[λe[dui(e)∧ Ag(e)=x
∧Th(e)=yi ge xueren∧(∃e')[(BECOME(gaogao-de))(e')
∧ Arg(e')=yi ge xueren∧τ(e)=τ(e')]](by predication formation)

h. [gaogao De dui le yi ge xueren]I' → λxλe.[dui(e)∧ Ag(e)=x
∧Th(e)=yi ge xueren∧(∃e')[(BECOME(gaogao-de))(e')
∧ Arg(e')= yi ge xueren∧τ(e)=τ(e')]∧ PAST(e)]

i. [Haizimen gaogao De duile ge xueren]IP→λxe. [dui(e)∧Ag(e)=x
∧Th(e)=yi ge xueren∧(∃e')[(BECOME(gaogao-de))(e')
∧Arg(e')= yi ge xueren∧τ(e)=τ(e')]∧ PAST(e)] (haizimen)
=λe[dui(e)∧Ag(e)=haizimen∧Th(e)=yi ge xueren
∧ (∃e') [gaogao-de(e')
∧Arg(e')=yi ge xueren]∧τ(e) =τ(e')]∧Past(e)]

j. Existential quantification leads to:
∃e [dui(e)∧Ag(e)=haizimen∧Th(e)=yi ge xueren

∧ (∃e') [(BECOME(gaogao-de))(e') ∧ Arg(e')=yi ge xueren]
∧ τ(e)=τ(e')]∧Past(e)]

All these components will be combined to get the detailed derivation tree in (88):

(88) ∃e [dui (e)∧Ag (e)= haizimen ∧Th(e)= yi ge xueren
∧(∃e')[(BECOME(gaogao-de))(e')∧Arg(e')=yi ge xueren
∧τ(e)=τ(e')]∧Past(e)]
(Existential Quantification)

IP, λe[dui (e)∧Ag(e)= haizimen ∧Th(e)= yi ge xueren
∧(∃e')[(BECOME(gaogao-de))(e')
∧ Arg(e')=yi ge xueren∧τ(e)=τ(e')]∧ PAST(e)]

DP, haizimen

VP, λx[λe[dui (e)∧Ag(e)=x∧Th(e)= yi ge xueren
∧(∃e')[(BECOME(gaogao-de))(e')
∧ Arg(e')=yi ge xueren∧τ(e)=τ(e')]]
(Predicate Formation)

V', λe [dui (e)Ag(e)=x∧Th(e)= yi ge xueren
∧(∃e')[(BECOME(gaogao-de))(e')
∧ Arg(e')= yi ge xueren∧τ(e)=τ(e')]]

DeP, λP[λe[P(e)∧Ag(e)=x
∧∃e'[(BECOME(gaogao-de))(e')
∧Arg(e')= Th(e)∧τ(e)=τ(e')]]]

V', λe. dui (e) ∧Ag(e)=x
∧Th(e)= yi ge xueren

De'

V. λyλe.dui(e)
∧Ag(e)=x∧Th(e)=y

DP. yi ge xueren

AP, x λe.[gaogao-de(s)∧Arg(s)=x]
(Predicate Formation)

A, λs.gaogao-de(s)∧Arg(s)=x

De₅,λQ[λP[λe[P(e)∧Ag(e)=x
∧∃e' [(BECOME(Q))(e')
∧Arg(e')=Th(e)∧τ(e) =τ(e')]]]]

5.4.6 VP-oriented AAs

We have stated that the presence/absence of *-De* will cause the semantic difference. In this part, we will illustrate the difference in the derivation process. First, we will take (89a) as an example to illustrate the derivation process of VP-oriented AA with *-De*:

(89) a. Shibing men xunsu De zhanling le na ge chengshi.
        soilders   rapid De occupy Perf that CL city
        'Solders occupied that city rapidly.'
   b. $\exists e$ [zhanling(e)$\land$Ag(e)=shibingmen$\land$Th(e)=na ge chengshi
$\land \exists e'$[(MANIFEST(xunsu))(e')$\land$Arg(e')=e] $\land \tau(e) > \tau(e') \land$ PAST(e)]
   c. De_6: $\lambda Q[\lambda P[\lambda e[P(e) \land Ag(e)=x \land \exists e'$[(MANIFEST(Q))(e')
$\land$ Arg(e')=e $\land \tau(e) > \tau(e')$]]]]
   d. zhanling: $\lambda y \lambda e$ [zhanling(e) $\land$Ag(e)=x$\land$Th(e)=y]
   e. xunsu: λx. xunsu (x)

(89b) is the logic form of (89a). (89c) is the functional head of this kind of AA. (89d) is the logic form of the verb and (89e) is the form of the adjective.

(90) a. [zhanling]$_V$ → $\lambda y \lambda e$.zhanling(e) $\land$Ag(e)=x$\land$Th(e)=y
   b. [zhanling na ge chengshi] $_{V'}$ →$\lambda y \lambda e$.zhanling(e)
$\land$Ag(e)=x
      $\land$Th(e)=y(na ge chengshi)
=λe.zhangling(e) $\land$Ag(e)=x$\land$Th(e)=na ge chengshi
   c. [xunsu]$_A$ →λx. xunsu (x)
   d. [xunsu]$_{AP}$ →λx s.[sunsu(s)$\land$Arg(s)=x](by predication formation)
   e. [xunsu-De]$_{DeP}$→$\lambda Q[\lambda P[\lambda e[P(e) \land \exists e'$[(MANIFEST(Q))(e')
$\land$Arg(e')=e$\tau(e)>\tau(e')$]]]] (xunsu)
=$\lambda P[\lambda e[P(e) \land Ag(e)=x \land \exists e'$[(MANIFEST(xunsu))(e')

$\wedge \text{Arg}(e') = e \wedge \tau(e) > \tau(e')]]]$

f. [xunsu De zhanling na ge chengshi]$_{V'}$ → $\lambda P[\lambda e[P(e)$
$\wedge \exists e'[(\text{MANIFEST}(xunsu))(e') \wedge \text{Arg}(e') = e$
$\wedge \tau(e) > \tau(e')]]]$(zhanling na ge chengshi)
= $\lambda e [zhanling(e) \wedge Ag(e) = x \wedge Th(e) = na\ ge\ chenghsi$
$\wedge \exists e'[(\text{MANIFEST}(xunsu))(e')$
$\wedge \text{Arg}(e') = e \wedge \tau(e) > \tau(e')]]$

g. [xunsu De zhanling na ge chengshi]$_{VP}$ → $\lambda x \lambda e.$
[zhanling(e)
$\wedge Ag(e) = x \wedge Th(e) = na\ ge\ chengshi$
$\wedge \exists e'[(\text{MANIFEST}(xunsu))(e')$
$\wedge \text{Arg}(e') = e \wedge \tau(e) > \tau(e')]]$(by predication formation)

h. [xunsu De zhanling le na ge chengshi]$_{I'}$ →
$\lambda x \lambda e.[\ zhanling(e) \wedge Ag(e) = x \wedge Th(e) = na\ ge\ chengshi$
$\wedge \exists e'[(\text{MANIFEST}(xunsu))(e')$
$\wedge \text{Arg}(e') = e \wedge \tau(e) > \tau(e')] \wedge \text{Past}(e)]$

i. [Shibing men xunsu De zhanling le na ge chengshi]$_{IP}$→
$\lambda x \lambda e.[\ zhanling(e)\ \wedge Ag(e) = x \wedge Th(e) = na\ ge\ chengshi$
$\wedge \exists e'[(\text{MANIFEST}(xunsu))(e')$
$\wedge \text{Arg}(e') = e \wedge \tau(e) > \tau(e')] \wedge \text{Past}(e)]]$(shibing men)
= $\lambda e[zhanling(e)\ \wedge Ag(e) = shibingmen \wedge Th(e) = na\ ge\ chengshi$
$\wedge \exists e'[(\text{MANIFEST}(xunsu))(e')$
$\wedge \text{Arg}(e') = e \wedge \tau(e) > \tau(e')] \wedge \text{Past}(e)]$

j. Existential quantification leads to:
$\exists e\ [zhanling(e) \wedge Ag(e) = shibingmen \wedge Th(e) = na\ ge\ chengshi$
$\wedge \exists e'[(\text{MANIFEST}(xunsu))(e') \wedge \text{Arg}(e') = e]$
$\wedge \tau(e) > \tau(e') \wedge \text{PAST}(e)]$

(91) ∃e [zhanling(e)∧Ag(e)=shibingmen∧Th(e)=na ge
chengshi
∧∃e'[(MANIFEST(xunsu))(e')
∧Arg(e')=e]∧τ(e)>τ(e')∧PAST(e)]
(Existential Quantification)

IP, λe[zhanling(e)∧Ag(e)=shibingmen∧Th(e)=na ge chengshi
∧∃e'[(MANIFEST(xunsu))(e')
∧Arg(e')=e∧τ(e)>τ(e')]∧Past(e)]

DP, shibingmen   VP, λxλe.[zhanling(e) ∧Ag(e)=x∧Th(e)=na ge chengshi
∧∃e'[(MANIFEST(xunsu))(e')
∧Arg(e')=e∧τ(e)>τ(e')]](shibingmen)
(Predicate Formation)

V', λe [zhanling(e)∧Ag(e)=x∧Th(e)=na ge chenghsi
∧∃e'[(MANIFEST(xunsu))(e')
∧Arg(e')=e∧τ(e)>τ(e')]]

DeP, λP[λe[P(e)∧Ag(e)=x∧Th(e)=y   V', λe. zhanling(e) ∧Ag(e)=x
∧∃e'[(MANIFEST(xunsu))(e')   ∧Th(e)= na ge chenghsi
∧Arg(e')=e∧τ(e)>τ(e')]]]

De'   V. λyλe.zhangling(e)   DP. na ge chenghsi
                 ∧Ag(e)=x∧Th(e)=y

A λx λs.[xunsu(s)∧Arg(s)=x]   De₆, λQ[λP[λe[P(e)∧Ag(e)=x
(Predicate Formation)   ∧∃e'[(MANIFEST(Q))(e')
A, xunsu(x)   ∧Arg(e')=e∧ τ(e)>τ(e')]]]]

When *-De* is absent, (89a) is interpretated as (91), and (91b) is the derivation tree:

(91) a. ∃e [zhanling(e)∧Ag(e)=shibingmen∧Th(e)=na ge chengshi
∧xunsu(e) ∧PAST(e)]

(91) b. ∃e [zhanling(e)∧Ag(e)=shibingmen∧Th(e)=na ge chengshi ∧xunsu(e)∧PAST(e)]

(Existential Quantification)

```
              IP,    λe[zhanling(e)∧Ag(e)=shibingmen
             /  \         ∧Th(e)=na ge chengshi ∧xunsu(e) ∧Past(e)]
            /    \
   DP, shibingmen  VP,  λxλe.[ zhanling(e) ∧Ag(e)=x
                         ∧Th(e)=na ge chengshi ∧xunsu(e)]
                        **(Predicate Formation)**
                   V',   λe [zhanling(e)∧Ag(e)=x
                         ∧Th(e)=na ge chenghsi∧xunsu(e)
           /           \
   V', λe. zhanling(e)∧xunsu(e)    DP. na ge chenghsi
        ∧Ag(e)=x ∧Th(e)=y
       /        \
  A, λx, xunsu (x)   V. λe.zhanling(e)
```

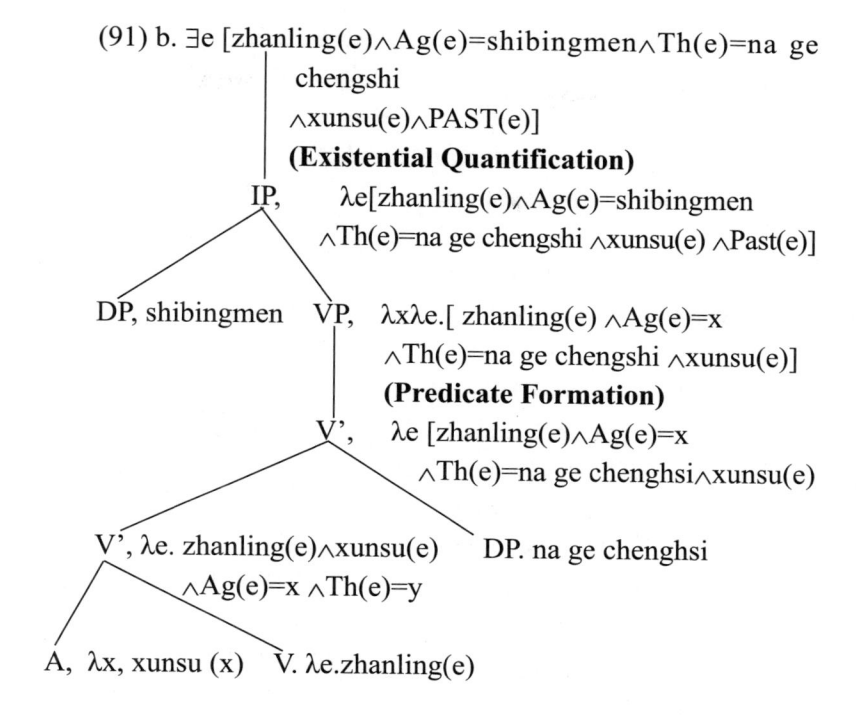

The derivation tree in figure (91b) indicates that, when -*De* is absent, adjective *xunsu* just dente a property, which combine with the verb as a conjunct to classify the denotation of the verb.

5.4.7 Clause-oriented AAs

The representations of the components (92a) have been given: (92b) is the representation of the whole sentence, (92c) is the representation of the functional head of Clause-oriented [−concomitance] [−participant] [−homogeneity] AAs, (92d) is the logic form of the main verb, and (92e) is the form of the adjective:

(92) a. Li Si yihan De cuoguole mobanche.
　　　　p.n regrettable De miss last bus
　　　　'It is regrettable that Li Si missed the last bus.'
　　b. ∃e [cuoguo(e)∧Ag(e)=Li Si∧Th(e)=mobanche
　　　　∧(∃e') [(MANIFEST(yihan))(e')∧Arg(e')=(cuoguo(e)∧
　　　　Ag(e)=Li Si

$\wedge$Th(e)=mobanche$\wedge$τ(e) >τ(e')$\wedge$Past(e))]]

c. De₇: λQ[λP[λe[P(e)$\wedge$∃e'[(MANIFEST(Q))(e')
$\wedge$Arg(e')=P $\wedge$τ(e) >τ(e')]]]]

d. cuoguo: λyλe [cuoguo(e) $\wedge$Ag(e)=x$\wedge$Th(e)=y]

e. yihan: λx. yihan (x)

These components will be combined in the derivation process in (93) and the derivation tree is as (94):

(93) a. [cuoguo]ᵥ → λyλe.cuoguo(e) $\wedge$Ag(e)=x$\wedge$Th(e)=y

b. [cuoguo mobanche] ᵥ' →λyλe.cuoguo(e) $\wedge$Ag(e)=x
$\wedge$Th(e)=y(mobanche)
=λe. cuoguo(e)$\wedge$Ag(e)=x$\wedge$Th(e)= mobanche

c. [yihan]ₐ →λx. yihan (x)

d. [yihan]ₐ →λx λs.[yihan(s)$\wedge$Arg(s)=x] (by predication formation)

e. [yihan-De]_DeP→λQ[λP[λe[P(e)$\wedge$∃e'[(MANIFEST (Q))(e')
$\wedge$Arg(e')=P $\wedge$τ(e) >τ(e')]]]](yihan)
=λQ[λP[λe[P(e)$\wedge$∃e'[(MANIFEST(yihan))(e')
$\wedge$Arg(e')=P $\wedge$τ(e) >τ(e')]]]]

f. [yihan De cuoguole mobanche]ᵥ' →λP[λe[P(e)$\wedge$
Ag(e)=x
$\wedge$∃e'[(MANIFEST(yihan))(e')
$\wedge$Arg(e')=P$\wedge$τ(e)>τ(e')]]](cuoguo mobanche)
=λe [cuoguo(e)$\wedge$Ag(e)=xTh(e)=mobanche
$\wedge$ ∃e'[(MANIFEST(yihan))(e')
$\wedge$Arg(e')=(cuoguo(e)$\wedge$Ag(e)=x$\wedge$Th(e)=mobanche)
$\wedge$τ(e)>τ(e')]]

g. [yihan De cuoguo mobanche]ᵥᴘ →λx[λe[cuoguo(e)$\wedge$
Ag(e)=x
$\wedge$Th(e)=mobanche$\wedge$ ∃e'[(MANIFEST(yihan))(e')
$\wedge$Arg(e')= (cuoguo(e)$\wedge$Ag(e)=xTh(e)=mobanche)
$\wedge$τ(e)>τ(e')]]

(by predication formation)

h. [yihan De cuoguole mobanche]ᵢ' →λx[λe[cuoguo(e)$\wedge$

Ag(e)=x
∧Th(e)=mobanche∧ ∃e'[(MANIFEST(yihan))(e')
∧Arg(e')= (cuoguo(e)∧Ag(e)=xTh(e)=mobanche)
∧τ(e)>τ(e')]]∧Past(e)]

i. [Li Si yihan De cuoguole mobanche]$_{IP}$→λx[λe[cuoguo(e)∧Ag(e)=x
∧Th(e)=mobanche∧ ∃e'[(MANIFEST(yihan))(e')
∧Arg(e')= (cuoguo(e)∧Ag(e)=xTh(e)=mobanche)
∧τ(e)>τ(e')]]∧Past(e)](Li Si)
=λe[cuoguo(e)∧Ag(e)=Li Si∧Th(e)=mobanche
∧ ∃e'[(MANIFEST(yihan))(e')∧Arg(e')= (cuoguo(e)
∧Ag(e)=Li Si∧Th(e)=mobanche)∧τ(e)>τ(e')]]∧Past(e)]

j. Existential quantification leads to:
∃e [cuoguo(e)∧Ag(e)=Li Si∧Th(e)=mobanche
∧ (∃e') [(MANIFEST(yihan))(e')∧Arg(e')= (cuoguo(e)
∧Ag(e)=Li Si∧Th(e)=mobanche)∧τ(e)>τ(e')∧Past(e))]]

(94) is the derivation tree:

(94) ∃e [cuoguo(e)∧Ag(e)=Li Si∧Th(e)=mobanche
∧ (∃e') [(MANIFEST(yihan))(e')∧Arg(e')= (cuoguo(e)
∧Ag(e)=Li Si∧Th(e)=mobanche)∧τ(e) >τ(e')∧ Past(e))]

(Existential Quantification)

IP, λe[cuoguo(e)∧Ag(e)=Li Si∧Th(e)=mobanche
∧ (∃e') [(MANIFEST(yihan))(e')∧Arg(e')= (cuoguo(e)
∧Ag(e)=Li Si∧Th(e)=mobanche)∧τ(e)>τ(e')
∧Past(e))]

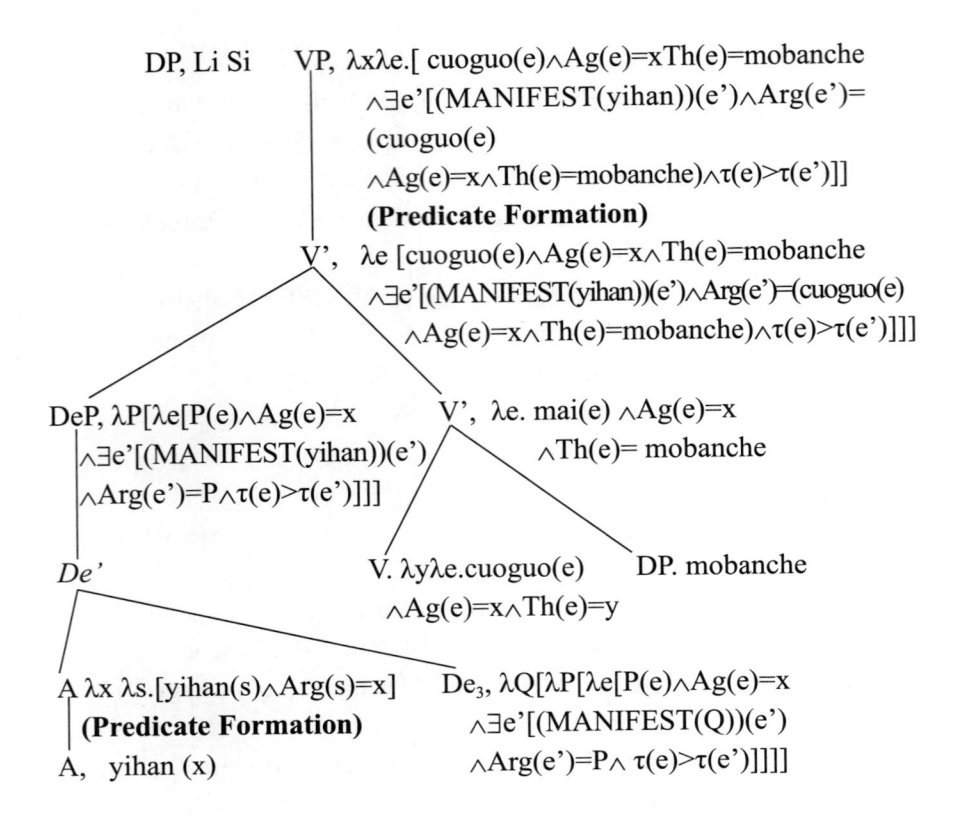

```
DP, Li Si      VP, λxλe.[ cuoguo(e)∧Ag(e)=xTh(e)=mobanche
               ∧∃e'[(MANIFEST(yihan))(e')∧Arg(e')=
               (cuoguo(e)
               ∧Ag(e)=x∧Th(e)=mobanche)∧τ(e)>τ(e')]]
               (Predicate Formation)
           V', λe [cuoguo(e)∧Ag(e)=x∧Th(e)=mobanche
               ∧∃e'[(MANIFEST(yihan))(e')∧Arg(e')=(cuoguo(e)
               ∧Ag(e)=x∧Th(e)=mobanche)∧τ(e)>τ(e')]]]

DeP, λP[λe[P(e)∧Ag(e)=x        V', λe. mai(e) ∧Ag(e)=x
    ∧∃e'[(MANIFEST(yihan))(e')       ∧Th(e)= mobanche
    ∧Arg(e')=P∧τ(e)>τ(e')]]]

De'              V. λyλe.cuoguo(e)      DP. mobanche
                  ∧Ag(e)=x∧Th(e)=y

A λx λs.[yihan(s)∧Arg(s)=x]   De₃, λQ[λP[λe[P(e)∧Ag(e)=x
 (Predicate Formation)          ∧∃e'[(MANIFEST(Q))(e')
 A, yihan (x)                   ∧Arg(e')=P∧ τ(e)>τ(e')]]]]
```

In this section, the dynamic derivation process of the sentences containing seven kinds of AAs has been provided. The derivation process accurately reflects the principle of compositionality. The incremental process of the interpretation of AA and the process of the specification of semantic orientation of AA is clearly represented in the derivation tree. Furthermore, the information included in the functional head -*De* is vital for the interpretation of AAs. However, there is no rigid one-to-one match between adjective and the kind of functional head -*De*.

5.5 AAs with Multi Orientations

It is a controversial issue whether AAs can have multi semantication orientation. We assume that on the condication of semantic compatibility, it is possible for AA to have more than one semantic orientation. According to the target that adjective modify, adjectives are classified into object adjectives and event adjectives. Object adjectives can be further divided into adjectives modify human being and adjectives modify objects. However, some adjectives are not that typical so they can modify both human or object, or they can modify both event and object, or even human, object and event. As we have stated that subject₃-oriented AAs regularily have both agent-oriented reading and VP-oriented reading. Clause-oriented AAs also have VP-oriented reading. Such regular phenomena are easy to explain.

For example, AA in (95) is assumed to have object2-reading and subject1-oriented reading:

(95) a. Chu qiu de yangguang nuanhonghong De zhao zhe
early autumn of sun   warm   De shine ASP
ta de houbei.
his of back
'In early autumn, the sun shined his back warm.'

$\qquad$ Zheng (2000: 163)

b. ∃e [zhao(e)∧Ag(e)=chuqiu de yanguang∧Th(e)=ta de houbei

∧(∃e')[nuanhonghong-de(e')∧Arg(e')=chuqiu de yangguang

∧τ(e) ⊆τ(e')]∧HOLD(e)]

"There was a singular event e *Chuqiu de yangguang zhaozhe ta de houbei* in which another event e' *Chu qiu de yangguang nuanhonghong de* is embedded, and the run time of e overlaps the run time of e'"

(96) ∃e [zhao(e)∧Ag(e)=chuqiu de yanguangTh(e)=ta de houbei

∧(∃e')[(BECOME(nuanhonghong-de))(e')∧Arg(e')=ta de houbei

∧τ(e) ⊆τ(e')]∧HOLD(e)]

"There was a singular event e *Chuqiu de yangguang zhaozhe ta de houbei* in which another event e' ta de houbei (BECOME(nuanhonghong-de)) is embedded, and the run time of e overlaps the run time of e'".

In (96), the under adjective *nuanhonghong-de* 'warm' incorppotates with functional head De_1:$\lambda Q[\lambda P[\lambda e[P(e) \wedge Ag(e)=x \wedge \exists e'[Q(e') \wedge Arg(e') = Ag(e) \wedge \tau(e) \subseteq \tau(e')]]]]$; consequently, *nuanhonghong-de* is interpreted as Subject$_1$-oriented [+homogeneity] [+concomitance] AA. In (96c), the under adjective *nuanhonghong-de* 'warm' incorppotates with functional head De_5: $\lambda Q[\lambda P[\lambda e[P(e) \wedge Th(e)=x \wedge \exists e'[(BECOME(Q))(e') \wedge Arg(e')=Th(e) \wedge \tau(e) \subseteq \tau(e')]]]]$; as a result, the adjective *nuanhonghong-de* 'warm' is interpretated as object$_2$-oriented [+concomitance] [−homogeneity] AA.

There are a few AAs are ambiguous between sebject$_2$-oriented [+concomitance] [−homogeneity] reading and object$_1$-oriented [+concomitance] [+homogeneity] reading, for such adjectives can express the transitory state of certain object, and also express the temporary physical state of persons. Take (97a) as as example:

(97) a. Zhang San rehuhu De chile wan bian.
      p.n   hot De eat bowl noodle
    'Zhang San got hot while he ate that bowl of noodle.'
    'Zhang San ate a bowl of noodle hot.'
b. $\exists e\ [chi(e) \wedge Ag(e)=Zhang\ San \wedge Th(e)=yi\ wan\ mian \wedge (\exists e')[(BECOME(rehuhu-de))(e') \wedge Arg(e')= Zhang\ San \wedge \tau(e)=\tau(e')] \wedge Past(e)]$
    'Zhang San got hot while he ate that bowl of noodle.'
c. $\exists e\ [chi(e) \wedge Ag(e)=Zhang\ San \wedge Th(e)=yi\ wan\ mian \wedge (\exists e')[rehuhu-de(e') \wedge Arg(e')=yiwanmian] \wedge \tau(e) \subseteq \tau(e')] \wedge Past(e)]$
    'Zhang San ate a bowl of noodle hot.'

The AA *rehuhu-De* in (97a) is ambiguous. In (97b), the under adjective *rehuhu-de* incorporates with functional head De_2: $\lambda Q[\lambda P[\lambda e[P(e) \wedge Ag(e)=x \wedge \exists e'\ [(BECOME(Q))(e')Arg(e')=Ag(e) \wedge \tau(e) \subseteq \tau(e')]]]]$, and AA has sebject$_2$-oriented [+concomitance] [−homogeneity] reading. In (97c), the under adjective *rehuhu-de* incorporates with functional head De_4: $\lambda Q[\lambda P[\lambda e[P(e) \wedge Th(e)=y \wedge \exists e'[Q(e') \wedge Arg(e') =Th(e) \wedge \tau(e) \subseteq \tau(e')]]]$, and the AA has object$_1$-oriented[+concomitance] [+homogeneity] reading.

It is indicated in the logic forms that when an adjectival adverbial has more than one interpretation, semantic orientation is not the only difference, there are corresponding differences caused by the different interpretations of AA. Following the combinatorial nature of AA, I propose that the different interpretation of AA is not always the polysemy of the adjectives, but the result of the combination of the under adjective together with different functional head De.

What's more, AAs with multi-interpretation express more information with less language, which is in agreement of economy of language.

5.6 Beyond Compositionality

We have been focusing on the combinatorial property of AAs in Mandarin, and analyze AA as composing of an under adjective and a functional head *-De*. It seems that the combinatorial account works effectively. Before proceeding, a comment is in order on the nature of units which do not lend themselves to such a perfectly combinatorial account. Their interpretations are not derived compositionally from the meaning of their parts.

In Mandarin, some combinations of monosyllabic adjective and monosyllabic verbs are lexicalized, and these two parts of the words are integrated. *-De* can not be inserted. We have stated that the reduplication of the monosyllabic adjective can permit more adjectives occur as adverbials. However, even the reduplication of the monosyllabic adjective in such compounds still can not permit the insertion of the particle *-De*:

> (98) Compounds composed of monosyllabic adjective +monosyllabic verb:
> a. *qingchang* 'sing a cappella',   * *qingqing –De chang*
> b. *anxi* 'feel happy secretly',   * *anan-De xi*
> c. *danwang* 'fade from one memory',   * *dandan –De wang*
> d. *haokan* 'good looking',   #*haohao –De kan*

e. *xugou* 'make up'.   * *xuxu –De gou*

Such compounds are different from monosyllabic adjectival adverbial. Although the number of such monosyllabic adjectives is small, they exhibit strong production and compositionality.

(99) a. *kuaipao* 'run fast'   kuaikuai –*De* pao
     b. *jinwo* 'grasp tightly'   jinjin –*De* wo
     c. *xikan* 'look carefully' xixi –*De* kan
     d. *shenwa* 'dig deep'   shenshen –*De* wa

What's more, some monosyllabic adjectives in some idioms also cannot be analyzed in a compositional pattern:

(100) a. pingqipingzuo
         flat stand flat sit
         'on an equal footing'
      b. piantingpianxin,
         partial listen partial believe
         'be biased'
      c. xihuofengshou
         glad get harvest
         'get a harvest gladly'

Whether an adjective can combine with a verb to constitute a -*De*-less adverbial, sometimes, is dependent on real world knowledge, which might be culturally motivated. In this book, we tend to treat combinations in (98) and (100) as a whole, which can not be included in the pattern of analysis we proposed here.

5.7 Summary

In this Chapter, the pattern of analyzing different kinds of AAs proposed in Chapter 4 is evaluated and improved. The event e' denoted by AA is analyzed as an embedding event, which reflects the syntactic nature of the AA as an adjunct. The aspectual feature of the event e' is expressed compositionally as the result of different combination with different predicates, including BECOME and MANIFEST. The overt modification marker De is analyzed as the head of the DeP, in which all the information is included, including the grammatical relationship between events, the temporal relation, and the shared element of the two events. We have classified AAs into seven kinds; accordingly, there are seven types of functional head -De. As an overt modification marker, -De relates AA to the event denoted by the main verb. Its type is always <<e,t>,<<e,t>,<e,t>>>. Adjectives are inherently predicative, and most adjectives in Chinese occur as predicates. The default denotation of an adjective is a stative event. But the context provided by -De can coerce the under adjective into a particualr aspectual class.

The semantic dedivation of the sentences containing different AAs exhibits the dynamic and incremental process of how the under adjective is getting semantically saturated. In this process, the syntactic status of the under adjective, the semantic orientation of the undera djective and the temporal feature of the AA is decided compositionally.

Such a pattern of analysis also provide a satisfying explanation for AAs with ambiguity. Some AAs have more than one interpretation due to the polysemy of the under adjective, whereas some AAs' multi-interpretation is the result of the incorporation of the under adjective with different functional head –De.

The advantages of such a proposal are that the semantic of an adjectival adverbial is not pre-decided, and the tempotal realtion between the AA and the main event is decided dynamically in the combining process, which strictly conforms to the compositionality principle, which asserts that the meaning of an expression is built up from the meaning of its components and the operations by which these components are combined together.

Chapter Six

Conclusive Remarks

In this book, a formal study of the semantics of adjectival adverbials in Mandarin has been made within the framework of event semantics. This study aims to identify and represent the semantic restrictions that adjectives undergo when they occur as adverbials. Generally speaking, the objectives of the research have been realized and the questions on adjectival adverbials that we put forward in Chapter 1 have been answered. However, when adjectives occur as adverbials, too many factors, including prosodic, morphologic, syntactic, semantic and pragmatic ones, should be taken into consideration. This study mainly focuses on semantic factors, so it is unavoidable to miss some interesting and valuable data. However, this is the beginning of future researches.

6.1 Important and Innovative Features of the Research

The innovative features of this research include theoretical contributions to widening the application of event semantics. This research also clarifies understanding about adjectival adverbials in Mandarin.

Firstly, based on the features of AAs in Mandarin, we have adapted Parsons' subatomic event semantics and Rothstein's predicate theory to make it suitable for the analysis of AAs. The event e' denoted by the AA is analyzed as an embedded event in Parsons' style. The dynamicity and the free variable x of Rothstein's predicate theory have been kept. Due to the overt modification marker –*De*, the TOCONNECT in Rothstein's predicate theory has been given up. Finally, we have constructed a model that is suitable for the syntactic and semantic feature of AAs in Mandarin. With this newly-constructed model, AAs are analyzed in a dynamic and incremental process. Classical Davidsonian approach is assumed to be applicable only in action sentences and some prepositional adverbials, and Parsons included some attributive adverbs into the neo-Davidsionian approach. However, the application of this theory has largely still been restricted to the VP-oriented adverbials. In this research, not only subject-oriented AAs, but also object-oriented AAs, and even some clause-oriented AAs are analyzed in the framework of event semantics. Including AAs in Mandarin as the targets of event semantic research greatly enlarges the application of this theory.

Secondly, in this book, AAs have been studied from the perspective of formal semantics. A natural language like Chinese can be considered as an abstract system analogous to formal language of logic or mathematics. Both natural and formal languages are compositional in the sense that the meaning of any syntactically well-formed expression is uniquely determined by the meaning of its constituent parts, and the pattern used to combine these constituents. With the model we constructed in this paper, the semantic properties of adjective adverbials elucidated in this study are clearly represented in a compositional pattern.

Thirdly, there are two kinds of mismatches when some adjectives occur as adverbials: one is the mismatch between the syntactic positions of the adjectival adverbials and their semantic orientations; the other mismatch is between the temporal feature of adjectives and that of verbs. The research in this paper is centered on how to explain and represent these two mismatches. In addition, it has long been observed that when adjectives occur as adverbials, the meaning of the adjectives will shift. However, the motivation and the manner of such meaning shift have not been clearly indicated yet. The research on AA in this paper is not limited to a certain layer of grammar, but conducted in an integrated incremental process. In this process, the meaning shift of the under adjectives is indicated as the combination of the under adjective with different predicates such as BECOME and MANIFEST, and the orientation of the AA is indicated as the element that is co-indexed with the free variable of the event e'.

Fourthly, the proposed criteria for classification of AAs in this research not only take the semantic of adjective per se, but also the adverbial function of the under adjective into consideration. Based on the classification of AA, the restriction on the morphological features of adjectives, the dependency on –De, and the semantic shift process of each kind of AA are studied specifically and presented clearly..

Fifthly, this research is helpful to understand the nature of the structural subordinator –De. Generally speaking, less attention has been paid to the research on –De. The existing research on the structural subordinator focuses on the description of the function and the distribution of it. In this book, -De is analyzed as a functional head, which is the vehicle of the information that decides the compositional pattern of the two events denoted by these predicates in a sentence containing AA. When adjectives combine with different functional head –De, AAs will obtain different interpretation on condition of semantic compatibility. Such an explanation of AAs with multi-interpretation also adheres to the compositionality principle.

6.2 Further Questions

This book lays the groundwork for a further investigation into the semantics of adverbials in Mandarin. Although seven kinds of AAs have been studied, more remains to be done for a complete account of adverbials in Mandarin.

Firstly, the model we constructed in this book is effective in analyzing AAs and it is feasible to analyze –De following adjectival adverbial as a functional head. However, -De also appears following other words besides adjectives, such as adverb in (1), noun in (2), and number + Classifier adverbials in (3), and –De is free to be absent or present in (1) and (3), and indispensable in (2):

> (1) Li Si feichang (De) xingfen.
>   p.n very   De excited
>   'Li Si is very excited'

(2) Xiaoming benneng *(De) zuochu le fanyin.
    p.n   instinct De make Perf reaction
    'Xiaoming reacted instinctively.'
(3) Xiaoli yibu   yibu (De) zouxiang jiangtai.
    p.n   one step one step De walk toward teaching table
    'Xiao li walked toward the teaching table step by step.'

It is a very interesting and challenging to ask if it is possible to apply the model we proposed in this paper to analyze other kinds of adverbials.

Secondly, the research of AAs in this book is mainly in comparison with secondary predicates and predicational adverbs in English and other languages occasionally. In order to understand AAs well, we must study AAs from a typological perspective.

Thirdly, AAs in Mandarin can be stacked together. In this book, we have only briefly mentioned the relative order of multiple AAs in a sentence, but we have not discussed the derivation process of multiple AAs in the model proposed in this paper.

The study in this book is just a beginning of research on adverbials in the framework of event semantics. The main hope is that the model proposed in this book can be applied to the analysis of a diverse collection of languages.

References

Alexiadou, A., 2010, Reduplication and Doubling Contrasted: Implication for the Structure of the DP and the AP. *Linguistica-Revista de Estudos Lingusticos da Universidade do Porto* 5: 9-25.

Barwise, J., and Perry, J., 1983, *Situations and Attitudes,* Cambridge, Massachusetts: MIT Press.

Bayer, Samuel Louis, 1996, *Confessions of a Lapsed Neo-Davidsonian: Event and Arguments in Compositional Semantics,* Ph.D. dissertation of Brown University.

Bellert, Irena, 1977, On Semantics and Distributional Properties of Sentential Adverbs, *Linguistic Inquiry.*

Birner, B., and G. Ward, 1998, *Information Status and Noncanonical Word Order in English,* Amsterdam: John Benjamins.

Blank, A., 2001, Pathways of Lexicalization, In *Language Typology and Language Universals* (Vol. II), H. Martin, et al. (eds.), 1596-1608, Berlin/New York: Walter de Gruyter.

Bolinger, D., 1967, Adjectives in English: Attribution and Predication. *Lingua* 18:1-34.

Bolinger, D.,1968, Entailment and the Meaning of Structure, *Glossa* 2:119-127.

Borer, H. 2005, *The Normal Course of Events,* Oxford University Press.

Brinton, L.J., and E.C.Traugott, 2005, *Lexicalization and Language Change,* Cambridge: Cambridge University Press.

Carlson. G.N., 1977, *Reference of Kinds in English,* Ph.D. dissertation, University of Massachusetts.

Carlson. G.N., 1980, *Reference of Kinds in English*, Garland, New York.

Caudal, Patrick, and Nicolas, David, 2005, Types of Degree and Types of Event Structure. In E*vent Arguments: Foundation and Applications,* Claudia Maienborn, and Angelika Wöllstein (eds.), 277-299. Tübingen: Niemeyer.

Chao Y. R. 1968. *A Grammar of Spoken Chinese,* Berkeley: University of California Press.

Chen Baoya. 1999. *Methodology of Linguistic Research in China in 20th Century*. Jinan: Shandong Educational Press.

Chen-Sheng Luther Liu, 2013, Reduplication of Adjectives in Chinese: a Default State, *East Asian Linguist* 22:101-132.

Chen Yi, 1987, Reconsideration of adjectival adverbial, *Beifang luncong* 5: 77-82.

Chen Yi, 1993, The constrains of combination of adjective and verb as well as the subcategories of adjectives, *Qiushi xuekan* 2: 86-90.

Chierchia, G., 1984, *Topics in the Syntax and Semantics of Indefinites and Gerunds*. Dissertation of Amherst: University of Massachusetts.

Chierchia, G., 1985, Formal Semantics and the Grammar of Predication, *Linguistic Inquiry*. 3:417-443.

Chierchia, G., 1989, 'structured Meanings, Thematic Roles, and Control'. In *Properties, Types, and Meaning*, Vol. II. Chierchia, G. *et al.* (eds.), 131–166. Kluwer, Dordrecht.

Chierchia, G., 1995, Individual Level Predicates as Inherent Generics. In *The Gennetic Book,* Chicago, G. Carlson and F.J. Pelletier, eds., 175-223, The University of Chicago Press.

Chierchia, G., 1998, Reference to Kinds Across Language, *Natuural Language Semantics*, 6(4), 339-405.

Chomsky, N., 1965, *Aspects of the Theory of Syntax,* The M.I.T. Press, Cambridge.

Chomsky, N., 1981, *Lectures on Government and Binding,* Foris: Dordrecht.

Chomsky, N., 1986, *Barriers,* MIT Press: Cambridge, Mass.

Chomsky, N., 1995, *The Minimalist Program*. Cambridge: MIT press.

Cinque, G., 1999., *Adverbs and Functional Heads, A Cross-linguistics Perspective,* Oxford University Press, New York.

Cong Yingxu, 2013, *Mismatched Modification in Chinese and English: A Grammatical Metaphor Perspective*. Ph.D. dissertation of Shanghai International Studies University.

Creswell, M.J., 1977, The Semantic of Degree. In *Montague Grammar,* Partee. B.H. ed., 261-292. Academic Press, New York.

Cristophor, Piňón, 2007, Manner Adverbs and Manners, Handout, URL http:// pinon. sdf-eu.org/covers/mam.html.

Cristophor, Piñón, 2010, What to Do with Agent-oriented Adverbs, "Speaking of possibility and time"-The 7th Workshop on Inferential Mechanisms and Their Linguistic Manifestation Göttingen, 4-5 June 2010.

Croft, W., 1984, Semantic and Pragmatic Correlates to Syntactic Categories, In *Papers From the Parasession on Lexical semantics,* Testen D., V. Mishra and J. Drogo, eds., 53-70, Chicago: Chicago Linguistic Society.

Creswell, M.J., 1977, The Semantic of Degree, In *Montague Grammar*, Partee. B.H. ed., 261-292, New York:Academic Press.

Dai Haoyi, 1988, Temporal Sequence and Chinese Word Order, *Linguistics Abroad* 1:10-20.

Daria Protopopescu, 2007, Remarks on Transparent Adverbs. *Bucharest Working Papers in Linguistics* Vol. IX No.1, 188-195.

Davidson, D., 1967, The Logical Form of Action Sentences. In *The Logic of Decision and Action,* N. Rescher, ed., 105-122, Pittsburgh: University of Pittsburgh Press,1980.

De Swart. H., 1998, *Introduction to Natural Language Semantics*, CSLI Lecture Notes 80, Standford, CA: CSLI.

Ding Shengshu, Lü Shuxiang, et al., 1961, *Lectures on the Syntax of Modern Chinese*, Beijing: The Commercial Press.

Dong Jinhuan, 1991, *Semantic* Orientation of Adjectival Adverbial, *Jilin University Journal Social Science Edition* 1:91-97.

Dowty, David R., 1979, *Word Meaning and Montague Grammar: The Semantic of Verbs and Times in Generative Semantics and in Montague's PTQ,* Dordrecht: Reidel.

Dowty, David R., 1991, Thematic Proto-roles and Argument Selection. *Language* 67: 547-619.

Ernst, Thomas, 1984, *Towards an Integrated Theory of Adverb Position in English*. Bloomington, Ind: Indiana University Linguistics Club.

Ernst, Thomas, 1987, Why Epistemic and Manner Modifications are Exceptional. In *Proceding of the 13th Annual Meeting of the Berkeley Linguistics Society*, J. Aske, N.Beery, L. Michaelis and H. Filip, ed., 77-87. Berkeley: Berkeley Linguistics Society.

Ernst, Thomas, 1995, Negation in Mandarin Chinese. *Natural*

Language and Linguistics Theory 13, 665-707.

Ernst, Thomas, 2002, *The Syntax of Adjuncts,* Cambridge University Press.

Fang Li, 2000, *Logical Semantics: An Introduction,* Beijing: Beijing Language and Cultural University Press.

Feng Shengli, 1997, *Prosody, Morphology and Syntax in Chinese*, Beijing: Peking University Press.

Fernald, Theodore B., 2000, *Predicates and Temporal Arguments,* Oxford, New York: Oxford University Press.

Frey, Werner, 2003, Syntactic Conditions on Adjunct Classes. In *Modifying adjuncts*, Ewald Lang, Claudia Maienborn, and Cathrine Fabricius-Hansen, ed., 163-209. Berlin: Mouton de Gruyter.

Gallego, A., and J. Uriagereka, 2011, *The Lexical Syntax of ser and ester,* Ms., University Autónoma de Barcelona and University of Maryland.

Gan Yulong, 1986, Discussion on the Unification and Division of de and De, *Xuzhou Normal University Journal Social Science Edition* 1:144-146.

Gao Mingkai, 1948, *On Chinese Grammaer*, Beijing: The Commercial Press.

Gärdenfors, Peter, 2000, *Conceptual Spaces.* Cambridge MA: MIT Press.

Geuder, Wilhelm, 2000, *Oriented Adverbs: Issues in the Lexical Semantics of Event Adverbs.* Doctoral dissertation, University Tubingen.

Geuder, Wilhelm, 2004, Depictives and Transparent Adverbs. In *Adverbials: The Interplay between Meaning, Context and Syntactic Structure,* J, Austin, S. Engelberg and G. Rauh, eds,, 131-166. Amsterdam: Benjamins.

Geuder, Wilhelm, 2005, Manner Modification of States. In 10th annual meeting of the Gesellschaft für Semantik October: Christian Ebert and Cornelis Endriss, eds., 13-15.

Greenberg, Y., 1994, *Hebrew Nominal Sentences and the Stage/Individual-level Distinction.* MA thesis, Bar-Ilan University.

Gu,Y., 2007, Reduplication, Atelicity and Pluractionality. Paper presented at the City University of Hong Kong, August 2007.

Gu, Y., 2008, From Adjective Reduplication, Atelicity and

Plurationality and Analyticity. Talk given at Beijing Language University, June 8, 2008.

Guo Rui, 2002, *Research on Part of Speech in Mandarin Chinese*, Beijing: The Commercial Press.

Haider, H., 1997, Precedence Among Predicates. *Yje Journal of Comparative Germanic Linguistics* 1, 2-41.

Haiman, J., 1985, *Natural Syntax: Iconicity and Erosion* Cambridge: Cambridge University Press.

Halliday, M.A.K., 1967, Notes of Transitivity and Theme in English, Part I, *Journal of Linguistics* 3: 37-81.

Han Yuguo, 2001, *The subdivision and syntactic functions of Chinese adjectives, Language Teaching and Linguistic Study* 2: 47-54.

He Hongfeng, 2006, *A Study of Manner Adverbial in Chinese*, Ph.D. dissertation of Central China Normal University.

He Hongfeng, 2010, The Semantic Nature of Descriptive Object-oriented Adverbial sentences, *Studies in Language and Linguistics* 4:51-58.

He Hongfeng, 2012, *Manner Adverbial in Mandarin Chinese*, China Social Sciences Press.

Heim, Irene, 1985, *Notes on Comparatives and Related Issues*, Ms., University of Texas, Austin.

Heim, Irene and Angelika Kratzer, 1998, *Semantics in Generative Grammar*, Oxford: Blackwell.

He Yang, 1996, Investigation on Property Adjectives Occurring as Adverbials, In *Inverstigation on Part of Speech*, Hu Mingyang, ed.. Beijign Language Institute Press.

Higginbotham, James, 1985, On semantics, *Linguistics Inquiry* 16(4), 547-593.

Higginbotham, James, 2000, On Event in Linguistic Semantics. In *Speaking of Events*, J. Higginbotham, F. Pianesi and A. Varzi, eds., Oxford, New York: Oxford University Press.

Higginbotham, James and Gillian Ramchand, 1997, The stage-level/individual-level Distinction and the Mapping hypothesis. Oxford University Working Papers in Linguistics, Philology and Phonetics 2, 53-83.

Huang Borong and Liao Xudong, 2002, *Contemporary Chinese*, Higher Education Press.

Huang, C. -T. James, 1982, *Logic relations in Chinese and the theory of grammar,* Ph. D dissertation, MIT; edited version published by Garland, New York, 1998.

Huang, C. -T. James. 1988. *Wo pao de kuai* and Chinese phrase structure. *Language* 64:274-311.

Huang, S, Z., 2006, Property Theory, Adjectives, and Modification in Chinese. *Journal of East Asian linguistics*, 15(4) 343-369.

Hu, J. H, Pan and L. Xu, 2001, Is There a Finite vs Nonfinite Distinction in Chinese? *Linguistics*, 39(6): 1117-1148.

Hu Mingyang, 1991, Reclassification of Adjectives in Beijing Dialect, *Selected Works On Linguistics,* Renming University of China Press.

Hu Yushu, 1987, *Contemporary Chinese*, Shanghai: Shanghai education Press.

Iden Landau, 2010, Saturated Adjectives, Reified Properties, *Lexical Semantics, Syntax, and Event Structure,* Malka Rappaport Hovav, Edit Doron, and Ivy Sighel, eds., 204-225, Oxford University Press.

Irena Bellert, 1977, On Semantic and Distribution Properties of Sentential Adverbs. *Linguistic Inquiry* 8:337-350.

Jackendoff, Ray S., 1972, *Semantic Interpretation on Generative Grammar*. Cambridge, MA, The MIT Press.

Jesperson, O., 1924, *The Philosophy of Grammar*, London: Allen and Unwin. Ltd.

Jin Lixin, 2009, A Possible Analysis of Chinese Buyu, *Zhongguoyuwen* 5:387-398.

Kamp, Hans, 1975, Two Theories About Adjectives, In *Formal Semantics of Natural Language*, E. Keenan, ed., 125-155, Cambridge: Cambridge University Press.

Katz, Graham, 2003, Event Arguments, Adverb Selection, and Stative Adverb Gap, In *Modifying Adjuncts, Interface Explorations*, Ewald Lang, Claudis Maienborn, and Cathrine Fabricius-Hansen, eds., vol.4,455-474, Berlin: Mouton de Gruter.

Katz, Graham, 2008, Manner Modification of State Verbs. In *Adjectives and Adverbs: Syntax, Semantics, and Discourse, Studies in Theoretical Linguistics,* Louise McNally and Christopher Kennedy, eds., Oxford: Oxford University Press.

Ke Hang, 2006, A Study on Haplology in Chinese, *Chinese Language Learning* 4: 36-44.

Kennedy, C., and McNally. L., 2005, Scale Structure, Degree Modification, and the Semantics of Gradable Predicates, *Language* 81(2) 345-381.

Kennedy, Christopher, 2007, Vagueness and Grammar: the Semantics of Relative and Absolute Gradable Adjectives. *Linguistics and Philosophy* 30(1):1-45.

Kong Lei, 2015, *A Constrastive Study of Speaker-oriented Expressions in English and Chinese: An Event Semantics Perspective,* Ph.D. dissertation of Beijing Foreign Language University.

Kratzer, Angelika, 1989, An Investigation into the Lumps of Thought, *Linguistics and Philosophy* 12:607-653.

Kratzer, Angelika, 1995, Stage-level and individual-level predicates, In *The Gennetic Book,* G. Carlson and F.J Pelletier, eds., 175-223. Chicago: The University of Chicago Press.

Kratzer, Angelika, 1996, Serving the External Argument from its Verb. In *Phrase Structure and the Lexicon,* Johan Roorych and Laurie Zaring, eds., Dordrecht: Kluwer Academic.

Krifka, Manfred, 1989, Nominal Reference, Temporal Constitution and Quantification in Event Semantics, In *Semantics and Contextual Expressions*, Renate Bartsch, John van Benthem, and Peter Van Emde Boas, eds., 75-115, Dordrecht: Foris Publications.

Krifka, Manfred, 1992, Thematic Relations as Links Between Normal Reference and Temporal Constitution, In *Lexical Matter*, Sag, I.A., and Szabolcsi, A., eds., 29-53, Stanford: Center for the Study of Language and Information.

Krifka, Manfred, 1998, The Origins of Telicity, In *Events and Grammar,* S. Rothstein, ed., 197-235, Dordrecht: Kluwer.

Landau, I., 2010, Saturated Adjectives, Reified Properties, In *Lexical Semantics, Syntax, and Event Structure*, M. Rappaport Hovav, E. Doron and I. Sichel, eds., 204-225, Oxford University Press.

Landman, Fred, 1996, *Plurality,* In *Handbook of Contemporary Seamtics*, Shalom Lappin, ed., 425-457, Oxford, UK: Blackwell Publishing.

Landman, Fred, 2000, *Event and Plurality: The Jerusalem Lectures,*

Dordrecht: Kluwer.

Landman, Fred, 2004, *Indefinites and the Type of Sets,* Malden, MA: Blackwell.

Larson.R., 1995, Olga is a Beautiful Dancer, *LSA-New Orleans,* Jauuary 5-8.

Leech, George, 1983, *Semantics: The Study of Meaning,* Second Edition Hamondsworth: Penguin.

Lepore, Ernst, 1985, The Semantics of Action, Event, and Singular Causal Sentences. In *Action and Events: Perspectives on the Philosophy of Donald Davidson,* E. LePore and B. McLanghlin, eds., 151-161, Oxford: Blackwell.

Li, Charles N. and Sandra Thompson, 1981, *Mandarin Chinese: A functional reference grammar*, 2nd edn, Berkeley, CA: University of California Press.

Li Jinrong, 2007, A functional analysis of sentence with objected-oriented adverbial, *Studies of the Chinese Language* 4:331-342.

Li Jinxi, 1924, *Newly-written grammar of Chinese,* Beijing: The Commercial Press.

Li, Guohong and Liu Ping, 2014, On the Subjectivity of Adverbial Qualitative Phrases and Their Semantic Characteristics, *Modern Foreign Languages* Vol.37 No.2 157-167.

Li Quan, 2005, *The Study of Prototypical Features for the Monosyllabic Adjectives.* Dissertation, Beijing Foreign Language and Culture University.

Li Yuming, 1996, The meaning of reduplication, *Chinese Teaching in the World* 1:10-19.

Liao Qiuzhong, 1985, The Identification of Reference of the Kuangling Relation in Text, *Research and exploration of Grammar,* Beijing: Peking University Press.

Lim, Jeong-Hyun, 2004, *Secondary Predication in Chinese,* Ph.D. dissertation, Tsinghua University, Taiwan.

Lin, Jo-wang, 2003. Event Decomposition and the Syntax and Semantics of Duratice Phrase in Chinese, paper presented at the workshop in formal syntax and semantics in academia sinica in Taipei.

Ling Hongmei, 2011, *The Research on the Function of Adjectives Used as Adverbs*, Dissertation for Master of Shanghai Normal University.

Link G, 1983, The Logical Analysis of Plurals and Mass Terms: a Lattics-Theoretic Approach. In *Meaning, Use and Interpretation of Language*, Rainer B., Christophe Schwa, and Arnim von Stechow, eds., 303-323, Berlin: de Gruyter.

Liu. Chen-Sheng Luther, 2013, Reduplication of Adjectives in Chinese: a Default State, *East Asian Linguist* 22:101-132.

Liu Dawei, 1992, Seamntic Entailment and the Movement of the Modifying Constituent, *Chinese Teaching in the World* 1:17-22.

Liu Danqing, 1986, Research on Reduplication of Suzhou Dialect, *Studies in Language and Linguistics* 1:7-28.

Liu Danqing and Xu Liejiong, 1998, Focus and Background, Topic and Sentence Containing 'Lian', *Studies of the Chinese Language* 4: 243-252.

Liu Wei and Li Zhe, 2011, A VP-shell Analysis of Adjective Adverbials Semantically Oriented to Objects, *Chinese Language Learning* 6: 24-31.

Liu Yuehua, 1983, The Classification and Linear Order of Adverbials, *Research and exploration of Grammar II,* Beijing: Peking University Press.

Liu Yuehua and Pan wenyu, 1983, Applied Contemporary Chinese Grammar, Beijing: Foreign Language Teaching and Research Press.

Liu Yuehua, Pan Wenyu, Gu Hua, 2004, Chinese Grammar for Teaching and Learning, Beijing: The Commercial Press.

Liu Zhenping, 2007, *Comparative Study on Mono-syllable-adjective as Adverbial and Complement,* Ph.D. dissertation of Beijing Foreign Language and Culture University.

Lu Bingfu, 2003, The Basic Function and Derived Function of 'de' Viewed from its Distribution, *Chinese Teaching in the World* 1:14-30.

Lu Bingfu, 2004, Distance-marking Correspondence as a Language Universal, *Studies of the Chinese Language* 1: 3-15.

Lu Jian, 2003, An Analysis on the Syntactic Realization and Function of Chinese Depictive Adverbial Modifiers, *Studies in Language and Linguistics* 1: 99-106.

Lu Jianming, 1963, The Unification and Division of 'de' and Relevant Problems, *Esays on Linguistics* 5.

Lu Jianming, 1983, The Distinction of Attributive and Adverbial, *Chinese Language Learning* 2

Lu Jianming, 1999, About Semantic Orientation Analysis, *Chinese Linguistic Reviews*, 34-471, Beijing: Beijing Language and Cultural University Press.

Lu Jianming and Shen Yang, 2004, *Fifteen Lectures on Chinese and Researches on Chinese*, Beijing: Peking University Press.

Lu Yingshun, 1995, On Semantic Orientation Research, *Chinese Teaching in the World* 3: 22-26.

Lü Shuxiang, 1954, Some Principle Issues on the Word Classes in Chinese, *Studies of the Chinese Language* 9: 16-22.

Lü Shuxiang, 1962, About the Unification of Unit of Language, *Studies of the Chinese Language* 11: 483-495.

Lü Shuxiang, 1963, Initial Research on Monosyllabic and Disyllabic in Contemporary Chinese, *Studies of the Chinese Language* 1.

Lü Shuxiang, 1966, On the Usage of Monosyllabic Adjective, *Studies of the Chinese Language* 2.

Lü Shuxiang, 1978, On Grammar Analysis of Chinese, Beijing: The Commercial Press.

Lü Shuxiang, et al., 1980, Eight Hundred Words in Modern Chinese, Beijing: The Commercial Press.

Lü Shuxiang, 1986, The Flexibility of Chinese Syntax, *Zhongguo Yuwen* 1.

Ma Zhen and Lu Jianming, 1997, Study on Adjectives as Complement, *Hanyu Xuexi* 6: 3-7.

Maienborn, C., 2003, Die Logische Form von Kopula-Sätzen, Berlin: Akademie-Verlag.

Maienborn, C., 2005, Eventualities and Different Things: A reply, *Theoretical Linguistics,* 31(3), 383-396.

Marcin Morzycki, To appear, *Modification*. To appear for the Cambridge University Press series *Key Topics in Semantics and Pragmatics*.

Martin Schafer, 2008, Resolving Scope in Manner Modification, In *Empirical Issue in Syntax and Semantics,* O.Bonami and Cabredo Hofherr, eds., 7: 351-372.

Matsui, Ai, To appear, 'Transforming Manner Adverbs into Subject-oriented Adverbs: Evidence from Japanese', Ms,. Michigan State University, To appear in a special issue of *Natural Language and Linguistic Theory*.

McConnell-Ginet, Sally, 1982, Adverb and Logical Form: a Linguistically Realistic Theory, *Language* 58, 144-184.

McNally, Louise, To appear, 'Modification', In *Cambridge Handbook of Semantics,* Maria Aloni and Paul Dekker ,eds., Cambridge University Press, Cambridge.

Michael Richter, Roeland van Hout, 2010, Why Some Verbs Can Form a Resultative Construction While Others Cannot: Decomposing Semantic Binding, *Lingua* 120: 2006-2021.

Milada Walkova, 2012, Dowty's Aspectual Tests: Standing the Test of Time But Failing the Test of Aspect, *Poznan Studies in Contemporary Linguistics* 48(3) 495-518.

Milsark,G.L., 1974, *Existential Sentence in English,* Ph.D. Dissertation, MIT, Published in 1976 by Bloomington, IN: Indiana University Linguistics Club.

Moens, M and Steedman, M., 1988, Temporal Ontology and Temporal Reference, *Computational Linguistics* 14: 15-28.

Moore, Robert C, 1995, Event, Situations and Adverbs, *Logic and Representation*, PP: 159-170, Standford, CA: CSLI Publications. (Originally published in 1989)

Ning Chunyan, 1993, *The Overt Syntax of Relativization and Topicalization,* Ph.D. diss, University of California, Irvine.

Ning Chunyan, 1996, De as a Functional Head in Chinese. In *UCL Working Papers in Linguistics* 1, B Agbayani K. Takeda and Sze-Eing Tang, eds., 63-79. ILSA, University of California, Ivine.

Pan, Haihua, 1993, Interaction Between Adverbial Quantification and Perfective Aspect, In *Proceedings of the Third Annual Linguistics Society of Mid-America Conference, Northwestern U.,* Stvan L. S., ed., 188-204, Bloomington: Indiana U Linguistics Club Publications.

Pan Haihua and Lu Shuo, 2013, The Problems of the DeP Analysis and its Possible Solution, *Studies in Languages and Linguistics* 4: 53-60.

Pan Haihua, Handout, For Linguistics Institute of China, LINC 2014.

Pan Guoying, 2010, *A Study on Word Order of Adverbials in Modern Mandarin Chinese,* Ph.D. dissertation of East China Normal University.

Pan Guoying, 2012, The Statue of Modifiers as a Downgraded Predication Constituent, *Shijie Hanyu Jiaoxue* 1. 54-64.

Pan Xiaodong, 1981, About the Relocation of Attributives, *Studies of* the Chinese Language 4.

Papafrago, Anna, 2006, Epistemic Modality and Truth Conditional, Lingua 116:1688-1702.

Partee, B.H., Meulen, A. and Wall, R.E., 1990, *Mathematical Methods in Linguistics,* Dordrecht: Kluwer Academic Publishers.

Partee, Barbara H. and Vladimir Borschev, 1998, Integrating Lexical and Formal Semantics: Genitives, Relational Nouns, and Type-shifting, In R. Cooper and Th. Gamkrelidze,eds..

Partee, Barbara H., 2003, Are There Privative Adjectives? Conference on the philosophy of Terry Parsons, Notre Dame, 7 and 8 February, 2003.

Patee, Barbara H., 2007, Compositionality and Coercion in Semantics: The Dynamics of Adjective Meaning, In *Cognitive Foundations of Interpretation*, G. Bouma et al., eds., 145-161, Amsterdam: Royal Netherlands Academy of Arts and Sciences.

Patee, Barbara H., 2009, Formal Semantics, Lexical Semantics, and Compositionality: The Puzzle of Private Adjectives, *Philologia* 7:7-19.

Parsons, T., 1980, Modifiers and Quantifiers in Natural Language, *Canadian Journal of Philosophy, Suppl. vol* 6, 29-60.

Parsons, T., 1985, Underlying Events in the Analysis of English, In LePore and McLaughlin, eds., 235-267.

Parsons, T., 1990. *Events in the Semantics of English: A Study in Subatomic Semantics,* Cambridge, MA: Massachusetts: The MIT Press.

Paul, W., 2010, Adjectives in Mandarin Chinese: The Rehabilitation of a Much Ostracized Category. In *Adjectives, Formal analyses in syntax and semantics,* Cabredo-Hofherr, P. and Matushansky, O., eds., 115-152, Amsterdam: Benjamins.

Paul, W., 2006, Zhu Dexi's Two Classes of Adjectives Revisited, In *Studies in Chinese Language and Culture, Festschrift in Honour of Christoph Harbsmeier on the Occasion of His 60th Birthday*, Christoph Anderl and Halvor Eifring, eds.,303-315, Oslo: Hermes Academic Publishing.

Pelletier, F.J., 1979, Non-singular Reference, In *Mass Terms: Some Philosophical Problems*, F.J. Pelletier, ed., 1-14, Kluwer, Dordrecht.

Pustejovsky, J., 1995, *The Generative Lexicon,* Cambridge: MIT Press.

Pylkkänen. Liina, 2008, *Introducing Arguments,* The MIT Press.

Qi Huyang, 1997, The Adjacent Adjective in Subordinate Phrase, *Explanations in Chinese Grammar* 8, Beijing: The Commercial Press.

Ramsey, Frank P., 1927, Facts and Propositions, Reprinted in *The Foundations of Mathematics,* Paterson, New Jersey: lottlefield, Adams and Co., 1960.

Rapoport, Tova, 1990, Secondary Predication and the Lexical Representation of Verbs, *Machine Translation* 5, 31-35.

Rapoport, Tova, 1991, Adjunct-predicate Licensing and D-structure, Syntax and Semantics, In *Perspectives on Phrase Structure: Head and licensing,* vol 25: Susan D. Rothstein,ed.,159-187, New York: Academic Press.

Rappaport Hovav, M. and Beth. Levin, 1998, Building Verb Meaning, In *The Projection of Arguments: Lexical and Compositional Factors*, M. Butt and W.Geuder,eds., 97-134, CSLI Publication, Stanford, CA.

Reichenbach, H., 1947, *Elements of Symbolic Logic,* New York: Free Press.

Rothstein,S., 1999, Fine-grained Structure in the Eventuality Domain: the Semantics of Predicative Adjective Phrase and *be, Natural Language Semantics* 7: 347-420.

Rothstein, S., 2001, *Predicates and Their Subjects,* Dordrecht: Kluwer.

Rothstein, S., 2004, *Structuring Events,* Blackwell, Oxford.

Schmitt, C., 1992, *Ser and estar: A matter of aspect,* NELS 22, GLSA.

Sera, M., 1992, To be or to be, *Journal of Memory and Language* 31: 408-427.

Shangtianliulizi, 1995, Investigation on the Disyllabic Adjectival Adverbials, *Chinese Teaching in the World* 3:27-34.

Shen Jiaxuan, 1995, Bound and unbounded, *Studies of the Chinese Language* 5: 367-380.

Shen Jiaxuan, 1997, The Pattern to Mark the Syntactic Function of Adjectives, *Studies of the Chinese Language* 4:242-250.

ShenJiaxuan, 2004, Reconsider Bound and Unbound, *Essays on Linguistics* 30:40-54. Beijing: The Commercial Press.

Shen Jiaxuan, 2007, My Opinion on the Word Class in Chinese, *Language Science* 1: 1-12.

ShenJiaxuan, 2011, Rhythmic Structure and Adjective in Chinese, *Chinese Language Learning* 3:3-10.

ShenKaimu, 1996, On Semantic Orientation, *Journal of South China Normal University (Social Science Edition)* 6: 69-74

Shen Yang, 1994, The Semantic Reference of Proform in Syntactic Structure, *Linguistic Study* 2: 25-44.

Shi Qin, 2010, *Development of Reduplicated Adjective in Chinese*, Beijing: The Commercial Press.

Shi Yuzhi, 2000, Unification of Grammar Function of de, *Chinese Teaching in the World* 1: 16-27.

Shui Changxi, 2004, Evolution of Semantic Orientation Analysis and its Prospect, *Language Teaching and Linguistic Study* 1:62-71.

Siegel. M., 1976, *Capturing the Adjective,* Ph.D. dissertation of University of Massachusetts-Amherst.

Si Fuzhen, 2004, Head theory and DeP in Chinese, *Contemporary Linguistics* 1: 26-34.

Si Fuzhen, 2005, Hapology in Chinese, *Language Teaching and Linguistic Study* 2: 56-62.

Simpson,J., 1986, *Resultative Attributes,* MS, MIT.

Smith, Carlota S., 1997, *The Parameter of Aspect*, 2nd edition, Dordrecht: Kluwer.

Stowell, T., 1981, *The Origins of Phrase Structure,* Ph.D. dissertation. MIT.

Stowell, T., 1991, Small Clause Restructuring, In *Principles and Parameters in Comparative Grammar*, R. Frieden, ed., 182-218. MIT Press: Cambridge, Mass.

Su Ying and Yang Rongxiang, 2014, The Identification of Adjectives Used as Adverbials in Ancient Chinese, *Studies in Language and Linguistics* 1:90-95.

Sui Na, 2014, The Syntax of Reduplication, Ph.D. dissertation, Chinese Academy of Social Sciences.

Sun Rujian, 1995, The Unification or Division of de and De, *Journal of Yangzhong Normal University* (Social Science Edition) 1: 80-82.

Swan, Toril, 1990, Subject-oriented Adverbs in 20th-century English,

Nordlyd 9:14-58.

Swan, Toril, 1997, From Manner to Subject Modification: Adverbialization in English, *Nordic Journal of Linguistics*, 20: 179-195.

Tang Tingchi, 1979, De Construction in Mandarin Chinese, *Paper Collection on Grammar of Mandarin Chinese,* Taipei: Student Books.

Tang, Ting-Chi, 1988, Reduplication of Adjectives in Chinese, In *Studies on Chinese morphology and syntax,* 29-57. Taipei: Student Book Company.

Tao Yuan, 2009, The Syntactic Constraints on Argument-oriented Adverbials, *Chinese Language Learning* 5: 50-58.

Taylor, J. R., 2002, *Cognitive Grammar* [M]. Oxford University Press.

Thomason, R and Stalnaker, R., 1973, A Semantic Theory of Adverbs. *Linguistic Inquiry* 4: 195-220.

Tsai, D., 1998. Tense Anchoring in Chinese, *Lingua* (118):675-686.

Valera, S., 1998, On Subject-orientation in English –ly Adverbs, *English Language and Linguistics*, 2, pp263-282.

Vendler, Z., 1967, *Linguistics in Philosophy,* Ithaca: Cornell University Press.

Vendler, Z., 1968, *Adjectives and Nominalizations,* MOUTON The Hague Paris.

Verkuyl, Henk. J., 1972, *On the Compositional Nature of the Aspects,* Dordrecht: Kluwer.

Von Stechow, A., 1984, Comparing Semantics Theory of Comparison, *Journal of Semantics* 3 (1), 1-77.

Wang Huan, 1991, Buyu Following DE, *Chinese Teaching in the World* 1:1-2.

Wang Junyi, 2006, Declarative and Descriptive: Two Types of Adjective as Adverbial. *Chinese Teaching in the World* 4:26-32.

Wang Li, 1943, Modern Chinese Grammar, Beijing: The Commercial Press.

Wang Lidi and Gu Yang, 2000, Subject-oriented Adverbial Modifier, in *The Grammar Research on Chinese Grammar Facing the Challenges of New Century*, Jinan: Shangdong Education Press.

Wang Xin, 2012, Context-free Semantics and Semantic Orientation, *Journal of Foreign Languages* 3: 75-81.

Wen Binli, 1996, *The Syntax of Chinese and English Free Relatives,* Ph.D. diss, Guangdong University of Foreign Studies.

Wierabicka, A., 1988, *The Semantic of Grammar,* Amsterdam: John Benjamins.

Williams, E., 1980, Predication, *Linguistic Inquiry* 8:203-238.

Wu Ping, 2007, *Formal Semantic Analysis and Computation of Constructions,* Beijing Language and Culture University Press.

Wu Ping and Jin Hui-ling, 2008, A Review of Parsons' Subatomic Semantics, *Journal of Hebei University (Philosophy and Social Science)* 4: 133-137.

Wu Ping, 2009, *Event Semantic Analysis and Computation of Selected Constructions in Mandarin Chinese,* Beijing: China Social Sciences Press.

Wyner, Adam, 1994, *Boolean Event Lattices and Thematic Roles in the Syntax and Semantics of Adverbial Modification,* Ph.D. dissertation, Cornell University.

Wyner, Adam, 2008, Towards Flexible Types with Constraints for Manner and Factive Adverbs, In McNally and Kennedy, eds., 249-273.

Xing Fuyi, 1996, *Grammar of Mandarin Chinese,* Northeast Normal University Press.

Xiong Zhongru, 2005, DP Structure Headed by De, *Contemporary Linguistics* 2: 148-165.

Xiong Zhongru, 2013, Syntactic Analyses of Sentence with Object-oriented Adverbials, *Modern Foreign Language* 1: 25-32.

Xu Shu, 1993, Semantic Restrictions and the Condition of Construction Formation, *Chinese Teaching in the World* 4:279-284.

Xu Yangchun, 2003, *A study on Form Word 'de' and Its Related Matters,* Ph.D diss, Fudan University.

Xu Yangchun, 2011, Chunking, Prominese and Usage of "*De*", *Language Teaching and Linguistic Study* 6:76-82.

Xuan Yue, 2007, Natural Focus of the Descriptive Adverbial-verb Configuration Functioning as Predicate, *Chinese Teaching in the World* 3. 64-78.

Yang Yongzhong, 2014, The Syntactic Structure and Derivation of Sentence with Object-oriented Adverbials, *Modern Foreign Language* 1: 32-41.

Yuan Yulin, 1995, Implying Predicate and its Syntactic Consequence, *Studies of the Chinese Language* 4:241-255.

Yuan Yulin, 2006, The Information Structure of the Lian-construction in Mandarin, *Linguistics Sciences* 2:14-28.

Yuan Yulin, 2010, *A Cognitive Investigation and Fuzzy Classification of Word-class in Mandarin Chinese,* Shanghai Educational Publishing House.

Zhao Chunli and Shi Dingxu, 2011, Some Principle on the Co-occurrence of Affective Adjectives and Verbal-constructions, *Chinese Language Learning* 1: 12-21.

Zhao Mingqin, 2008, The Function of Semantic Orientation Analysis in Syntactic Analysis, *Modern Chinese* 2:44-45.

Zhang Bojiang and Fang Mei, 1996, *Functional Grammar of Mandarin*, Nanchang: Jiangxi Education Press.

Zhang Bojiang, 2011, Predicate Adjectives in Modern Chinese, *Chinese Teaching in the World* 1:3-12.

Zhang Guoxian, 1991, Semantic Orientation of Predicational Adverbials, *Chinese Learning* 2: 13-16.

Zhang Guoxian, 1993, *Study on the Selectiveness of Adjectives in Mandarin*, Ph.D. dissertation of Shanghai Normal University.

Zhang Guoxian, 1995, Dynamic Adjectives in Mandarin, *Studies of the Chinese Language* 3: 221-229.

Zhang Guoxian, 2000, Typical Feature of Chinese Adjectives, *Studies of the Chinese Language* 5:447-458.

Zhang Guoxian, 2005, Rule of Semantic Orientation and the Pragmatic Motivation of Syntactic Mismatch, *Studies of the Chinese Language* 1:16-28.

Zhang Guoxian, 2006, Attribute, State and Change, *Language Teaching and Linguistic Study* 3:1-11.

Zhang Lijun, 1990, Semantic Orientation of A in "NP1+A+VP+NP2" Construction, *Journal of Yantai University (Social Science Edition)* 3:87-96.

Zhang Jing, 1988, Contemporary Chinese, Higher Education Press.

Zhang Min, 1998, *Cognitive Linguistics and NP in Mandarin*, Beijing: China Social Sciences Press.

Zhang Niina, 2000, The Syntactic Structure of the Secondary

Predication in Chinese, Paper present at German Society for Linguistics (DGLS) University of Marbung March 1-3.

Zhang Niina, 2001, The Asymmetry Between Depictive and Resultatives in Chinese. In Anns Maria Di Sciullo, eds., *Asymmetry in Grammar,* John Benjamins.

Zhang, Niina, 2002, The Asymmetry Between Depictives and Resultatives in Chinese. In *Asymmetry in Grammar* (Vol,1), Anna Maria Di Sciullo, eds., 165-186. Amsterdam /Philadelphia: John Benjamins Publishing Company.

Zheng Guiyou, 2000, Study the Relations of Adjectival Adverbials of Contemporary Chinese, Central China Normal University Press.

Zheng Huaide and Meng Qinghua, 2003, *Dictionary of Adjectives in Chinese*, Beijing: The Commercial Press.

Zheng Yuanhan, 2005, On the Omission of the Adverbial Marker "DE" from the Perspective of the Discourse Restrictions, *Chinese Linguistics* 3: 65-72.

Zhou Guoguang, 2006, On the Principle and Method of Semantic Orientation Analysis, *Linguistics Sciences* 4: 41-49.

Zhu Dexi, 1980, A Study of Adjectives in Modern Chinese, *Yuyan Yanjiu* 1, 83-112.

Zhu Dexi, 1980, *Studies in Modern Chinese Syntax*, Beijing: Commercial Press.

Zhu Dexi, 1961, On 'de', *Zhongguo Yuwen* 12: 1-15.

Zhu Dexi, 1966, On discussion of 'de', *Studies of the Chinese Language* 1, Beijing: The Commercial Press. 131-151.

Zhu Dexi,1982, *Lectures on syntax*, Beijing: The Commercial Press.

Zhu Dexi, 1984, *Attributive and Adverbial*, Shanghai: Shanghai Education Press.

Zhu Dexi, 1985, *Questions on Grammar*, Beijing: The Commercial Press.

Zhu Dexi, 1993, Nominalization of State Adjective from the Dialect and History perspective, *Dialect* 2: 81-100.

Zhu Jingsong, 2003, The Syntax and Semantics of Reduplicated Adjectives, *Yuwen Yanjiu* 88(3):9-1.

Acknowledgements

This book has been many years in the making, and I could never adequately thank everyone to whom I am indebted in various ways for helping me write this book. First and foremost, I would like to thank Prof. Wu Ping, for being an advisor, mentor, and friend to me over the last ten years.

I particularly thank Prof. Shen Jiaxuan, Prof. Zou Chongli, Prof. Yuan Yulin, Prof. Zou Chongli, Prof. Pan Haihua, Prof. Hu Jianhua, Prof. Gao Mingle, Prof. Si Fuzhen, Prof. Wen Weiping, Prof. Chen Qianrui, Prof. Liu Wei, and Prof. Wang Zhenya. for their invaluable comments and suggestions.

I have many friends whose encouragement and support I would like to acknowledge, among them Ferreira Martins. Dina, Hao Xiangli, Hu Bo, Chen Hong, Sun Hongbo, Zhang Chi, An Fengcun, Wang Changsong, Meng Fanjun, Wang Xiaona and Xu Wei for their contributions towards making my graduate experience a memorable and enjoyable one. Sun Hongbo and Hu Bo have made an invaluable contribution to the completion of this work. I am also grateful to my colleagues form Guangdong Ocean University for their help and thanks especially go to Prof. Guo Suihong for having been so encouraging

Finally, I offer my gratitude and love to my parents, and all my sisters and brothers. Special thanks to An Shengxi, my wife, and An Baicheng, my son, for their love, encouragement, perseverance and patience with me.

Li Mo at China Social Science Press made the publication process painless and quick, for which I am very grateful.

All mistakes and errors in this book are entirely mine.